Malpractice: A Trial Lawyer's Advice for Physicians

Walter G. Alton, Jr., LL.B.

Malpractice

A Trial Lawyer's
Advice for Physicians
(How to Avoid,
How to Win)

Little, Brown and Company
Boston

To My Father

Contents

Preface

As a physician* practices his profession, he unavoidably exposes himself daily to potential claims from his patients and their relatives. Nevertheless, most physicians have no real understanding of what medical malpractice is all about. As a result, the average physician does not know how to practice medicine so as to reduce the chances that a claim against him will be made and, if a claim is made, to increase his chances of defeating it. In fact, because of this general lack of understanding, the average physician not only makes unnecessary mistakes that are prejudicial to his defense, but often unwittingly causes a patient to commence a claim or unintentionally helps a patient to prosecute a claim against him.

The purpose of this book is to provide a basic understanding of medical malpractice from a legal and practical point of view that can be related to the practice of medicine. Such an understanding will not, of course, guarantee immunity from claims or from adverse verdicts, but it can reduce the possibility of a malpractice claim and greatly enhance the chances of the physician's winning if he is sued. In light of years of medical malpractice defense experience, it is my considered opinion that the practitioner who has a good grasp of what medical malpractice is all about can protect himself from malpractice claims and win those claims that are prosecuted against him.

This book is based primarily on my experience as a trial attorney defending medical malpractice suits in the State of New York. Although the principles of law explained here are of general application, they are unavoidably rooted in my New York experience. As a result, there may be minor variations in these principles as enunciated and applied by the courts of some state jurisdictions; nevertheless, such variations are inconsequential to the basic understanding that the book seeks to impart.

W. G. A.

*Although this book utilizes the terms *physician* and *medical malpractice*, its content applies equally to dentists and dental malpractice.

Acknowledgments

I wish to express my appreciation and thanks to Steven C. Mandell, Esq., for his assistance with this book.

W. G. A.

Malpractice: A Trial Lawyer's Advice for Physicians

1   What Is Medical Malpractice?

The Legal Definition—What Does It Mean?

The legal definition of medical malpractice can be expressed in many ways. If you asked me about it at a cocktail party, I would define malpractice simply as a deviation from the approved and accepted standards of medical practice for the medical specialty in question under the circumstances of the particular case, producing an injury. Very often it is defined in terms of duty to a patient. In trying to explain medical malpractice to juries, judges tend to wander about in their definitions. A judge might define malpractice in his instructions (charge) to the jury in one or more of the following ways:

It is the duty of a hospital and of a doctor to adhere to that standard of care and of conduct to be expected of reasonably prudent people in the same or similar circumstances and that standard is that which is accepted generally in medical practice and in hospital practice and is called for by the particular circumstances in the particular case; it is the duty of a doctor or a hospital or both to use the methods and practice known and used ordinarily in the community by the average of those performing the same services or a similar service and by the average of those carrying on the same specialized practice or a similar practice; it is a duty to exercise judgment based on careful consideration of all the surrounding circumstances; it is a doctor's duty to do what he thinks best after he has carefully considered the surrounding circumstances.

The fact is that the law does not attempt to make the definition precise. Perhaps what the term is intended to connote defies precision by its very nature. In any case, lawyers and judges defining medical malpractice use "that which a reasonably prudent physician would do" or "that which the average physician would do" or "that which is generally accepted in medical practice" or "that which is in accordance with the accepted standards of practice" as interchangeable equivalents.

This imprecision does not arouse much concern, since, practically speaking, the expert testimony adduced at trial will determine the specific standards against which the defendant physician's treatment will be measured in each individual case. If the definition of medical malpractice is to be equitable, however, it must measure treatment against standards of practice that are generally accepted in the medical community. Without attempting to determine what the reasonably prudent physician would do, or what the average physician would do, a physician's treatment should be judged simply by determining whether or not it would be considered acceptable by the medical community.

Thus I believe in defining medical malpractice in terms of what is acceptable within the medical community, irrespective of its popularity or degree of acceptance. Nevertheless, in the final analysis, the standards against which a physician's treatment will be measured are set by the credible expert testimony. Using the judge's instructions at the end of the case as a guide, the jurors will decide the question of malpractice by measuring what they believe took place against the standards laid down by the expert testimony they believe. The following case is an example.

A duly qualified surgeon was called in as a consultant on the fourth day after admission to the hospital of a 35-year-old married female patient with a three-year history of stomach pain, incidents of tarry stool, and fatty-food intolerance. At the time of admission, the stomach pain had become constant and was unrelieved by food or antacid. The pain radiated to the lumbar spine and caused the patient to be awakened at night. In the six weeks prior to admission, she had lost fifteen pounds as a result of anorexia, nausea, and vomiting. Fifteen months prior to this admission, she had been hospitalized for approximately twelve days because of ulcers and had been treated conservatively with medication and diet.

At the time our surgeon was called in as a consultant, the patient's internist had hospitalized her because of her intractable pain, unrelieved by diets, tranquilizers, medication to reduce acid production, antispasmodics, or antacids. This conservative regimen had been continued after the patient's admission, but had given her no relief. She continued to be awakened at night by the pain, cried frequently, and begged her physician for an operation to relieve her of the pain.

The surgeon read the patient's chart, questioned her, and had a hospital resident verify that her prior admission had indeed been for ulcers and not another ailment. The surgeon's physical examination revealed midepigastric pain radiating to the patient's lower back. Despite the radiologist's report of an upper gastrointestinal series that unequivocally confirmed the presence of a duodenal ulcer, the surgeon himself read the films. He then sought out the radiologist and together they reread the films and confirmed the x-ray diagnosis of a duodenal ulcer.

The patient was continued on conservative therapy for several more days, without relief from pain. The surgeon then decided to operate. He made a thorough exploration of the abdomen, pylorus, and duodenum through a gastrostomy incision. He did not find evidence of an ulcer. The only abnormality found was enlarged mesenteric nodes. During the surgery he removed one node, for pathological examination, and the appendix. Incidental removal of the appendix had not been discussed with the patient before the surgery. Nothing else was done.

The patient did well after the operation except for the development of an infection at the site of a retention suture. Strangely, her stomach complaints disappeared. She was discharged home. The infection was followed in the surgeon's office but required that she be rehospitalized for ten days of treatment before it healed. The patient was left with an ugly hypertrophic scar extending vertically down her midriff.

The patient retained an attorney and sued everyone connected with her treatment. She sued the internist who had admitted her to the hospital, ordered conservative treatment, and called the surgeon in consultation. The patient alleged that the internist's diagnosis of an ulcer was incorrect, that he should not have called in the surgeon when he did, and that he should not have permitted the operation so soon after her admission.

She sued the surgeon, alleging that the operation should not have been performed, that the preoperative diagnosis was incorrect, that the surgery was improperly performed, and that the appendix was removed without informed consent.

She sued the hospital for the acts of the radiologist who read the x-rays, alleging that he improperly read the films as a duodenal ulcer.

Was there malpractice on anyone's part? One can understand the reasoning that prompted the lawsuit. The patient was operated on for an ulcer and nothing was found. She reasoned that *all* the physicians caused her to have a large ugly scar on her belly for nothing, and that she unnecessarily underwent the pain and discomfort of the operation, the recovery period, the treatment, and the second hospitalization for the infection. Why shouldn't these physicians pay for their mistake? The patient alleged that if she had been continued on conservative treatment without the operation, she would have improved, as she had during her prior hospitalization.

The patient's line of reasoning does possess a certain logic and appeal to a lay jury—that is, a jury composed of lay persons, who are, of course, all patients. One advantage the plaintiff always has is that, at some time during their deliberation, the members of the jury will put themselves in the plaintiff's shoes. "What if this had happened to me?" "What if that ugly scar were on my belly?" "What a shame." These kinds of thoughts have to be overcome with logic, reason, a basic understanding of the medical problems involved, and an appreciation of the limitations of medicine. This will be the task of the defense lawyer, defense experts, and the defendant.

I have defined malpractice in terms of measuring treatment against standards of practice that are generally accepted in the medical community. The essential question is, as it is most often put, whether the treatment deviated or departed from accepted practice. In order for the plaintiff to prevail, she will have to prove a deviation from accepted practice under certain rules of law I shall discuss later. Suffice it to say here that, in order to prevail against a defendant, the plaintiff must prove that the defendant deviated from the accepted standards of practice and that this deviation was a substantial factor in producing the injuries complained of. She will have to prove this assertion with respect to each defendant sued if she wishes to succeed against that defendant.

Of course, determining whether or not there has been a deviation from accepted practice will depend on what the expert witnesses testify are the accepted standards of practice under the circumstances. The jurors will hear each expert testify about the accepted standards of practice in the medical community under the circumstances of the case and about whether or not each defendant's treatment was in accordance with or deviated from these standards. These opinions may or may not accurately reflect what actually takes place in the medical community. The plaintiff's expert could be taking into account advances that were not common knowledge or generally used at the time of the alleged malpractice. He could be holding the defendant to higher standards than those considered acceptable at the time. He could be condemning an acceptable mode of treatment merely because hindsight shows it failed. He could be just plain wrong or intentionally perjuring himself. By the same token, a defense expert could be guilty of comparable abuses. Being overprotective, he may classify subpar treatment as acceptable. He may mistakenly assume, because of the excellence of the defendant's qualifications, that certain steps have been carried out.

You, as the physician being sued, must realize that the plaintiff will succeed in convincing the jury with his claim as long as his expert testifies that in his opinion, with a reasonable degree of medical certainty, there was a deviation from accepted practice that caused the injuries complained of—whether or not his opinion is unrealistic or even outrageous. The jurors have no independent knowledge with which to judge the quality of the opinion. The weight they assign to it will depend on such factors as the demeanor of the witness, the ability of the witness to hold up under cross-examination, the credibility of the opposing expert opinion, the demeanor of the opposing expert, and such intrinsic evidence as hospital records and x-rays, not to mention the testimony of the parties and other witnesses.

In effect, then, your treatment is being measured not against what you know to be the accepted standards in the community, but against the testimony of the plaintiff's hired expert as to these standards. On the other side of the case, your treatment is measured against what your defense expert testifies are the standards. The jury must decide which opinion it believes. Quality and credibility of expert testimony are therefore essential in any malpractice action.

Consider our example. For the plaintiff to fulfill the legal requisites that entitle her to have a jury deliberate on her case,[1] she will have to adduce expert testimony establishing the defendants' deviations from accepted practice and the causal connection between these deviations and her injuries. As for the internist, the expert will probably testify that calling the surgeon in when he did

---

1. The plaintiff's *burden of proof.* See *prima facie case* and *burden of proof* in the Glossary; also see Chapter 10, pp. 178, 182-187.

was a deviation from accepted practice. He will surely state that the patient should have been continued on conservative therapy for a longer period to determine whether the stomach would respond without surgery. The expert will then add that, even after the consultation and recommendation for surgery, the internist should not have permitted surgery without a longer trial of conservative therapy. To permit surgery at that point in the hospitalization was, he will testify, a deviation from accepted practice.

Turning to the radiologist and the x-ray interpretation, the plaintiff's expert must state that in his opinion the films were not only misread but so negligently read as to constitute malpractice. His opinion must be that the proper reading of the films was so obvious that to read them as showing an ulcer constituted a deviation from the accepted standards of the practice of radiology, not just an error in judgment. In the case from which the example is taken, the plaintiff's expert testified that a first-year intern could not have misread the films as showing an ulcer. The expert stated that the films clearly showed a diverticulum and not an ulcer. He concluded that the hospital radiologist had deviated from the accepted standards used by radiologists in reading films.

As to the surgeon, the plaintiff's expert testimony is obvious. He will testify that, under the circumstances, the surgeon had no business recommending surgery, much less performing it. In the actual case the criticism of the surgeon was broad in scope. The expert stated that instead of merely checking to see if the prior admission had been for ulcers, the surgeon had an obligation to obtain and review all the prior records and x-rays; that there had been an insufficient trial of conservative therapy; that the surgeon had misread an x-ray that obviously showed a diverticulum, not an ulcer; and that there was no bleeding or other indication for surgery. For the plaintiff to prevail, his expert must make clear that the decision to operate was not just an error in surgical judgment but a "negligent" judgment: a judgment no reasonably prudent surgeon would make when faced with the same circumstances; a judgment that could not have been reached if the accepted standards of surgical practice had been followed.

As you can see, these criticisms sometimes overlap. The expert could choose to say that it was the responsibility of the internist to obtain the prior hospital records for review and the responsibility of the radiologist to obtain the prior films. In this case the expert chose to focus on the surgeon, but the division of responsibility among multiple defendants is within his discretion with regard to some aspects of treatment.

What about the incidental appendectomy and the question of lack of informed consent? In this case the plaintiff's attorney did not attack that aspect of the treatment. The subject of lack of informed consent will be covered at length in Chapter 4. Suffice it to say here that the plaintiff's attorney and probably his expert concluded that they could show no real damage caused by the "uninformed" removal of the appendix and chose to concentrate on the decision to operate.

This brings up an essential point that is often overlooked. It must be remembered that in addition to testifying to deviations from the accepted standards of practice, the plaintiff's expert must state with a reasonable degree of medical certainty that in his opinion such deviations "proximately caused"—or, in nonlegal language, were substantial factors in causing—the injuries complained of. In our example this is self-evident. If the internist had forbidden surgery at the time, or the radiologist had not read an ulcer on the x-rays, or the surgeon had not read the same thing, or the surgeon had concluded that there were no indications for surgery, there would have been no operation, no scar, no related pain and discomfort, no infection, and no subsequent hospitalization. If, therefore, the jury in this case chose to believe the plaintiff's expert on the question of the various deviations from accepted practice, the causation element would follow naturally. This is often not so, however, and the causation element can be the major issue for a jury to decide.

The importance of the causation factor can be illustrated by imagining a wrinkle in our case. Suppose that on cross-examination the surgeon was asked whether he relied at all on the radiologist's conclusion in deciding whether to operate, and that his answer was that he gave the radiologist's report and opinion no consideration but made his decision solely on his own reading of the films. The radiologist's attorney would argue to the judge at the time of his motion to dismiss[2] that the causation element was missing as to the claims against the radiologist and that his client was thus entitled to dismissal. His argument would be that even if the allegations that the radiologist negligently read the films were true, the radiologist's interpretation did not affect the treatment, since the surgeon relied solely on his own interpretation. In other words, the radiologist's treatment did not "proximately cause" the injuries complained of. Under these circumstances, the judge would dismiss the claim against the radiologist due to the lack of the causation element.

When there is conflicting expert testimony on the question of causation, an intelligent jury can choose to agree with the plaintiff's expert on the question of a deviation from accepted practice but disagree with him on the question of the effect of that deviation on the patient, and can render a verdict for the defendant on that basis.

The plaintiff presents his case first. Thus the plaintiff's experts have the advantage of giving the jury its first exposure to expert medical opinion on the accepted standards of practice, how the defendant's treatment measures up, and the effect of the defendant's deviation from accepted practice on the plaintiff. This can be a significant advantage for the plaintiff, since the lay jurors know no medicine and defer to the experts on these matters. They have only these initial opinions to chew on until either the cross-examination of the plaintiff's experts or the testimony of the defense experts convinces them to the contrary.

The key, then, to the definition of malpractice is what the expert medical witnesses in *your* case testify to. Who are they? What about their integrity? Expert medical witnesses are usually paid for their time in court. This remuneration is supposed to compensate them for the time spent away from

2. See Chapter 10, pp. 182-185, 186-187.

their practices, which costs them money. However, there are certain "experts" who spend a large part of their time testifying—some who testify more than they practice, and some who do nothing but testify. Certain physicians become professional expert testifiers due to compulsory retirement because of age, sickness, bad conduct, or poor ability; the lure of the money; or merely the challenge of the courtroom. These professional medical expert witnesses come in all shades of integrity. Some are honest. Some try to get away with what they can but yield when confronted with the truth on cross-examination. Some lie and never recant their testimony no matter what they are confronted with. The latter type is known to render his opinion in favor of whoever retains him first to review the case. Such an "expert" is sometimes hired by an attorney to review a case merely to prevent the other side from retaining him.

I am reminded of the case in which such an expert witness with excellent qualifications unwittingly rendered two conflicting opinions, one for each side. When this situation came to light at the time of trial, the case had to be adjourned by the judge to allow each side to obtain a new expert.

Because of the importance of expert testimony in a medical malpractice case, expert witnesses are usually subjected to strenuous cross-examination. Not all expert witnesses are polished testifiers or bright enough to cope with all lawyers. Even experienced professional expert witnesses can be caught lying, shown to be biased, and have their credibility destroyed. It is the goal of every trial attorney to impeach the adverse expert's opinion through effective cross-examination. From a defense point of view, if cross-examination can impeach the first-spoken expert opinion of the plaintiff's expert and destroy that advantage, the opposite opinion may be inferred by the jury and the stage set for its enunciation by defense experts. It is rare that a defense attorney is able to destroy the credibility of the plaintiff's expert to this degree. It is more realistic to hope that the cross-examination will erode the expert's credibility enough to keep the jurors' minds open and at least amenable to the opinion of the defense experts.

Since the pragmatic definition of malpractice revolves so much around expert testimony, the job of the defense expert is a key one. I think that he has more of a burden to be honest and credible than the plaintiff's expert. He must convince the jury that his opinions concerning the accepted standards of practice, causation, and the propriety of the defendant's treatment are correct after the jury has already heard a contrary expert opinion that explains the plaintiff's injuries. No longer is the jury without any knowledge on the subject, as was the case when the plaintiff's expert began to speak. If the plaintiff's expert came across well, the jury may already have made up its mind. The defense expert must then change the jury's mind. Sometimes jurors think that the plaintiff's expert is courageous to testify against another doctor or a hospital, and therefore tend to believe him. Sometimes, because the jurors identify with the patient, there is a subconscious sympathy for a physician who is siding with the patient against a defendant physician or hospital. In conjunction with this attitude, some jurors tend to be skeptical of a physician coming to the defense of another physician. They look more closely at what he says to see whether he is bending the truth to protect "one of his own." Many lay people believe that doctors stick together to the point of never conceding that another physician was negligent.

Despite this credibility burden, a good defense expert can often convince a jury that the defendant did not deviate from accepted practice despite the plaintiff's injuries. He explains to the jurors the reasons for the presence of any injuries that do exist. Once he does turn the tide of juror opinion in favor of the defendant, the plaintiff usually cannot turn it back in his favor. In order to convince the jury, the defense expert really has to defeat the opinion of the plaintiff's expert; and in doing so he defeats the heart of the plaintiff's case. How does the defense expert accomplish this? By being straightforward, unequivocal, definitive, clear, and honest.

To illustrate this, I will conclude my discussion of what medical malpractice really means by going back to our ulcer case and showing how the patient's claim that she should not have been operated on for nonexistent ulcers was defended.

Normally, each defendant would introduce expert testimony in support of his particular area of treatment. In this case the attorney for the internist felt that the claim against his client was particularly weak and that the expert testimony adduced on behalf of the surgeon would be enough to exonerate his client. Thus he did not call an expert to testify on behalf of the internist. If an expert had been called, he would have explained to the jury that the plaintiff presented a classic history and clinical picture of gastric ulcers. Since the patient's pain became intractable and unresponsive to diet and medication, and the presence of a duodenal ulcer was confirmed by x-ray, it was proper practice to request a surgical consultation. The expert would conclude that in light of the whole picture, including the severity of the patient's unrelieved pain, there was no medical basis to forbid surgery and that proper practice did not require him to do so.

The defendant radiologist in the case was a recognized expert in gastrointestinal roentgenography and testified both as a defendant and as his own expert. He used the films to demonstrate and explain to the jury why what was seen on the x-rays represented an ulcer, not a diverticulum. He pointed out that diverticula are not found in the area of abnormality shown on the films, that diverticula have a different appearance on x-ray, and that since the dye showed an erosion of the duodenal lining it was a classic x-ray picture of a duodenal ulcer. He reaffirmed his interpretation of the films and unequivocally asserted that there was no deviation from accepted radiological practice.

The concentrated attack by the plaintiff on the surgeon (my client) made strong expert testimony in support of his surgical judgment a necessity. This testimony came from the surgeon himself and one other expert. Both stated clearly and unequivocally that, on the basis of the history and clinical picture presented by the patient in conjunction with a positive x-ray, the surgeon had two classic indications for surgery: intractable pain and fear of perforation. They explained that the details of the prior hospitalization were not determinative in the face of the current symptoms and their duration in the current history. The prior films and treatment details were not relevant because the ulcer condition could easily have developed during the time between admissions. Both explained why the reading of the x-ray films as an ulcer and not a diverticulum was correct in terms of location, etiology, and configuration of diverticula, as well as what the surgeon actually visualized when he operated. The expert testimony on behalf of the surgeon definitively asserted that the surgical judgment exercised was within good accepted surgical practice.

The defense lawyers faced one challenge greater than all the other problems inherent in the case: to elicit testimony that would explain to the jury how it could be that history, symptoms, and x-ray all indicated an ulcer, yet none was found at surgery. It was this apparent inconsistency the plaintiff was counting on to win the case.

The doctors involved were positive that good medical practice had been followed. What had occurred was very unusual. The only reasonable explanation was that the ulcer had been small and accompanied by a great deal of spasm, and that during the interval between the taking of the x-ray films and the surgery the ulcer had healed without leaving any distinguishable scar. Despite this healing process, the patient had continued to feel severe pain as a result of spasm. Due to the continued presence of pain, no one suspected that the ulcer had resolved itself; but when the surgeon opened the patient he found no ulcer. It was not considered accepted practice to x-ray the patient again before surgery when only five days had elapsed and the patient was continuing to complain of severe pain.

Explaining this situation became the task of the surgeon. In putting this explanation before the jury, the surgeon had to point out that medicine is not perfect. In replying to direct questions asked by the judge himself, he testified that it has happened that a patient writhing on the floor of the emergency room with all the classic signs and symptoms of a ruptured appendix is rushed to the operating room and opened only to find a benign appendix.

What was the result of all this testimony? The judge dismissed the claims against the internist and the hospital's radiologist due to the insufficiency of the plaintiff's proof, which in this case amounted to inadequate expert testimony against these two defendants. The case against the surgeon went to the jury. The jury decided that it could not find that his surgical judgment constituted a deviation from accepted surgical practice and rendered a unanimous verdict in his favor. The jury had been able to focus correctly on the issue of whether or not his treatment had been a *deviation from accepted surgical practice*, rather than reasoning in hindsight that since no ulcer was found at surgery, the decision to operate must have been negligent. The jurors had kept their minds on the *legal definition* of medical malpractice.

The Nature of the Lawsuit

When we talk about a medical malpractice suit, what are we talking about? What kind of suit is it? In legal terminology, it is a civil suit for money damages, not a criminal action. It is not brought by the state to jail or disenfranchise a physician. It is brought by a patient or his relatives to recover monetary compensation for injuries or death alleged to have resulted from the physician's or hospital's malpractice.

This distinction is important in terms not only of the relief sought but also of the different rules that apply to each category of lawsuit. For example, the burden of proof in criminal cases is greater than that in civil cases. The concept of the burden of proof has been touched on and will be discussed at length in Chapter 10, "The Trial," but at this point it can be characterized as the amount of proof necessary for the plaintiff to prevail.[3]

Some types of treatment can give rise to both an action in civil malpractice and a criminal action. Treatment that involves euthanasia, molestation, abortion, assault, battery, and similar matters *may* be the subject of both civil and criminal actions, depending on the facts, the criminal statutes involved, and the public policy of the state.

For example, the performance of an abortion may be illegal in your state and the subject of a criminal action by the district attorney. In addition, the woman who requested the abortion may decide to bring a civil malpractice suit for damages when she discovers that her uterus was perforated. She sues to be compensated for the damage she claims was caused by improper performance of the procedure. Subjecting herself to an illegal procedure may not necessarily bar her from bringing the civil malpractice suit.[4]

Whether you would have insurance coverage for such a civil suit arising from an illegal act would depend on the terms of your policy. Most policies provide that the company has the right to disclaim under such circumstances. Despite such provisions, some companies will reserve decision on their right to disclaim until there is an actual conviction, depending on the criminal act involved. Other insurance companies will provide legal counsel to defend a physician from a suit arising from activity not covered under his policy, whether criminal or not, with the understanding that the physician will pay all expenses other than the attorney's fee, and will pay any judgment that may be rendered against him. Such service could apply to such activities as seducing a patient, impregnating a patient, libeling a patient, causing a patient to lose his job, causing a patient to become divorced, and the like. Such claims are not covered under most policies but, to promote goodwill, some insurance carriers will help their insureds to defend suits alleging such activities.

The Statute of Limitations

How long are you exposed to a malpractice suit for money damages by any given patient? The length of time you are exposed to suit as a result of treatment is the subject of a constantly changing body of law. It is not uniform; it is subject to each state's individual policy.

3. See *burden of proof* in the Glossary.
4. It does in New York. See *Reno v. D'Javid*, 85 Misc. 2d 126, (Sup. Ct. 1976), *aff'd as modified*, 55 App. Div. 2d 876, (1st Dept. 1977).

There are three basic approaches to the question of the statute of limitations for medical malpractice claims other than wrongful death, which usually has a separate statute of limitations. Each approach has its own problems of fairness and application. These approaches have evolved over the years through statutes and court decisions. This evolutionary process has taken place in each state, and very often one approach is rejected in favor of another or somehow modified so as to become a given state's treatment of the subject. Modifications usually involve incorporating part of a different approach for certain situations in an effort by the legislature or the courts to deal with a situation equitably. Since this book cannot survey the law of each state on medical malpractice, it is up to you to find out your own state's policy.

The crucial question with regard to the statute of limitations is when the period of time *begins to run*. Whether the statute says the period is two, three, or six years, the question is, When do you start the clock running? In legal jargon this is the same as asking when the cause of action[5] "accrues." The statute of limitations starts running when the cause of action accrues.

The Oldest Rule

The oldest rule in this regard is that the statute of limitations (or time) starts running from the commission of the alleged malpractice. Thus, if you treat a patient from August 1, 1967, to August 1, 1976, but the allegations of malpractice are directed at a surgical procedure performed on December 1, 1970, the statute will begin to run from December 1, 1970. If the statute of limitations is three years, it will expire as of midnight December 1, 1973, barring any lawsuit in regard to that surgery, whether or not you are still treating the patient for the same condition, or the patient has had an opportunity to discover, say, that an instrument was left behind. Thus, after December 1, 1973, he can no longer successfully sue you in regard to that act of malpractice—his right to do so has expired.

One problem in applying this rule is determining to what date the allegations of malpractice refer. In the surgical situation one can pin down a specific date, but it becomes more complicated when the allegations refer to negligent postoperative care or failure to observe certain signs and symptoms. Such allegations cover more than one date of treatment, and when the expiration of the statute of limitations can be a matter of days or even hours, determining exact dates is imperative. To isolate within a series of x-ray treatments the date of an alleged improper administration of treatment that caused burns can be extremely difficult, if not impossible. Often the question of the expiration of the statute of limitations cannot be decided until the trial. Sometimes the last possible date the alleged malpractice *could have* occurred must be used in order to be fair to the plaintiff.

Further problems are created in cases involving different allegations of malpractice occurring at different times during the course of treatment. If, for

5. See *cause of action* in the Glossary.

example, a patient alleges not only that the surgery was improperly performed but also that the postoperative care was negligently administered, it is possible that the plaintiff could be barred from prosecuting the allegations concerning the actual surgery but not those concerning the postoperative care. Of course, the postoperative care is usually inextricably connected to the operation, and it is difficult to separate them for purposes of trial, especially in regard to proof as to the cause of the plaintiff's injuries. To keep inferences about the operation out of the case is next to impossible. To ask a jury not to consider the operation itself in its deliberations is unrealistic.

Despite these types of problems, the rule that the statute of limitations begins to run from the "commission of the malpractice" is still used in some states.

The Continuous-Treatment or Last-Related-Treatment Rule

Because of the problems inherent in applying the rule that the statute of limitations begins to run from the commission of the malpractice, and such public-policy considerations as fairness to the patient, many states apply the "continuous-treatment" or "last-related-treatment" rule in regard to the statute of limitations. If after the date of the alleged act of malpractice you continue to treat the patient for the same ailment or a related one, the statute of limitations will not begin to run until the last date of related treatment: the date you last treated the patient for the same ailment or a related one.

If, therefore, the treatment after the date of surgery, December 1, 1970, was related to the surgery, the three-year statute of limitations will not begin to run until August 1, 1976, the date of the last related treatment, and will not expire until midnight August 1, 1979. Thus the patient will not be barred from suing you for any alleged act of malpractice having to do with your treatment from 1967 through 1976 until August 1, 1979, assuming that all the treatment you rendered during this period was for the same ailment or a related one. If the treatment prior to the operation of December 1, 1970, was for an unrelated ailment, the statute of limitations for a claim in regard to the treatment for that ailment would begin to run from the last date of treatment for that ailment or a condition related to it.

Let us assume that the treatment from August 1, 1967, to August 1, 1976, including the surgical procedure of December 1, 1970, was for the same condition. Under the continuous-treatment rule the statute of limitations would not expire until August 1, 1979, even if during 1972 the patient was treated by another physician for the same condition and then came back to you. The statute of limitations applying to this second physician's period of treatment would begin to run from the last date of his treatment in 1972 and expire three years later, in 1975, despite the fact that the patient is still under your care for the same condition. Under this rule you could conceivably be sued in 1979 for something you did in 1967, while the statute of limitations applying to the second physician's treatment in 1972 would have expired some four years earlier, in 1975.

However, there is some authority for the principle that a practitioner such as a pathologist, who should reasonably have expected that his work would be relied on by other practitioners in determining the subsequent mode of treatment, will be deemed as having constructive participation in that subsequent treatment as long as it continues. Thus the statute of limitations as to his treatment will not begin until that subsequent treatment by the other practitioners has ended.[6]

It is less difficult to apply the continuous-treatment rule than the "date-of-the-commission-of-the-malpractice" rule. Though a doctor is exposed to a lawsuit in regard to all his related treatment for a long period if he treats for a long period, the last date of related treatment can be pinpointed with accuracy. Thus the question of whether the suit is barred because of the expiration of the statute of limitations can usually be decided in the early stages of the lawsuit.

You might wonder whether any difficulty arises in deciding what constitutes related treatment. This decision does not usually present much of a problem; if the subsequent treatment can be connected in any logical way to the treatment under attack, the extension of time for the period of subsequent treatment will be granted.[7] The subsequent treatment cannot have had anything to do with the condition for which the earlier treatment was rendered if the commencement of the running of the statute is not to be delayed. For example, if a general practitioner treats a patient for a severe laceration and subsequently for influenza, the statute would begin to run in regard to a malpractice claim for improper suturing of the laceration as of the last office visit when the doctor checked the wound, not the last visit for the flu.

One difficulty with this rule is that a patient may try to circumvent the expiration of the statute of limitations by returning to you for a phony checkup after several years have gone by. He then claims that he is not barred from suing you in regard to treatment rendered years earlier because the statute does not begin to run until the date of the last checkup. It is not always easy to prove the fraudulent nature of such subsequent visits, especially if you see the patient and render some form of treatment for the condition.

In order to prevent such fraudulent circumvention of the statute of limitations, you should be circumspect with any patient who comes to see you after a long absence for no logical reason. Also, the last-related-treatment rule in your state may provide that any such checkup examination performed at the patient's request does not constitute last related treatment so as to extend the statute of limitations.[8]

The main difficulty in applying the continuous-treatment or last-related-treatment rule involves the concepts of agency and partnership. If a person who is your agent renders treatment subsequent to yours, the statute of limitations as to your treatment will not begin to run until the last date of related treatment by

6. See *Fonda v. Paulsen*, 46 App. Div. 2d 540 (3d Dep't 1975).
7. When there is a genuine dispute as to whether the subsequent treatment is "related" to the prior treatment or whether it is "continuous," the issue is decided by the jury after a trial on the issue. See *Fonda v. Paulsen*, 46 App. Div. 2d 540 (3d Dep't 1975).
8. Such a provision was added to the rule in New York in 1975; see N.Y.C.P.L.R. §214-a.

your agent. This means that the statute of limitations as to your treatment is extended by subsequent treatment rendered by your employees or partners. In fact, the statute of limitations as to treatment by any partner in a group would not begin to run until the last date of related treatment by *any* partner or employee of the partnership. If the subsequent treatment by an employee or partner is unrelated to the earlier treatment, the running of the statute of limitations in regard to any claim directed at the earlier treatment will not be delayed.

Consider what this rule means for hospitals. The hospital is responsible for the acts of its employees. If a patient is hospitalized in 1972 and rehospitalized at the same institution in 1976 for the same or a related condition, the statute of limitations as to allegations concerning treatment rendered during the first admission will not begin to run until the last date of related treatment during the second admission (assuming it is the last admission to this hospital for the condition), usually the date of discharge. What if the patient comes back for physical therapy as an outpatient? If the therapy is for the same condition for which he was treated during his hospitalizations, or a related condition, the statute will not begin to run as to any claim directed at any aspect of the entire treatment rendered by hospital personnel until the last date of therapy.

The Discovery Rule

The most recently adopted rule in regard to the statute of limitations is the "discovery" rule. It developed from the argument that in many cases the patient has no way of discovering that malpractice has occurred for a long time. A patient often does not understand what is being done to him, and the results of negligent treatment may not manifest themselves for years. This being so, it is argued that a patient should not be penalized by having the statute of limitations running during his period of ignorance concerning the treatment rendered to him. It is pointed out that in other types of lawsuits the prospective plaintiff is aware of possible grounds for a claim, or at least has had a reasonable opportunity to become aware of such grounds, as the statute of limitations runs, and therefore cannot complain when the statute runs out and he is barred from suing. It is urged that a patient cannot be put in the same position in regard to the malpractice statute of limitations until he is aware of, or has had a reasonable opportunity to discover, possible grounds for a malpractice claim.

The discovery rule is more liberal than either of the other rules. The major problem it raises is the determination of when the patient has had a reasonable opportunity to discover possible grounds for a malpractice claim. Assuming both that the patient has had a reasonable opportunity to discover possible grounds for a malpractice claim *prior to* the date of actual discovery and that the discovery rule is being assiduously followed, the statute of limitations cannot begin to run before establishment of a date when a reasonable opportunity to discover occurred. Except in certain obvious cases, it is extremely difficult to determine when a patient has had a reasonable opportunity to discover possible grounds for a malpractice claim.

Because of this difficulty, there is a temptation to consider the date of actual discovery as the date when the patient had a reasonable opportunity to discover, although the date when the patient had a reasonable opportunity to discover may in fact have preceded the date of actual discovery by a substantial period. In such a case, the running of the statute of limitations would be unduly delayed.

The discovery rule and its rationale have been adopted by some states in regard to *specific* areas of treatment where it is felt that the rule is called for as a matter of equity and that safeguards exist to protect the physician from belated, false, or frivolous claims. New York is such a state, and an examination of its limited application of the rule is valuable.

In regard to medical malpractice claims, New York applies the continuous-treatment or last-related-treatment rule to a two-and-one-half-year statute of limitations.[9] The period was shortened from three years in 1975. In 1969, by means of a court decision, New York adopted the discovery rule in regard to foreign objects left in the patient. The case involved the leaving behind of surgical clamps, undiscovered until after the statute of limitations had expired. The rationale for adopting the discovery rule as to foreign objects left in the patient was explained by the New York appellate court in this way:

Where a foreign object is left in the patient's body, it was pointed out that no claim may be made that the patient's action is feigned and frivolous, that the danger of "belated, false or frivolous claims is eliminated" and that the patient's action rests not "on professional diagnostic judgment or discretion" but upon the actual physical presence of the foreign object in her body . . .[10]

After explaining its reasoning, the court held that a hip prosthesis qualified as a foreign object and that the discovery rule should apply. Thus the statute of limitations would not start running until the patient had discovered, or had had a reasonable opportunity to discover, whichever came first, that something was wrong with the insertion of the hip prosthesis that could be a possible ground for a malpractice claim.

In 1972 another appellate court extended the application of the discovery rule to a case in which an injured pancreas was not discovered until four years after the operation during which it was injured. In extending the application of the rule to this case, the court held that the rationale for application of the rule to foreign objects was operative. That is, the act of malpractice was committed internally, making discovery difficult; real evidence of the malpractice (such as the clamps, prosthesis, or hospital record) was available at the time of the suit; professional judgment was not involved; and there was no danger of false claims.[11] The New York court would not apply the rule to a claim of misdiagnosis based on mistaken readings of biopsy slides.[12]

In 1975 the New York legislature stepped in and tried to clarify the limited

9. N.Y.C.P.L.R. §214-a.
10. *Flanagan v. Mount Eden General Hospital*, 24 N.Y. 2d 427 (1969).
11. *Dobbins v. Clifford,* 39 App. Div. 2d 3 (4th Dep't 1972).
12. *Schiffman v. Hospital for Joint Diseases*, 36 App. Div. 2d 31 (2d Dep't 1971).

application of this rule by amending Section 214-a of its Civil Practice Laws and Rules to read as follows:

An action for medical malpractice must be commenced within two years and six months of the act, omission or failure complained of or last treatment where there is continuous treatment for the same illness, injury or condition which gave rise to the said act, omission or failure; provided, however, that where the action is based upon the discovery of a foreign object in the body of the patient, the action may be commenced within one year of the date of such discovery or of the date of discovery of facts which would reasonably lead to such discovery, whichever is earlier. . . . For the purpose of this section the term "foreign object" shall not include a chemical compound, fixation device or prosthetic aid or device.[13]

This action by the legislature constituted a retrenchment in the application of the discovery rule, in that it eliminated its application to cases involving chemical compounds, fixation devices, or prosthetic aids or devices. Without exploring the reasons for this action in detail, a logical argument can be made that the use of any fixation device or prosthetic aid or device requires careful monitoring, so that the discovery rule should not be required, and that the effect of chemical compounds is so hard to judge that the application of the discovery rule to such cases could unduly extend the statute and lend itself to false and belated claims. Since the amendment does not cover the injured pancreas situation, the implication is that application of the rule to this situation is also withdrawn; however, this is still open to question.

No matter what the scope of the application of the discovery rule, there is no doubt that it can expose you to the possibility of suit for extremely long periods. To return to the original example, if the patient could not have discovered, or did not have a reasonable opportunity to discover, until September 1, 1980, that the surgery of December 1, 1970, had been improperly performed, the statute would not begin to run until that date and would not expire until September 1, 1983, if we assume the normal three-year statute of limitations. Even if the application of the discovery rule required the use of a shorter period, such as one year, the statute still would not expire until September 1, 1981, eleven years after the commission of the alleged malpractice and five years after the last related treatment, which was rendered on September 1, 1976.

Wrongful Death

In addition to the three rules I have discussed for application of the statute of limitations, there is usually a separate statute of limitations for claims alleging wrongful death. If the plaintiff (the next of kin) is alleging that the treatment hastened or caused the death of the patient, he will usually be required to sue within a specific number of years from the date of death. The time period is usually less than the period applicable to other malpractice claims. The reasons for a separate statute of limitations for wrongful death actions are obvious. One cannot sue for wrongful death until the death occurs. This is a date that presents

13. N.Y.C.P.L.R. §214-a.

no difficulties in determination. There can be no further treatment or complication. Once the death has occurred, the plaintiff is put on notice to accomplish his investigation for possible malpractice claims and to sue within the specified period.

Most malpractice actions involve claims (for monetary compensation) for pain and suffering,[14] loss of services, and expenses. A wrongful death action is a claim for the pecuniary loss caused to the next of kin by the negligently caused death of the patient. Sometimes there is a period of pain and suffering before the patient dies. The patient and his family are not precluded from suing for both pain and suffering (including loss of services and expenses) and wrongful death. If they do so, two different statutes of limitations are applied. It can happen that a cause of action for pain and suffering alleging improper treatment can be viable as a result of application of the last-related-treatment rule or one of the other rules, while the cause of action for wrongful death involving allegations against the same treatment is barred by the running of the wrongful death statute of limitations.

Let us consider an example. Suppose your state applies the last-related-treatment rule to medical malpractice claims for pain and suffering caused by improper treatment. The statutory period is three years. The statute of limitations for claims for wrongful death caused by improper treatment is two years from the date of death. The plaintiff is the husband of your former patient, who died after a period of treatment. The husband is suing on his wife's behalf as the administrator of her estate, on his own behalf, and as the next of kin. He is suing on his wife's behalf, or rather on behalf of her estate, to obtain money damages for her pain and suffering. He is suing as her husband to collect money damages for expenses he alleges he incurred for medical care and for the loss of his wife's services as a result of improper treatment. These claims are made in conjunction with the claim for pain and suffering, and the same statute of limitations applies. He is suing as the next of kin for the pecuniary loss he claims he has incurred as a result of his wife's death. The wrongful death statute of limitations applies to this cause of action.

The husband alleges that you misdiagnosed cancer, resulting in pain and suffering for his wife and finally her death on May 1, 1973, which was also the last date of related treatment by you. On April 30, 1976, the husband serves a summons and complaint on you containing his causes of action for pain and suffering, loss of services, expenses, and wrongful death. Your attorney moves to dismiss the cause of action for wrongful death as barred by the statute of limitations. The judge dismisses the wrongful death cause of action, although the other causes of action involving the same treatment are still viable. Why? The wrongful death statute of limitations expired two years from the date of death, or May 1, 1975. The plaintiff husband was one day shy of being one year late in commencing his suit as to the wrongful death cause of action. The normal malpractice statute of limitations would have expired three years from the last date of related treatment, or May 1, 1976; thus the husband plaintiff started his suit in respect to the other causes of action one day before the statute expired.

14. This includes loss of earnings caused by the alleged malpractice.

The Effect of the Patient's Status

What if the patient who wishes to sue was an infant, imprisoned for less than life, or insane for a period of time? Each state handles these situations in its own manner, usually delaying (tolling) the running of the statute of limitations for a certain period. In most states the statutory period will not begin to run until the disability ceases or the patient dies, whichever comes first. For example, in the situations mentioned the statute of limitations will not begin to run until the patient reaches the age of majority, is released from prison, or becomes competent. Using a three-year last-related-treatment rule, if the patient was ten years old when the last related treatment was rendered and the age of majority is eighteen years old, you could still be sued up to eleven years after the last date of your related treatment—that is, up to three years after the patient had reached the age of eighteen. If on the date your last treatment was rendered the patient was institutionalized for insanity for six years, regained sanity, and was released, the three-year period would begin on the date of release and the statute could run for a total period of nine years.

Sometimes the period the statute is allowed to run past the date when the disability or infancy ends is limited. It could be less than the normal period the statute runs. For example, the normal statutory period could be three years but the rule that applies to a disability or infancy situation might allow the statute to run for only one year after the disability or infancy ends. When there is no such limitation, the normal statutory period is merely extended by the period of disability.

There can also exist an overall time limitation that does not allow the extension of the statute of limitations because of infancy or disability to exceed a fixed number of years after the cause of action accrues. Suppose in the above infancy example there was a ten-year limitation of this type. If the last date of related treatment was the infant patient's tenth birthday, the running of the statute of limitations could not be extended beyond the patient's twentieth birthday because of his infancy, notwithstanding the normal three-year statutory period. Without the ten-year (or any other) limitation, the normal three-year period would have started to run from the age of majority, eighteen, and expired when the patient was twenty-one, extending the statute a total of eleven years beyond the accrual of the cause of action (the last date of related treatment).

Each state also has its own rules regarding the existence of the disability at the time the cause of action accrues, rules regarding the commencement of the disability after the cause of action has accrued and the statute has started running, and rules regarding any interruption of the disability. If you have a question regarding one of your patients, you should contact an attorney.

The Importance of Understanding the Statutes of Limitations

It is important that you be aware of, and understand, the application of the statutes of limitations where you practice, so that you know how long to preserve your records and prevent fraudulent circumvention of the statute. This is crucial to malpractice defense, since it is almost impossible to defend yourself without your records of treatment, especially if you are forced to testify that you destroyed your records. Whatever reason you may give for the destruction of your records, it is very easy for a jury to conclude either that you never made any records, which is shoddy practice, or that you destroyed them because they were damaging. The plaintiff's lawyer will encourage such conclusions.

This means, of course, that in certain instances, such as the treatment of infants or incompetent or imprisoned patients, records will have to be kept for a long time. Most records involving foreign bodies will normally be hospital records, and thus the hospital's responsibility. Nevertheless, it will reflect badly on both you and the hospital if those records are nonexistent at the time of trial. You should do what you can to see that they are preserved for the appropriate length of time. Any office records concerning a patient whose treatment included the use of any foreign object must be kept by you for the appropriate length of time, notwithstanding the preservation of the hospital records. A careful study of the applicable statute of limitations in your state for the type of patient and the treatment rendered should dictate how long to preserve your medical records and help you prevent fraudulent circumvention of the statute.[15] If you have any questions about the statute as it applies to the treatment you are rendering or have rendered to a patient, it is worth a phone call to your insurance carrier or attorney.

15. Records should be microfilmed if storage becomes a problem.

2   The Doctor-Patient Relationship

The Legal Principles Governing Your Duty to Your Patients

Implied Representations and Duties to the Patient

The landmark medical malpractice case of *Pike* v. *Honsinger*, decided in 1898, set out in remarkable fashion the implied representations and duties of a physician to his patient:

A physician and surgeon, by taking charge of a case, impliedly represents that he possesses, and the law places upon him the duty of possessing, that reasonable degree of learning and skill that is ordinarily possessed by physicians and surgeons in the locality where he practices, and which is ordinarily regarded by those conversant with the employment as necessary to qualify him to engage in the business of practicing medicine and surgery. Upon consenting to treat a patient it becomes his duty to use reasonable care and diligence in the exercise of his skill and the application of his learning to accomplish the purpose for which he was employed. He is under the further obligation to use his best judgment in exercising his skill and applying his knowledge. The law holds him liable for an injury to his patient resulting from want of the requisite knowledge and skill, or the omission to exercise reasonable care, or the failure to use his best judgment. The rule in relation to learning and skill does not require the surgeon to possess that extraordinary learning and skill which belong only to a few men of rare endowments, but such as is possessed by the average member of the medical profession in good standing.[1] Still, he is bound to keep abreast of the times, and a departure from approved methods in general use, if it injures the patient, will render him liable, however good his intentions may have been. The rule of reasonable care and diligence does not require the exercise of the highest possible degree of care; and to render a physician and surgeon liable, it is not enough that there has been a less degree of care than some other medical man might have shown, or less than even he himself might have bestowed, but there must be a want of ordinary and reasonable care, leading to a bad result. This includes not only the diagnosis and treatment, but also the giving of proper instructions to his patient in relation to conduct, exercise and the use of the injured limb. The rule requiring him to use his best judgment does not hold him liable for a mere error of judgment, provided he does what he thinks is best after careful examination. His implied engagement with his patient does not

---

1. If you are a specialist, this phrase should be interpreted to mean the average specialist in your field.

guarantee a good result, but he promises by implication to use the skill and learning of the average physician, to exercise reasonable care and to exert his best judgment in the effort to bring about a good result.[2]

Despite the age of this opinion, it remains one of the best outlines of your obligations and duties to your patients. It is often used by judges to instruct jurors on the law of medical malpractice. If every physician were compelled to read it after taking the Hippocratic oath, rather than hearing it for the first time from the lips of the judge instructing the jurors deciding his first malpractice suit, there would be a better understanding of the duties and obligations involved in becoming a physician. Understanding medical malpractice has to be a part of every physician's training if he is to render the best possible care and protect himself.

The opinion does mention that a physician must possess "that reasonable degree of learning and skill that is ordinarily possessed by physicians and surgeons in the locality where he practices." It is my opinion that today the locality where you practice can almost never be the basis for a meaningful distinction in respect to the standards against which your treatment will be measured in a malpractice suit. Pragmatically speaking, there is no longer a viable distinction between standards of care in a rural area and an urban area. Except for access to sophisticated machinery, the quality of care in the United States is more or less standard in terms of what is considered acceptable practice in a malpractice context. At one time an expert might have conceded that the standards of care in a small town were lower than those in a large city, but this is no longer true. With better schooling, widespread dissemination of information, and the growth of community hospitals, an expert from the city will come to court in a small town and testify that there is no difference in the standards of care between the two localities and that the defendant cannot hide behind lower standards of care because he practices in a small town. For a defendant to take such a position after such expert testimony has been elicited is next to impossible. The defense must assert that the treatment rendered would be considered within the accepted standards of practice anywhere.

As I stated, the only exception would be a situation in which a smaller community did not have certain sophisticated machinery available for treatment of the patient. The questions then would be whether the physicians involved realized the necessity of the use of such equipment when they should have and whether there was enough time for the patient's transfer to a locality where such equipment was available. If the necessity of the use of the machinery was not recognized when it should have been, or if the necessity was recognized but the patient was not transferred despite the ability to do so, allegations of malpractice will be made.

It is wise to keep your duties and obligations in mind as a general guide when you treat, because you will be held to them if you are sued.

2. *Pike* v. *Honsinger*, 155 N.Y. 201 (1898).

Privileged Information

What has transpired between you and your patient in your professional relationship with the patient as a physician is confidential. It is privileged information. No one is entitled to that information unless the patient has released you from that privilege by means of a release or waiver, such as by bringing or defending a personal injury action in which the mental or physical condition of that patient is affirmatively put in issue.

This means that none of your records, test results, or memory of conversations, events, or treatment—nothing involving your treatment of a patient—can be divulged by you without proper authorization by the patient or the patient's waiver of the privilege. The patient does waive this privilege when he puts his physical or mental condition ''in issue'' in a personal injury action. For example, if the patient sues in a civil action for malpractice, or automobile negligence, or whatever, and claims he has sustained mental or physical injury, or if he is being sued in a civil action for personal injuries and is interposing a defense involving his physical or mental condition (thereby putting it affirmatively in issue), he waives his privilege.

If your patient is suing someone for a whiplash back injury and you are treating the condition, he has technically waived his privilege concerning your treatment of his back. You could be subpoenaed to court by the defendant to testify about your patient's back condition and your treatment without authorization from your patient. The privilege is also waived if, for example, your patient is being sued in a civil action for assault and battery in which it is alleged that your patient punched the plaintiff in the mouth, breaking four teeth, and your patient is defending himself by stating that he is physically incapable of having done so because of a partial paralysis of both arms, which you are treating.

As a matter of practice you must make sure that the patient's physical or mental condition (such as emotional anguish and the like) has been put in issue in a lawsuit before releasing any privileged information. If you are not sure, you should as a precaution request a written authorization from your patient to release the information.

Who Owns the Records?

Notwithstanding the physician-patient privilege, you should not be misled concerning the ownership of the records of treatment. The information is privileged but the records of treatment are your property, not the patient's. The patient is entitled to have copies of these records forwarded to subsequent treating physicians or institutions, but he is not entitled to demand the originals for his own purposes. This principle also applies to x-rays. You may make arrangements for a subsequent treating physician to view your original x-rays if it is too difficult or expensive to have them copied, but the films belong to you. The patient pays for the treatment, not the records. The records are for you to keep track of history, prior conditions, medications, progress, and treatment—in other words, to help you render treatment. They are also yours to substantiate your fee and *defend yourself* against a malpractice action.

All original records, test results, letters, x-rays, and any other data relative to the patient's treatment must be retained *by you* until the statute of limitations applicable to the treatment rendered has expired. The number of physicians whose defense has been prejudiced because they let the original x-rays or records out of their possession is astounding. You can try to claim that you gave them to the patient or sent them to Dr. Jones, but the patient can accuse you of destroying them or even of not making them; and when they are not in court to substantiate your treatment, there is nothing that can help. It is almost impossible to defend a physician who has no records or x-rays.

Medical Contracts and Guarantees

Physicians occasionally fall into the trap of contracting for, or guaranteeing, a cure. You must not contract or guarantee, orally or in writing, to achieve a certain result or cure. You are being retained *to treat*, not to cure. There are important reasons for this distinction. The obvious one is that you can be sued for failure to carry out your contractual obligation or guarantee. If you fail to cure the patient or achieve the result contracted for or guaranteed—at best a subjective determination—you can be sued. What you consider a cure or a good result may not be what your patient envisaged. If an unavoidable complication occurs, preventing the anticipated result, you have still breached your obligation and are liable. The fact that there was no negligence involved is irrelevant. All the patient must prove is your failure to achieve the result contracted for. Your only defenses to such a suit are to assert breach of contract by the patient, nullifying the contract and your obligation; to allege fulfillment of your obligation; and to deny the existence of the contract or guarantee. Remember that by suing for breach of contract the patient does not preclude his also suing for negligent treatment.

By making a contract or guarantee with a patient, you may also be lengthening the period of your exposure to a suit. You have subjected yourself to a possible suit for the duration of the *contract* statute of limitations, which is usually longer than the malpractice statute. Thus your patient could still sue you for breach of contract (a guarantee is a type of contract) after the malpractice statute of limitations has expired. This is unnecessary exposure.

When Does the Relationship Begin? (Refusing to Treat and Abandonment)

All your legal obligations as a physician begin when you accept someone as your patient. Under normal circumstances you do not *have* to agree to treat anybody. Nevertheless, many physicians are at a loss as to how to reject a patient. When someone comes into your office for the first time under nonemergency circumstances (circumstances in which immediate treatment is not required) and you prefer not to treat him, you should politely inform him that you cannot treat him and if possible provide him the names and addresses of several physicians who might be able to do so. You are under no obligation to divulge your reasons, but if he asks, you should attempt to remain friendly and polite. You should not give reasons or carry on an extended conversation. Your nurse or secretary can provide the person with the names and addresses of other physicians to contact. Never give the name and address of just one physician. You are not making an official referral, and your assistance must not be interpreted as such. This person is not your patient. Furthermore, if you give only one name and that physician also refuses to treat the person, there may be ill feeling directed at you. Always give several names and decline any request that you call another physician. This is not your responsibility. You must avoid getting involved in the person's attempts to secure treatment. The point is that if you never accept the person as your patient, you cannot be sued for abandonment. If you start rendering services for the person, such as calling other physicians or taking action that looks like a referral, it is more difficult to disclaim him as your patient. You only provide the names and addresses as a courtesy to prevent bad feeling.

When a person comes into your office with a condition that requires immediate attention, the situation becomes more complicated. Legally, you do not *have* to treat this person *provided* you do nothing to establish the person as your patient. This is totally unrealistic. Morally and ethically, you will be compelled under such circumstances to render some type of assistance that will constitute accepting the person as a patient. Because of the possibility of harm to the person in an emergency situation if you refuse to treat, in my opinion the law will reach to find some action on your part establishing the doctor-patient relationship. Once the relationship is established under the eyes of the law, you are open to a suit for abandonment if you refuse to treat or follow through with your care.

Consider this example. Suppose you were called into the waiting room by your nurse because a woman had come in with an arterial injury to the arm that was bleeding severely. You briefly examined the arm in the waiting room and said, "I can't treat this. You'd better get right over to the hospital." You then told the woman the name and location of the hospital and did nothing further. Did you establish a doctor-patient relationship? When the woman sues you for causing her paralysis, will you succeed with your defense that she was never your patient and that you never treated her? She alleges that if you had put a simple pressure dressing on her arm to stop the bleeding and arranged for her to be speedily admitted as your private patient, she would not have suffered an additional thirty minutes of heavy bleeding, which was enough to cause permanent nerve damage from ischemia. Quite frankly, you are not in a good position from a defense point of view. Your only defense is that the woman was never your patient. However, it is public policy to encourage treatment under such circumstances and the court will probably find that you entered into a doctor-patient relationship by looking at the person's arm, no matter how cursory your examination. The question then will be whether you should have done more for your patient under the circumstances.

It is conceivable that, had you entered your waiting room and done nothing besides asking your nurse who the injured person was and informing the woman that you do not treat such injuries, after learning that the woman came in from the street with an injured arm, you would have a viable defense that you never accepted her as your patient. To suggest that you should handle such an emergency situation this way would be morally and ethically improper. It might not even be legally safe, since a court could reach and find that the acts of your nurse (your agent) in asking the woman what was wrong constituted taking a brief history, and therefore treatment that could be attributed to you. In other words, your nurse's asking what was wrong constituted accepting the person as a patient, and therefore you were obligated to treat the person properly under the circumstances. If you refused to treat, you abandoned "your patient."

Such reasoning by a court is a definite possibility, so the answer is that morally, ethically, and *legally* you must treat under such circumstances. Even if you are a dermatologist, you must render what medical assistance you can and follow through until you are sure that the woman has come under the care of a qualified physician. You cannot leave anything to the patient. In other words, you cannot just come out of your office, take the woman into your treatment room, clean and examine the wound, apply a pressure dressing, instruct her how to get to the nearest emergency room, and send her out the door or put her in an ambulance your nurse has called. That is not being careful. What if the woman misunderstands you and goes to the wrong hospital, a hospital much farther from your office, causing much greater blood loss? What if she faints from loss of blood before she can summon a cab after leaving your office? What if she bleeds more profusely because she is sitting in a cab instead of lying down in an ambulance with an attendant rendering first aid? What if it takes much longer to get to the hospital because she is in a cab rather than an ambulance with a siren, resulting in greater blood loss? What if she gets to the emergency room in an ambulance but has trouble being seen right away without a private doctor, and thus loses more blood than she would have lost had you called and arranged for immediate admission? What if the emergency room is so crowded that the staff there refuses to treat the woman without a private physician and she is sent on to another hospital, resulting in greater blood loss? What if the emergency-room resident butchers her, rather than calling for an attending vascular surgeon, because she has no private physician? What if she is treated at the emergency room but is refused admission to the hospital because she has no private physician, and she starts bleeding again on the way home, resulting in unnecessary further blood loss? All these possibilities and others I have not mentioned could result in a malpractice claim against you because you did not follow through and cover yourself.

What should you do? You should do everything you would do if the person who came into your office with a bleeding arm was your sister. While rendering the best emergency care you can provide, have your nurse arrange for the fastest and safest method of taking the person to the hospital. This might be your nurse's car. It might be an ambulance. Phone ahead to alert the hospital to receive the person. Make whatever arrangements you can to insure speedy competent care. This depends on the procedure at the hospital. Even your choice of hospital is important. You must consider distance, your privileges, whether the hospital staff includes a physician qualified to take care of the emergency, whether the hospital has an adequate emergency room, and the like. If you must choose a hospital where you are not a member of the staff, you must phone ahead and make what arrangements you can as a physician without privileges. Phone a colleague who does have privileges in that hospital and ask him to make arrangements for the person's care. If you know someone in the appropriate specialty for the condition, call him and try to have the patient admitted on his service. If you don't know anyone in the appropriate specialty and you do have privileges, have the patient admitted as your patient but alert the appropriate department at the hospital and arrange for a physician in that department to see the patient as soon as possible. Inquire as to which physician should see the patient and request that he do so. In other words, you must do everything you can to put this person who has become your patient in competent hands, and you must stay with it until you are sure this has been accomplished.

The latter part of the preceding sentence is vital. It is in the follow-through that many physicians drop the ball and end up being sued. By means of the telephone you can make sure that the person has arrived at the hospital, has been x-rayed or whatever, has been seen, and is being cared for by the appropriate physician. Once you have done so and are sure that the care of the patient has been assumed by an appropriate physician, you can consider your obligation over. This sounds like a great deal of effort for someone who was a total stranger, but remember that it is a rare and special set of circumstances that has made the person your patient and entitled her to your best care and effort until she has been put under the care of another physician who is qualified to treat. You would do the same for a patient who had been seeing you for twenty years. Both patients must receive this careful attention and follow-through if you are to protect yourself in regard to any claims concerning your handling of the emergency. There must be no possibility of a claim that a failure by you in any way prejudiced the result or injured the patient.

Suppose you call a vascular surgeon you know, who you feel could treat the woman who has come into your office with a bleeding arm. His secretary answers and tells you that Dr. White is at the hospital and that she will call him there and ask him to see the patient when she arrives. If you think that you have done your job, you are wrong. And if you leave it at that, you are taking an unnecessary chance. Why allow the possibility of being sued to depend on the efficiency of Dr. White's secretary? You should try to contact Dr. White at the hospital yourself. What if you find that he is no longer at the hospital? Because you called yourself, you can immediately arrange for another physician to see the patient when she arrives at the hospital. You do not know whether Dr. White's secretary would have called you back when she found Dr. White was not at the hospital. You cannot expect her to arrange for another physician to receive your patient. Even after you have arranged for another physician to see your patient when she arrives at the hospital, you can call Dr. White later and ask him to see the patient. After you have arranged for a physician to see the patient, you should call the emergency room and inform them that your patient will be coming in and is to be seen by that doctor. Do not leave anything to chance.

You must always remember that your negligence in failing to make sure that a patient receives competent treatment is not excused by someone else's negligence. In other words, you will not be exonerated by the failure of Dr. White's secretary to call Dr. White at the hospital after you called her. You can protest "But I transferred the patient to Dr. White, who treats vascular injuries, and I can't help it if his secretary failed to call him at the hospital" as much as you like, but if you did not follow through, if you let the patient out of your hands after calling Dr. White's secretary, the secretary's negligence will not help you other than possibly to cause her to be a defendant with you. The secretary's negligence does not change the fact that you abandoned the patient before you knew that she was under the care of another physician. If the jury finds that the patient suffered because of your abandonment, you will probably be held most responsible. Similarly, negligence by hospital personnel in handling the patient will not exonerate you for any failure on your part. Rely as little as possible on others to do what you should to fulfill your obligation. Remember that you want to avoid being sued, not to have others joined with you as codefendants.

It is also important to remember that all your efforts to take care of your emergency patient should be recorded and kept as part of the patient's chart, which you have now begun.

A hospital is also subject to suit if some action by the hospital's personnel establishes a relationship with a patient. As you can imagine, a court will lean just as far, if not further, to consider contact by a hospital with a patient as establishing a doctor (hospital)-patient relationship. Even advice from the emergency-room nurse over the telephone may be considered sufficient. I was once forced to contribute toward the settlement of an action on behalf of a hospital I was representing because the hospital had refused to accept as a patient a woman who was hemorrhaging from a perforated uterus, sending her instead to a city institution. This refusal actually put the woman's life in jeopardy but did not cause the main injury for which she was suing, her permanent inability to carry a child as a result of the damage to her uterus from a negligently performed abortion. The woman had sued the abortion clinic where her uterus had been perforated, several physicians involved in the attempt on her, and my client, the private hospital that had refused to admit her for treatment.

The hospital's position was that it had never accepted the woman as a patient and that she was not a private patient of one of its physicians and thus rightfully belonged in a city institution. This position sounded good but was totally unrealistic. By taking the woman's history, examining her sufficiently to diagnose the condition, and advising her to go to the city hospital, the defendant hospital had established enough contact with her to create a hospital-patient relationship. By refusing to treat the woman, forcing her to endure another fifteen minutes in a taxi (she had arrived by taxi) when she was bleeding severely, and causing additional pain and suffering, not to mention endangering her life, the hospital had put itself in an indefensible position.

At the pretrial conference, the judge indicated that he was prepared to rule that the hospital personnel had had sufficient contact with the woman to establish a hospital-patient relationship. This meant that the judge would not dismiss the case against the hospital on the ground that the hospital had never accepted the patient for treatment and therefore could not be guilty of negligent treatment or malpractice. Without such a dismissal, the woman's allegations against the hospital would be decided by the jury. Once the jury heard what had occurred, it was quite likely to punish the hospital severely, no matter what it decided in regard to the other defendants. Under these circumstances, the hospital had to contribute to the settlement despite the fact that the *primary* negligence was that of the incompetent physicians who had ripped the plaintiff's uterus and the abortion clinic that had established no procedures for handling such foreseeable emergencies. Thus, by not understanding its obligations, the private hospital had become involved in a terrible case in which the defendants had to pay a young unmarried woman a great deal of money not only for her immediate pain and suffering, but also for her permanent inability to bear children and all its consequences to her life.

The Good Samaritan Law and the Emergency Situation

At this point you might ask, "What about the Good Samaritan Law?" The Good Samaritan Law applies only to situations outside places of treatment, such as your office or a hospital or clinic. It is designed to encourage the medical profession to render medical treatment to injured persons in emergency situations in which facilities for treatment are not available. It encourages physicians to treat injured persons they encounter in emergency situations as they go about their everyday lives, such as victims of car accidents or heart attacks. It provides that a physician who renders treatment to a person under such circumstances can be sued only for *gross* negligence. Allegations of *ordinary* negligence, which constitute the typical malpractice action, are not sufficient to bring a lawsuit. If, therefore, you stopped on the road upon seeing an accident and improperly set the fracture of one of the victims, you could not be sued successfully. Assuming your state has a Good Samaritan Law, you would invoke it and be granted immunity from such a suit for ordinary negligence. You would have to do something so blatantly improper as to be considered gross negligence (such as amputating the patient's arm for a broken hand) to lose the protection of the statute.

The reasoning behind the Good Samaritan Law is obvious. You, as a physician, must not hesitate or decline to "get involved" in emergency situations outside a medical facility because you fear being sued should the victim fail to recover or end up with a residual injury. Because of the beneficial effect of encouraging medical personnel to render treatment to injured persons in emergency situations outside medical facilities, many states have enacted Good Samaritan Laws. You should know whether the state where you live and work has enacted such a law so that you will understand exactly what rules apply to such treatment.

Notwithstanding the existence of a Good Samaritan Law, it is important that you continue to treat and stay with any injured person you help under such circumstances until other competent medical personnel have arrived and taken over, or until the person has been put under the care of an appropriate physician at a medical facility. If there is no Good Samaritan Law, following through until you are sure that the person has been put in competent hands and will be cared for prevents the possibility of a claim of abandonment. Whether you will desire to, or be able to, continue treating the person after he or she has arrived at a medical facility will depend on the circumstances. Despite the excitement and confusion of any emergency situation, it is important for you to make a record of what you did as soon as possible after your treatment. The record should state the time and date you are making it and contain a complete and accurate statement of your treatment and other related activity. The record should be carefully kept, like any other office record, so that it will be available to support you should there be a lawsuit.

What if the emergency occurs in the hospital where you practice, rather than in your office or on the street? Once you have rendered assistance to another physician's patient, you must continue to treat the patient until you are sure that his or her care has been taken over by another competent physician or until the emergency has passed and the hospital personnel can follow the patient. Suppose, for example, that you are making rounds of your own patients, and that while you are visiting with one of your patients the patient in the next bed begins to have a seizure. Obviously, you would immediately go to the aid of that patient. Once you do so, you must stay with the patient until you are sure someone qualified has taken over or until the emergency situation no longer exists. It is very important that you be sure the patient is no longer in danger before you leave the patient to be followed by hospital personnel without another physician in attendance. It is also important that you immediately make a note in the patient's chart stating what occurred, outlining your treatment, and carefully noting the condition of the patient at the time you left him or her in someone else's care. Always indicate the time and date of your note and the person who has relieved you or in whose care you have left the patient. If you feel that the patient has stabilized sufficiently to be left in the nurses' hands, make sure your note specifies the findings and observations on which you base your conclusion. All your orders should be put in the order sheet with time, date, and signature. All notes should be signed.

Once you are able to leave the patient, you must take steps to insure that the patient's regular physician is notified of what has occurred as soon as possible. This may mean either instructing a nurse to find out where he is and then making it your business to speak to him or seeking him out yourself. It is always best to speak to him personally as soon after the event as possible. You do have an obligation to make a reasonable effort to contact him. If you cannot reach him personally, you should leave word with his office or his service, and at the hospital. Your complete progress note should contain all the information the patient's physician needs. I also advise that you return later in the day or the next day (if the incident occured late in the day) to check on the patient and see if his doctor has been notified or has visited the patient. You should then make a second note in the chart recording what you found when you returned, your efforts to contact the patient's physician, and a description of your conversation with him if you did reach him.

The Covering Physician

Many physicians find themselves involved in malpractice lawsuits because of the acts of other physicians who treat *their* patients. This can happen in a variety of ways, and there is often substance to claims of negligence. When you have a fellow physician "cover" for you and treat your patients in your absence, you have certain obligations to your patients as well as to the covering physician.

Suppose you will be unavailable for a night because you must go to Philadelphia for your daughter's recital. You have two pregnant patients in the hospital who are ready to deliver at any moment. Each patient has special problems that you are monitoring. First, you must insure that the physician who covers for you is competent to handle these patients. You cannot leave these women in the hands of another obstetrician, no matter how qualified on paper, if you feel that he would not be able to handle these patients' special problems or conditions. The patients retained you for your expertise and are entitled to no less in your absence. You should have confidence in your replacement's ability to treat the potential problems you are leaving him.

Second, you must be sure that your replacement has available to him all the information he might need should any untoward complication arise. You must brief him not only on the current status of each patient he might have to treat in your absence, but also on the special idiosyncrasies of each, what to watch out for, what you would recommend or have done in the past for certain problems, where you can be reached if necessary, what persons in the patient's family should be notified in case of emergency, and anything else you deem relevant to the situation. Remember that even if it is unlikely that your replacement will have to treat a patient of yours who has very special problems, it will do no harm to brief him on that patient, just in case she does require care while you are away.

You must also make your office records on every patient available to the physician covering for you. Then if he gets a call from a patient you did not anticipate would need care, or if something you did not tell him about a patient suddenly becomes important, he will thus be able to obtain the information he needs from your office records without any delay. Remember that what he wants to know might not be in a hospitalized patient's chart. It might relate to a prior pregnancy. He might want information to help him decide on a medication or a dosage. If you were treating, you would remember your own past treatment—what you did, what you gave, and how the patient responded—but your replacement does not have the benefit of your prior experience and knowledge. It is impossible for you to give this physician orally all the information he might need, or for him to remember everything you tell him. You cannot foresee everything that might happen during your absence. Although your replacement may never have to look at your records, the benefit of the information therein must not be denied to him. It could save *your* patient's life. It could prevent a lawsuit against both you and your replacement.

Suppose one of the women you had in the hospital when you left for Philadelphia has an idiosyncratic adverse sensitivity to Pitocin. After you leave, she goes into labor. It becomes lengthy and your replacement wants to hasten delivery. He orders Pitocin after checking the patient's hospital chart to see if anything there contraindicates its use. You made no arrangement for him to have access to your office records. If you failed both to note in the chart her sensitivity to the drug and to bring it to the covering physician's attention when you spoke with him, he will think it perfectly proper for the patient to receive the drug. As a result, she loses the child and nearly dies. She sues you for abandonment; failure to retain a qualified substitute physician; failure to properly inform the covering physician of her idiosyncratic sensitivity to Pitocin; failure to prevent the improper administration of the drug Pitocin, causing the loss of her child and her extended illness; and reckless endangerment of her life. She also sues the covering physician, alleging failure to obtain adequate information about her idiosyncratic drug sensitivity, improper administration of the drug Pitocin, and all the rest. She asks for $3 million in damages, claiming that in addition to the extended pain and suffering from her illness and the physical and mental suffering in connection with the loss of her child, her whole life has been ruined. She claims that as a result of this incident she no longer desires sex, she is depressed all the time and must see a psychiatrist regularly, and her marriage is about to break up. Her psychiatrist is prepared to testify that as a result of this traumatic occurrence in her life she needs therapy four times a week at fifty dollars a session for at least the next five years, possibly much longer, and that in his opinion she will never completely get over this incident. Her lawyer will argue to the jury that a beautiful 22-year-old woman who had everything to live for and was expecting her second child has had her whole life, future, and happiness destroyed because you were too "busy" or lazy to inform the covering physician of her drug sensitivity, to provide access to your office records, or even to make the appropriate warning in the patient's hospital chart, before rushing off to Philadelphia for your daughter's recital, and because the covering physician was too incompetent to ask for the necessary information and records.

You can protect yourself from such a nightmare. Suppose that this woman received Pitocin even though you had made a point of discussing the drug sensitivity with the covering physician, recording the substance of the conversation in her office record, which was made available to the covering physician; that you had provided the covering physician a typed sheet listing the special problems and idiosyncrasies to watch for in the patients he was most likely to have to treat, and that the drug sensitivity was on the sheet; that, along with a separate note in the patient's office chart about the drug sensitivity, a copy of the typed problem sheet was included as part of her chart; and that you had entered a warning about the drug sensitivity in her hospital chart. Can you imagine your position when the lawsuit develops? You can testify with righteous indignation about all the precautions you took in regard to the administration of this drug. The covering physician and perhaps the hospital become the only real defendants. The plaintiff may try to pursue an abandonment claim against you, but it can only fail if your covering physician has any qualifications at all. No one can argue seriously that you should not have taken a night off under the circumstances. A good plaintiff's attorney would probably not even sue you. If he did, it would be only to obtain your testimony concerning your precautions to set the case against the covering physician and the hospital. Once he obtained this testimony, he would most likely either discontiue his action against you or submit no opposition to a motion by your attorney to dismiss the claims against you. The covering obstetrician and the hospital (we are assuming a nurse or other hospital employee administered the Pitocin) are in trouble because they did not heed your warnings. Whether the hospital can successfully defend itself by arguing that it was accepted hospital practice for its personnel to consider the covering physician's order as superseding your warning, and therefore to follow the order and administer the drug, will depend on the expert testimony the jury believes. It will not concern you because you protected yourself.

If such precautions are required for night coverage of your practice, they are obviously also required for vacation coverage. The longer the period involved, the greater the likelihood of your patients' individual peculiarities and special problems manifesting themselves, and of complications arising. This only underlines the necessity of securing a competent physician to replace you, providing your replacement with important information on your patients in writing, discussing with him relevant information on the patients he will cover, and allowing him access to your office records.

Legally the covering physician is responsible for his own treatment, because he is not your employee or partner. He is an independent contractor who bills independently for his services and is responsible for his own acts. An independent contractor who deviates from accepted standards of practice in treating your patients is liable for the injuries he causes; you are not. Nevertheless, you *are* responsible for your negligent omissions or commissions in turning over your patients to him. You may be included in a suit by a patient, or impleaded (brought in) by the covering physician on the grounds that you abandoned the patient or failed to supply important information to the covering physician, but if you took the proper precautions and left the patient in the hands of a qualified physician, such claims will not stand up. More often they will not even be made.

Keep in mind that if you give the covering physician *explicit* instructions as to what he must do in regard to a certain patient, rather than advising him of all the pertinent information and leaving it up to him to decide how to treat, you are leaving yourself open to inclusion in any lawsuit involving such treatment. By giving him orders how to treat, you are in effect making him your agent. Therefore, if he carries out your instructions negligently, not only is he liable for his negligence but so are you.

A crafty lawyer once attempted to use this principle incorrectly to force me to contribute toward a settlement of a lawsuit based on the negligence of a covering physician whom he represented. I represented a physician who had left his patients with a qualified covering physician whom he had trained but who was a private practitioner (independent contractor) and not a partner or employee. My client had discussed his patients and left the patients' records with the covering physician so that he would know exactly what the prior treatment had been. My client did not tell the covering physician how he should treat; he left that to the judgment of the covering physician. My client had been administering trigger-point injections to a given patient, using a method he credited himself with developing. He felt these injections had been successful in alleviating the patient's complaints. When this patient presented herself to the covering physician with the same complaints of pain she had made on prior visits to my client, the covering physician opted to administer the same type of injections my client had given, using the same method. Unfortunately, he caused a bilateral pneumothorax that caused the patient to be hospitalized, and he was sued, and with him my client.

I took the position that my client was on vacation at the time of the occurrence and could in no way be held responsible for the covering physician's negligence in administering the injections. The covering physician's lawyer cleverly argued to the judge during a pretrial settlement conference that my client had specifically instructed his client to continue giving these injections to this patient. The case was further complicated by the fact that the covering physician saw the patients in my client's office. He even billed them through my client's office. However, he did receive all the moneys for his services, minus an agreed-on deduction for the use of the office and billing of the patients. The covering physician's attorney used this strange arrangement to bolster his argument that there was an agency relationship. He argued that his client was, in effect, my client's employee, adding that my client had trained the covering physician in his method of giving the injections. The judge liked this argument and told me that I must make a contribution toward the settlement because my client would be held responsible if there were a trial. I admitted that my client had trained the covering physician in his method of injecting. I admitted that my client had agreed to an arrangement that all the patients would be seen by the covering physician in his office and billed by his staff for the services of the covering physician, and that the covering physician would receive all the fees except for a fixed percentage to pay for the overhead of my client's office. I then pointed out that none of these circumstances altered the fact that the covering physician was not a partner or employee of my client. Furthermore, the covering physician had admitted in his deposition that he was not an employee or partner of my client, and that he used his own judgment in deciding what treatment he should render to this patient. I refused to make a contribution toward a settlement on behalf of my client.

Because I made a claim against the covering physician asserting that my client would hold the covering physician responsible for any verdict rendered against him on the basis of the covering physician's acts, the case was eventually settled by the covering physician without any contribution from my client, much to the chagrin of the attorney representing the covering physician.

Obviously, you should leave the treatment up to the covering physician; it is also preferable to have him see the patients in his own office and, what is more important, to bill them himself. An important factor in determining whether the covering physician is your agent or an independent contractor is the billing of the patient. Your covering physician must be able to bill independently for his services. If you bill the patients he sees and then pay him a fixed stipend from the fees collected, he becomes your employee (agent); in effect, you are giving him a salary for seeing your patients while you are away. If you bill, collect the fees, and then share the proceeds with him after deducting expenses, he has become your partner. In other words, if you share in the profits generated by his seeing your patients, you have become partners for that period. Both arrangements must be avoided if you do not wish to be held responsible for any acts of malpractice your covering physician might commit.

Of course, if you are a partner in a partnership (whether it is called a professional corporation or not) and one or more of your partners cover for you while you are away, you as a partner are responsible for any malpractice committed by any other partner. (This would be true even if "your" patients were not involved.) The laws of your state will determine whether your personal assets, in addition to partnership assets, can be put in jeopardy by a suit against you as a partner.

If your covering physician is found to be your employee, you do have the right to sue him for any judgment you incur as a result of his malpractice. The value of this right depends on the insurance coverage or personal assets of your employee physician.

After you return to your patients, you are responsible for learning from the covering physician what treatment was rendered by him. You cannot count on receiving this information accurately from the patient. Whatever treatment was rendered must be entered on your patient's record. If your covering physician did not enter it, you must. If substantial treatment was rendered and the covering physician did not make entries in your records, copies of his records of treatment of your patients should be incorporated into your records. You should have a *detailed* discussion with the covering physician about the treatment he rendered in your absence. This discussion will enable you to decide how best to document the treatment rendered. It is good practice to note in your patient's chart that you had such a discussion and to outline its substance relative to that particular patient. This procedure may be in lieu of obtaining and incorporating copies of the covering physician's records, depending on the substance of the treatment rendered. What is important is that you have accurately documented the treatment for your information and consideration. If you are sued in regard to subsequent treatment, you will be able to prove by producing *your* office records that you were aware of, and took into consideration in continuing your own care, the treatment rendered in your absence. A record is one hundred times stronger than your word, since the record is made before any lawsuit.

If the covering physician has been treating patients who are hospitalized, his treatment should be completely documented in the hospital record. When you return you must make it your business to review the hospital record carefully and then to note in the record that you have spoken with the covering physician and reviewed the hospital record in regard to the treatment rendered in your absence. This can be part of your progress note for your first visit to the patient after returning. By documenting your diligence in this regard, you will be able to prove it should you need to.

If you are the covering physician, you should "cover" yourself by making sure that the vacationing physician does provide you with what you need to know and have at your disposal (such as x-rays and records) to render good care to his patients. If you are asked to cover for a friend but are too busy or not qualified to treat his patients, do not accept. Taking on more than you are able, or capable, to do could result in a malpractice suit against you.

Remember that, covering physician or not, you are responsible for the treatment you render; you must document it as carefully as you would under normal circumstances, in both hospital and office records. If you are sued, you will have access to hospital records; but if you are making entries in the vacationing physician's office records, you must make copies of these entries for yourself. Do not depend on having access to his records. His records may be lost or destroyed. You need those entries to substantiate your bill and to protect yourself. It is proof of your treatment. If you render substantial treatment or treat for a considerable period, you should make original records for yourself and provide copies to the returning physician. Whether you have copies of his records indicating minor or routine care rendered by you, or original records of your own indicating more substantial treatment, you must keep these records for the length of time dictated by the statute of limitations applicable to that treatment.

As a covering physician, you should also attempt to impart the details of your treatment to the returning physician. It is *his* obligation to obtain this information if he is going to continue treatment, but you as the covering physician may be included in any suit resulting from his failure to be aware of such information. In addition to making entries in his office records or providing him with copies of your records, it is always impressive to have a copy of a letter to him containing the important information about your treatment of his patients. I recommend this practice. It is also advisable to note in your records that you have spoken with the returning physician.

It is the responsibility of both the covering physician and the vacationing physician to insure that there is no gap in coverage, and thus no possibility of a claim of abandonment. The vacationing physician must not stop treating or leave for vacation until he is sure that the covering physician has assumed the responsibility of caring for his patients and is available; the covering physician must continue to treat and be available until he is sure that the vacationing physician has returned and resumed caring for his patients.

Direct Supervision

In addition to incurring liability for the negligence of a partner, employee, or agent who is treating according to your instructions, it is possible in some jurisdictions to be held responsible for the negligent acts of someone you are *directly* supervising. If, for example, you were in the operating room instructing a resident how to perform surgery in the pelvis when the resident inadvertently cut a ureter, you could be held responsible if you were standing right there telling him what to do. This is a very difficult principle to apply, and liability would depend on many factors, which could vary depending on the jurisdiction. Usually the resident or intern must be under direct supervision by you, the attending physician, and also he must be performing an act he could not be expected to do competently without supervision.

If such a rule could apply to you, ask your attorney whether it exists in any form in your state. Its existence should not affect your teaching other than to underline the necessity for extreme care in directly supervising your students.[3] Your discretion as to whether someone you are training should attempt a procedure under your direct supervision must be exercised cautiously.

The End of the Doctor-Patient Relationship

Because of the obligations involved in treating a patient, it is important that you understand when those obligations end and how you can end them if you want to. Your first concern must be the possibility of a claim of abandonment or premature discharge from your care. This matter was discussed earlier in connection with refusing to accept someone as a patient. The primary rule is that once you have established a physician-patient relationship, you cannot terminate it unless in your considered opinion no further treatment is required, the patient is being treated by a competent physician in your place, or you have made more than a reasonable effort to see to it that the patient is under the care of another qualified physician.

If treatment is still required but you no longer wish to treat a particular patient, you cannot merely discharge the patient from your care. You have an obligation to make *at least* a reasonable effort to put the patient in the hands of another qualified physician before you can stop treating. This effort can take several forms and will depend on the circumstances. It may involve a direct transfer to the care of a physician whom you know. This option is preferable,

---

3. In Chapter 5, see "Allowing a Resident to Operate on Your Private Patient," pp. 119-120.

and often occurs when a physician is terminating his entire practice. It may mean providing a list of alternative physicians and continuing to treat until a new physician is retained by the patient. You would be obligated to continue to treat only for a reasonable period of time under such an arrangement.

If you are rendering vital treatment that cannot be interrupted without jeopardy to the patient, you must *make sure* before you stop treating that the patient is under the care of another physician who will continue the treatment. The only exception to this principle would be if the patient (or his family) refused to cooperate. Under such circumstances, you must take great care to protect yourself. Your first step is to make all the necessary arrangements for the patient's transfer to another qualified physician's care. You should then inform the patient (or the family, if appropriate), in front of a reliable witness from your office and, if possible, a witness from the patient's family (if necessary, a friend of the patient), of your desire to stop your treatment, your arrangements for transfer to another physician's care, and the medical consequences should the patient (or his family) refuse to accept the transfer or to obtain treatment from another physician of his (or the family's) choosing. It is preferable to conduct this discussion in your office, if possible. It should be tape-recorded, with the patient's knowledge *if at all possible*. The tape is then kept as part of the patient's record. You must give the patient (or the family) sufficient notice of your desire to terminate the relationship to allow the patient a reasonable amount of time to secure a substitute physician of his own choosing if he does not accept the transfer you have arranged. You should then supplement your discussion by documenting your arrangements for transfer and your discussion (including the names and addresses of the witnesses) in the patient's office chart, and by sending your patient a registered letter (a copy of which is kept in his chart) reiterating all the important information already discussed. The letter and your note in the office chart must be carefully dated and must indicate how much notice you have given prior to the termination of your treatment. Once these steps have been taken, you can terminate your treatment on the noticed date, notwithstanding any adverse effect this may have on the patient because of his failure to arrange for continuation of the treatment by another physician.

If the patient wishes to terminate the relationship and leave your care, the situation is different. Although you are not obligated to take reasonable steps to put your patient under the care of another qualified physician or to make sure your patient has secured substitute care, you do have an obligation to inform the patient of your opinion about his or her condition, including prognosis, and the necessity of seeing another physician within a certain period, and to impress on the patient the importance of continuing treatment. This advice assumes you have the opportunity to speak with the patient before he discharges himself from your care. Obviously, it is best if your discussion can be tape-recorded. It should always be carefully documented by a note in the patient's office chart. When possible, it is a good idea to recommend other physicians who could treat the patient, and to include this in your note.

If you feel that leaving your care could have adverse effects on the patient, because you fear a gap in treatment or a failure on the part of the patient to secure the necessary treatment, you should take as many as you can of the precautionary steps outlined in the paragraph on terminating vital treatment, in order to protect yourself from any claim of abandonment or premature discharge. It may be impossible to take all the recommended steps, since the patient desires to leave your care and may not be cooperative; nevertheless, whatever steps you can take will be additional protection. For example, it is unlikely that a patient who wants to leave your care would allow you to transfer him to another physician; it may also be difficult to tape-record your conversation with him, but you can make a careful note in his office chart outlining your discussion and send him a registered letter containing all the necessary information.

If you have no opportunity to speak with the patient and you fear that his condition will be jeopardized because he will fail to obtain treatment, you should send a registered letter to the patient's last known address urging an immediate return to your care, and stating the condition and prognosis, the necessity of seeing a physician as soon as possible, and the importance of continuing treatment. Even if this letter never reaches the patient who has discharged himself from your care, you will have a copy of it in his chart to show that you tried to get the information to the patient and did not abandon him.

If the patient is leaving your care because he is moving to another area, you should do what you can within reason to help him find a new physician. Your efforts to do so must be commensurate with the seriousness of his condition. Obviously, you must work with a seriously ill patient who is going to a new area to insure that he will receive continuous care and that his condition will not be jeopardized. When your patient is not seriously ill, and you do not know a physician to whom to refer him, you must make sure the patient understands exactly what type of physician he must seek out. Offer to speak to the new physician or to send him what he requires, but do not give the patient his chart, x-rays, or other records, or copies thereof, to take with him.

If the relationship with your patient is strained and the patient informs you he wants to end it, it is important not to let pride prevent you from imparting the necessary information. If the patient is in your office, try not to let him walk out in a huff without the information. If he does so, or simply calls in and hangs up before he can be told, or fails to keep his appointment or respond to your follow-up[4] to urge him to come in, you must be sure to send a registered letter containing the necessary information.

I once represented a physician whose patient decided to leave his care because she felt his office was too far uptown and she wanted a physician closer to her apartment. The physician had received a suspicious Pap smear result from the lab, and had taken another smear at the time of the last visit when the patient informed him she did not wish to return. He told her that he had received a suspicious reading from the first smear, that he had not ruled out a malignancy,

_____
4. See pp. 40-41 and Chapter 3, p. 64.

and that she must be under the care of a gynecologist. The specimen taken on the last visit, which also came back from the lab as suspicious, was received after the patient had left the doctor's care. Unfortunately, the physician made no record of his conversation in his office chart and did not send the patient a letter informing her of the result from the last smear. As you can imagine, my client came under sharp attack when he attempted to testify about his warnings to his patient during the trial of her husband's suit for malpractice brought after she died of cervical cancer.

It is important that all meaningful information imparted to a patient, his family, or whoever is controlling treatment be carefully documented in the patient's office chart by means of dated notes. It is equally important that vital information, such as the result of the second smear in the above example, be sent to the patient by means of a registered letter, and that a copy be kept in the patient's record. If my client had taken the time to make an entry in the patient's chart describing his warnings to the patient, and to send the patient a registered letter containing the results of the second smear, reiterating the importance of seeing a gynecologist in light of this second suspicious reading, and explaining the possible consequences, he probably would not have been sued. Certainly no one would have had any reason to doubt his word that he advised the woman to see a gynecologist. No one could argue that he simply did not care and that he let her walk out of his office when he knew she might have a cancer that could, and later did, kill her.

In order to protect yourself from claims alleging abandonment or premature discharge—that is, that you prematurely ended your relationship with your patient—it is imperative that you institute a follow-up system that your secretary or nurse can use to remind a patient who misses an appointment to contact the office for a new one. Such notification should be in writing, by card or letter, and it should be noted in the patient's chart. At least two such cards should be sent in regard to a missed appointment, one immediately after the missed appointment and, if no response is received within two weeks, another indicating the failure to respond to the first card and the importance of making a new appointment. As noted earlier, if you fear that the patient's failure to be under the care of a physician may have serious consequences, a registered letter containing the appropriate information should be sent in lieu of cards.

Individualized follow-up letters, copies of which can be retained in your files, are more impressive than cards as proof of your effort to urge a delinquent patient to return to you and continue treatment. Whichever system you adopt, cards or letters, your overhead will be slightly increased. This minimal increase is well worth the protection from abandonment suits it affords. When you can state unequivocally that *as recorded in the chart* you took the time and trouble to send the patient two cards or letters in a two-week period urging him to make a new appointment after he missed a scheduled appointment, and you can produce the cards you use or carbons of the letters sent, the patient will be hard pressed to prove his claim that you never told him to come back or prematurely discharged him from your care, causing him to suffer a relapse or some other injury.

Remember that although telephone calls noted in the patient's chart can be used to *supplement* your follow-up system, they cannot replace cards or letters, since they are more difficult to prove and do not have the same impact on the patient or in court.

In a hospital situation too, you must be sure to protect yourself against any claim of premature discharge or abandonment. Before you discharge your patient from the hospital, it is essential that you perform a discharge physical examination and record your findings in an explicit note in the patient's chart. It is best to see the patient on the day of discharge and to have your note so dated. Doing so prevents a negative reply to the damaging question, "Did you bother to see the patient on the day you discharged him from the hospital?" It also makes more credible your concern for the patient and whatever instructions you are claiming you gave the patient to carry out on leaving the hospital.

If you see the patient the day or night before discharge, you are leaving yourself open to a claim based on a change in the patient's condition between the time you last see him and the time he is discharged. The resident's failure to pick up some change in the patient's condition occurring after your last visit that would contraindicate the discharge you ordered does not let you off the hook.

If you must see the patient before the actual day of discharge, make your visit as close to that day as you can, and make sure that you have checked all the most recent test results and films by the time of your last visit to the patient. If routine discharge lab tests or x-rays are performed, you must make sure that you have seen them and that you are satisfied the patient can leave the hospital. I stress this in order to eliminate the possibility of the following scenario occurring.

Routine pre-discharge x-rays are taken of a patient on whom you have performed a total hip replacement. Everything has gone beautifully and the patient is having a normal recovery in the hospital. You examine the patient the morning before the day you plan to discharge him and sign the order for discharge the next morning. The patient appears ready for discharge. The last x-rays you examined, taken several weeks earlier, showed normal healing. That afternoon, the radiologist's report of the routine pre-discharge films comes in to the nurse's station and is put in the patient's chart. The radiologist reports finding a suspicious spot on the femur, which he surmises could be Paget's disease or osteomyelitis, and he suggests that further specialized x-ray studies be taken. The resident on the floor does not notice the report. The radiological department does not notify you because it is late in the day, and the radiologist reading the films does not know the patient is to be discharged the following morning. You have left the hospital. The patient is discharged the following morning without your having seen him or his chart. He is driven home. He sits in a chair and then attempts to stand. He hears a loud snap and collapses on the floor in pain. His femur has snapped due to the presence of Paget's disease. After considerable distress, your patient is rushed back to the hospital. Both you and the hospital are sued.

Can you hear the patient's lawyer attacking you? "Doctor, did you bother to examine the patient and his chart before allowing him to leave the hospital?" "Did you examine the most recent films taken of the patient just prior to discharge?'' ''Did you at least call the x-ray department to find out the reading of the routine pre-discharge films before you ordered the patient's discharge?'' ''If you had known about the radiologist's report, or read the films yourself, you never would have discharged the patient, correct, doctor?'' ''You would have known about that x-ray report and had a chance to read the films yourself if you had bothered to see the patient and check his chart on the day of discharge, correct, doctor?'' ''If you had done this, you would have kept the patient in the hospital to ascertain the etiology of the spot shown on the femur and to treat the disease process, correct?'' ''This would have prevented not only all the pain and suffering the patient endured after he went home but also the severe fracture and all its consequences to the patient, correct?'' And on and on.

Furthermore, when a patient is being discharged but must continue his own care at home, it is much better if you examine him on the day of discharge and give him a typed instruction sheet outlining what he is expected to do. You can make a discharge note in the hospital record on the date of discharge stating that *on that day* you examined the patient and his chart, that you approved the discharge, and that you gave the patient oral and written instructions on what to do at home. Your note should list the findings of your examination, and a copy of your written instructions ought to be attached and made part of the record. By taking these steps, you eliminate the possibility of any change in the patient's condition between your last visit and discharge, and reduce the possibility of being sued for improper discharge, failure to give explicit instructions, or abandonment. The only basis for a claim involves your judgment in ordering the discharge at all.

The Patient's Duty to You

Contributory and Comparative Negligence

What if your patient is negligent in carrying out your instructions and thus injures himself? Does his negligence prevent him from suing you for your negligence in treating him? Doesn't the patient have a duty to you to carry out your instructions properly? These questions involve the legal principles of contributory and comparative negligence. You must understand both if you are to understand the effect of your patient's negligence on his malpractice claims against you.

In discussing the legal concepts of contributory and comparative negligence, we again encounter a body of law that has been changing considerably in recent years. In the past, generally speaking, it was the rule that in an ordinary negligence action, such as an automobile accident case, any negligence on the part of the person suing, the plaintiff, would bar his recovery. That is, if the evidence showed that the plaintiff himself was negligent in any way, the plaintiff would lose even if the defendant was also negligent.

Medical malpractice actions were not always treated as ordinary negligence actions when it came to the application of this contributory negligence rule. The question did not arise often, since most claims of contributory negligence involved the defendant's claim that the plaintiff failed to follow instructions or followed instructions improperly, and such allegations are usually difficult to prove. However, when a defendant could prove the plaintiff was negligent, the effect on the plaintiff's suit depended on the policy of the state where the action was being tried. Judges in some states would only allow such proof of the plaintiff's negligence to reduce the amount of the plaintiff's recovery when the defendant was found guilty of negligence. Some judges would permit such proof to be a complete bar to the plaintiff's recovery despite any negligence found on the part of the defendant. This was rare, however, because of the special nature of a medical malpractice suit. I believe that most judges in the past were reluctant to bar the plaintiff completely from any recovery as a result of his negligence because they felt that the parties were not really standing in the same shoes, as two automobile drivers might be, due to the relative ignorance of the plaintiff compared with the defendant physician. The effect of considering the plaintiff's negligence only in terms of mitigation of damages was really to allow the jury to apportion the respective negligence. In other words, it was a system of comparative negligence. This was commonplace no matter who had the burden of proof in respect to the plaintiff's negligence.

Because of this de facto system of comparative negligence being employed in malpractice cases, and the general feeling that contributory negligence as a complete bar to any recovery in a negligence action is unfair, many states have in recent years formally adopted systems of *comparative* negligence for all negligence actions, including malpractice.

Under a system of comparative negligence, the jury (or the judge, if the jury has been waived) apportions the negligence between the parties and determines the amount of damages the plaintiff will receive (as well as the responsibility for the payment of the damages between multiple defendants) in accordance with that apportionment, assuming, of course, that the jury determined that there was some negligence on the part of at least one defendant. If, for example, in a negligence case involving only a plaintiff and a defendant, the jury determined that the plaintiff was 20 percent at fault and the defendant 80 percent at fault, it would award the plaintiff 80 percent of what it decided the injuries were worth, and the defendant would have the responsibility of paying that amount. If there was more than one defendant, the jury would also apportion the fault, and therefore the responsibility, between the defendants. Consequently, if there were two defendants in the lawsuit responsible for the 80 percent awarded to the plaintiff, the jury might decide that one defendant was only 30 percent at fault and the other 50 percent, and therefore apportion the responsibility for paying the amount of the damages accordingly.

Many of the states that have adopted systems of comparative negligence have established the rule that the plaintiff can recover only if he is less than 50 percent responsible. This means that, if the plaintiff is found to be 50 percent or more responsible for his injuries, he cannot recover. (He is barred as if *contributory* negligence were in effect.) Therefore, if the plaintiff is found to be 75 percent responsible for his injuries, he will not be allowed to recover 25 percent of the value of those injuries. In states that apply the comparative negligence principle but have not established this rule, he would be allowed to recover this amount.

As you can see, the effect of the plaintiff's own negligence on his claims of malpractice against you will depend on whether the state where you practice applies the rule of contributory negligence or that of comparative negligence. Whichever principle is applied, the effect of the plaintiff's own negligence on his claim will probably only be to mitigate damages, rather than completely to bar him from recovery if you are found negligent in your treatment. Therefore, the key is still the quality of your care, and you cannot let any action or failure to act on the part of the plaintiff that you consider negligent affect the quality of the care you render. Never count on the plaintiff's negligence to protect you from being sued.

Paying Your Bill

If you render your services as a physician, you are entitled to be compensated. The patient has a duty to pay for the treatment he has received. Nevertheless, many physicians create unnecessary malpractice suits because they do not know how to proceed when a patient fails to pay his bill promptly. If you immediately sue for your bill, you expose yourself to the possibility of a counterclaim or a countersuit against you for malpractice. The amount sued for in connection with the claims of malpractice will greatly exceed the amount you sued for in your action to collect your bill. In addition, you may cause a patient who had not considered suing you in regard to a result he is not happy with to be spurred to action by your suit.

How should you handle this problem? Obviously, you cannot work for nothing. Nor can you afford to make general rules in regard to collecting all bills. You must consider each situation separately. Suppose you are an orthopedist who has performed an ankle arthrodesis on your patient to give him a better platform to walk on. Unfortunately the patient develops a severe infection and has a great deal of difficulty in healing. The result in terms of his walking is not as good as you had hoped for, and he is still being seen extensively for therapy. The patient has suffered much and is not happy. He has decided not to pay your bill of $3,000. Now the ball is in your hands. What are you going to do?

In such a situation you must weigh all the factors extremely carefully. You have spent a great deal of time and effort treating the patient. You feel that you should be compensated for it. At the same time, the patient has endured suffering beyond his worst fears and still has a less than satisfactory result. You yourself had expected a better result. The patient also must pay for and endure unanticipated physical therapy in an attempt to improve on the poor result achieved by surgery. He has not yet consulted an attorney; he just does not want to pay your bill, because he is so unhappy.

If you are sued, the plaintiff's expert will be able to criticize your treatment (fairly or unfairly) because of the complication that occurred and the poor result achieved. Even if you feel that there was absolutely no deviation from accepted practice on your part, whenever there is a complication and a poor result an expert will be able to pick at your judgment and testify that you should have done something differently. Had you done that which he states is proper practice, he will say, the patient would have healed without complication and ended up with a better result. If the plaintiff succeeds in convincing the jury, his pain and suffering, additional expenses, and poor result, which is permanent, will bring a large amount of money as damages.

What should you do? There really is no right and wrong here and I cannot give you a definitive answer, but under such circumstances it *may* be worth your while to let the $3000 go by the boards. You might make a conscious decision to do so after sending several bills and letters requesting payment. If you make such a decision, it is not a rule or a sign of weakness. It is a single decision based on the circumstances of this particular case: the complication, the poor result, the patient's extreme pain and suffering, the therapy required, the patient's dissatisfaction and unhappiness, the risk of being sued and losing, and the potential damages if you do lose. You must also consider the time and effort defending such a suit would cost you, time and effort away from your patients that you cannot bill for. It could, and probably would, cost a great deal more than the $3000 fee. There may also be insurance considerations. If your coverage for the treatment in question is low, you may not want to take the risk of prompting a malpractice suit. You may have a poor record with your insurance carrier and not want to risk losing your coverage. You may not want to risk the possibility of a large verdict on your record, which could increase your premium.

If you do not wish to give up your fee but you want to reduce the possibility of prompting a claim against you for malpractice, you should wait to sue until after the expiration of the malpractice statute of limitations for the treatment for which you are billing, which is usually years less than the statute of limitations for breach of contract. However, in certain cases (such as those involving infants and foreign bodies), this may not be possible because the time involved exceeds the contract statute of limitations within which you must sue for your bill. Consult your attorney if you wish to pursue this course of action.

Whichever course of action you choose, you *must* bill for your services. Even if you are fearful of a suit or suspect that the patient will not pay your bill, you should send it. The receipt of your bill will not normally bring on a malpractice suit by itself, but failure to send it will be considered unusual and a confirmation that you did something wrong. If the patient sues after receiving your bill, he was planning to sue anyway, but if he does not receive your bill he can only conclude that you feel the treatment was improper and not worth billing for. You must send the bill as usual and for an amount that is reasonable for the treatment rendered; the same inference will be drawn by the patient if the bill is unusually low. No bill or a low bill tells the patient that something is wrong and may prompt him to see a lawyer in regard to a possible malpractice claim.

In similar fashion, you must never *tell* a patient that you will not bill or that you will reduce your bill because you achieved a poor result or a complication developed. Such an offer is also a signal to the patient that you did something improperly; even if you are only trying to make a generous gesture out of sympathy, he may suspect your motive and investigate suing you.

You may be thinking that failure to follow up on a bill can also be interpreted as an admission of liability on your part. Not so. As long as you send your bill, you carry out normal procedure and no negative inference can be drawn. You have established in the patient's mind that as far as you are concerned you rendered proper treatment, for which you are entitled to be paid. If the patient is recalcitrant about paying because he is unhappy and you do not follow up on the bill, he may think that you forgot about the outstanding bill or missed following up on it, but he cannot infer that you do not think your treatment worth billing for. He may believe that you are not following up on it because of guilt about your treatment or its result, but he cannot be sure and will probably be satisfied simply not to pay what he owes you. Not paying your bill will probably satisfy his desire to punish you for causing his unhappiness. Obviously, if he wants more and really wishes to sue you, he is going to do so no matter what you do. At least, if he does sue you, no one will be able to ask you why you did not send a bill, in order to plant an inference of guilt or liability in the minds of the jurors. You should never be faced with such a question.

Please do not get the wrong idea. Patients should not be allowed to beat your bills willy-nilly. In the majority of cases many of the risks outlined above will not be present, and the advisable course will be to send your bill, send a dunning letter, turn the bill over to a collection agency, and then sue. This course may be appropriate despite a poor result, complications, the probability of prompting suit, and considerable verdict potential. In many cases you will be able to wait until the malpractice statute of limitations has expired before suing. You have to consider the facts of each case separately, carefully, and realistically. To help you make such a decision in a situation that is not clear-cut, it is always advisable to seek the advice of a medical malpractice defense lawyer.

3   Defensive Practicing

The Philosophy

It is obvious that the modern practitioner must practice carefully, in terms not only of treating patients but also of defending that treatment and protecting himself. This does not mean that you must do the unnecessary in treating your patients, as many people seem to think. Quite the contrary; it means rendering more complete treatment, not overreaching your authorization or ability, following your patients diligently, and the like, in a fashion that makes it easier for you to prove what you have done, if necessary. This will mean extra work for your staff. It will require you to be more conscientious in your note-taking and record-keeping, but practicing this way will improve the quality of your care and give you more confidence in treating, through the security it creates.

In learning to practice carefully, it is vital to recognize that one of the major factors responsible for the recent increase in the number of malpractice suits is the depersonalization of treatment, the lack of doctor-patient rapport. This development is in part due to the increased specialization of medicine and the decreased amount of time spent with patients. Patients are reluctant to sue physicians with whom they have good rapport. When a patient feels that his doctor cares about him, takes a personal interest in his welfare, and is doing his best to treat him, he often will not sue despite a poor result. Sometimes a patient will actually refuse to sue his physician in the face of his lawyer's advice to do so. He may agree to sue a hospital or a radiologist but refuse to allow his lawyer to include his regular physician.

How should this affect your treatment? It means being less greedy. You must make sure that you allot enough time to each patient. Many physicians today simply overload themselves. If a physician tells me that he sees forty patients a day, I know he is breeding a potential malpractice suit. There is no way he can allot enough time to each patient. Even if he works a ten-hour day without any break, he is allotting only fifteen minutes per patient. How can you possibly treat new and old patients, and create some kind of rapport, when you see so many patients and have so little time for each one? You can't. You must make it your business to schedule enough time for your patients, taking into consideration all your activities, including conferences, committee meetings, hospital duties, presentations, and research.

The Emergency Situation

I have already discussed the emergency situation involving a person who is not your patient at the time the emergency comes to your attention. Emergencies also arise involving persons you are already treating. Obviously the same rules apply, since there is no question about the status of these persons. They are already your patients; there is no issue about creating a physician-patient relationship. It goes without saying that you would do everything you could to render and obtain the best care for one of your patients, no matter what the circumstances surrounding the emergency.

If you are operating and an emergency arises, you can and must take the necessary steps to save the patient's life, possibly including surgery not mentioned or authorized in the operative consent. You have *implied* authorization when the emergency requires such a procedure. It is extremely difficult to sue a physician for attempting to save his patient's life in an emergency situation, even if he is not successful. Such a suit would have a basis only if the emergency procedure chosen was wrong or it was improperly performed. The patient or his next of kin can always attack the decision to perform the original surgery or the manner in which it was performed as having created the need for the emergency procedure, but this would not be a suit based on the decision to perform the *emergency* procedure.

Implied authorization or consent also applies to any emergency procedure you might have to perform on a patient in your office or on the street. Even if your patient has not authorized you, or refuses to authorize you, to perform a tracheotomy or give a transfusion in a life-threatening situation, you stand on better legal (not to mention medical and ethical) ground if you do what you must to attempt to save your patient, despite the fact that you can still be sued for assault and battery. If you succeed, the patient must sue you for saving his life. If you fail, you cannot be sued for not trying every proper emergency procedure to save the patient or his limb or organ. As in the hospital situation, you can always be sued in regard to the choice or performance of the emergency procedure, except when the emergency arises outside a medical facility and the Good Samaritan Law applies. If you fail to administer emergency care to the patient because he refuses the treatment, I believe you leave yourself more vulnerable to a lawsuit than if you proceed with the emergency care in an attempt to save life or limb. If you do not render the emergency care and are sued for that failure, you must prove the patient's refusal to have his life saved. This may be very difficult to prove, since it does not make any sense. In addition, you may be severely criticized for allowing a patient who is in extremis and probably not rational to stop you from rendering such important treatment. Do everything you can for your patient in *any* emergency situation, persist until the emergency is over or another qualified physician (either more qualified to handle the particular emergency or just a replacement for you) has taken over the care of the patient, and carefully document everything.

Office Treatment

When defending a case involving office treatment, a defense attorney always finds himself wishing his client had taken certain steps that would have helped to establish his defense. Some of the steps seem obvious, and very often the simplest of precautions are inexplicably not taken. The following section spells out what the malpractice defense lawyer always hopes to discover when he interviews his client for the first time about his treatment in the office.

The Initial Visit

Obtaining Information from the Patient   Office treatment can be subdivided into two categories: the initial visit and the follow-up treatment. When a patient sees you for the first time, it is essential that you have an efficient method for ascertaining and recording important information. There are many methods that can be used. Some physicians interview the patients themselves and either dictate their notes or record the information themselves. Another approach is to have the nurse question the patient initially, by filling in a form or in some other way, and then to interview the patient yourself, having the secretary take notes or making your own notes. Whatever method you devise, it is your responsibility to obtain the important information and to have it *legibly* recorded on the patient's chart.

Many physicians do not pay enough attention to this aspect of the initial visit, and this is a mistake. A great deal of relevant information that could have an important influence on how you treat can be obtained from the patient if you take the time to ferret it out. You should record the reason for the visit, who referred the patient to you, present complaints, a complete medical history, prior treating physicians, prior hospitalizations, prior operations, prior medications, current medications, and anything else you deem relevant. The person obtaining this information must ask sufficient questions to elicit as much as possible from the patient. Very often a new patient is too shy, embarrassed, or ignorant to volunteer information that could be very important to your treatment. This is why it is inadequate to have a patient fill out forms by himself. Patients need to be prodded to remember the past or yield certain information. If a patient is asked direct questions, he will make more of an effort to remember. Also, leading and suggestive questions put bluntly will often remind the patient of an event or medication he had forgotten, and will usually cut through any shyness he may feel about imparting information he considers personal or embarrassing.

For example, consider a patient who may previously have been treated for a heart ailment. He may have forgotten that he took a certain medication for several months. A knowledgeable interrogator will ask, "Did you take this, or this, when you were being treated?" Asking about certain common medications given for the ailment may cause the patient to remember taking them. Very often a patient will think a drug not worth mentioning; this cannot happen when he is being asked directly about various kinds of drugs. A patient may fail to mention drugs such as tranquilizers or birth control pills, but such medication may be important to you in making a diagnosis or deciding what medication the patient should take. If the patient is asked, "Do you take birth control pills?" or "Do you take any tranquilizers?" this information will not go unconsidered. You cannot leave it to the patient to volunteer relevant information.

If, under your system of obtaining and recording this information, someone in your office interrogates the patient and records the information before you see the patient, it is always advisable to put a few of the important questions to the patient yourself. This procedure serves as a check on the information recorded by the person who questioned the patient. Remember that you have more influence with the patient than does anyone else in the office, and that you may get a more complete or accurate answer. If the answers you receive are more accurate, you should question the patient until you are satisfied that your record accurately reflects the important information. You also show the patient you care by asking some questions prior to the physical examination, even if they are repetitive.

If possible, it is best to have the patient arrange for prior x-rays or the results of recent tests to be sent to you before the initial visit. If he has them in his possession, he can bring them with him. This procedure allows you the benefit of such information immediately. It can assist you in questioning and examining the patient, and can help you reach a diagnosis and prescribe treatment. Having such information at the initial visit can also help you decide what additional tests you must order. If these items cannot be sent or brought by the patient by the time of the initial visit, it is, of course, important that they be obtained as soon as possible. When the tests or x-rays are dated or irrelevant because of intervening time or events, or for other reasons, you must not hesitate to order new tests or x-rays. If more sophisticated tests or x-rays are required, make sure that you order them.

Even when you know from the history that prior tests or x-rays will probably not yield much useful information, it is still advisable to obtain the films or test results for comparison with the new tests and x-rays you order if possible. It is extremely impressive (to both a patient and a jury) when a physician has taken the trouble to obtain prior tests or films for purposes of comparison. Often the information thus acquired yields unexpected clues in regard to diagnosis or treatment. Obtaining these items can only help you and can never hurt.

If you find that the tests or films you had taken are inadequate, it is essential that they be repeated, or that different tests or x-ray studies that can better supply you the information you require be taken. Your definitive diagnosis should not be made before you obtain all the relevant information you can. Elective treatment must wait until you have all the data you need.

The Physical Examination   On the initial visit the physical examination is especially important. You should conduct a *general* physical examination before conducting your more specific examination focusing on the area of complaint. It is important for you to have some idea about the general health of your new patient, aside from the specific area you are concerned with as a specialist. Obviously, an internist or general practitioner should make a thorough general examination before concentrating on the area of complaint. By making such a general examination, you may discover a condition that is relevant to your treatment. Or you may discover that you cannot treat or prefer not to treat until the patient is seen by another physician.

I once defended a psychiatrist in an action in which the plaintiff claimed my client should have realized that his patient was suffering from Cushing's disease and therefore could not withstand the administration of mild shock therapy (Sedac), which caused multiple fractures. A reasonably thorough general examination on the initial visit (or a return to your care after a long absence) goes hand in hand with the taking of a complete history and will prevent such claims.[1] It also pays if you are a specialist to keep track of the general physical condition of your patients so that, if some disease develops, you at least have a chance to discover it. For example, the plaintiff in the above case alleged not only negligence in regard to the initial examination but also failure by the psychiatrist to recognize such signs of the disease as significant weight gain, rashes, and puffiness, which the patient developed during the course of his treatment.[2]

I want to make it clear that such a general examination is to be within reason and that, notwithstanding the above example, I do mean a *general* examination. Even an oral surgeon can perform a cursory general examination and note the general condition of the patient. If the patient seems sick or particularly weak, he may want to delay surgery in the mouth and refer the patient to an internist. Depending on the condition, the oral surgeon may want the general health of the patient to be improved through treatment by the internist before he performs oral surgery, in order to reduce the chance of complication. Obviously, if an internist finds a badly infected mouth on his general examination, he should refer the patient to an oral surgeon for treatment.

One method by which a surgeon can ascertain the general health of a patient he plans to operate on is to ask the patient to have his general practitioner or internist and his dentist send him letters stating that the patient is free from infection and an acceptable candidate for surgery. The letters should also include a list of the medications the patient is taking. Notwithstanding such precautions, it is still advisable to have the patient cleared by an internist prior to surgery. The amount of precaution to take in regard to the general condition of your patient (new or old) depends on the circumstances. If a patient is seeing

1. In some cases if you as a specialist (in psychiatry or any other field) feel it would be undesirable or harmful for you to perform a general examination you should insist on an examination by another physician and a report from him.
2. Obviously, if you as a specialist observe unusual signs or are told of unusual symptoms that may be caused by an ailment outside your specialty, you must refer the patient to a physician in the appropriate specialty for examination.

you, her new gynecologist, for a routine Pap test, the extent of the information about her general condition you will require is obviously less than that required by an orthopedic surgeon who is planning to perform a hip replacement.

Your specialized examination must be thorough and complete. Nothing can be taken for granted. If the patient is being seen for a hip replacement as a result of arthritis in the hip joint, you should still examine the entire body for arthritis.

I cannot emphasize enough the importance of carefully documenting what your examination consisted of and all significant findings.

Diagnosis or Working Impression? Sometimes great debates rage between lawyers and doctors as to whether the defendant physician made a definitive diagnosis or was treating with a working impression. This issue is important only in that when you treat with a working impression you are admitting that you have not definitely reached a diagnosis, you are still considering all the data, but for the present time you consider your working impression the most likely diagnosis. This means that you may change your working impression if something occurs that causes you to do so, and that you have not yet made up your mind what the definitive diagnosis is.[3] It is possible that the data will remain nebulous and never lead you to a definitive diagnosis, but this is rare. In most cases the information you collect will allow you to reach a diagnosis. The distinction is not profound and should never become a point of contention between you and an attorney because you use the terms carelessly in your office records or hospital records, or in testifying.

Your Ability to Treat—the Question of Referral After you compile all the information you can from history, materials from prior treating physicians (including prior hospital records, if relevant), examination, and testing (including x-rays), you must make an honest, realistic self-appraisal of your ability to treat the ailment. If the ailment is not within the realm of your expertise, or if you do not feel experienced enough to handle the particular problem, you *must* refer the patient to another physician who is better qualified to treat. If you reach this decision before the information-gathering process is complete, you should stop the process and make the referral. Depending on the circumstances (the uniqueness of the ailment, whether it is an emergency situation, and the like), you may or may not have difficulty finding the proper physician, and the patient may or may not return to your care. Nevertheless, depending on what the circumstances require, you have an obligation to take the appropriate steps to find a physician qualified to treat your patient's ailment and to refer the patient to him.

Communicating with the Patient Once it becomes time to discuss with the patient your diagnosis (or impression), prognosis, recommendations for treatment, possible complications, and risks, the keynotes must be truthfulness, completeness, and frankness. I cannot emphasize enough that the era of the physician who keeps the patient in the dark in order not to scare him away from the treatment is over. A frank and full discussion of such matters is part of allotting enough time to the patient. After you have submitted him to the battery

---

3. A diagnosis can also be changed, but the term connotes you have reached some kind of conclusion.

of questions, the physical examination, and various tests, it is vital to your rapport with the patient that you sit down with him and discuss your findings; your thoughts about prognosis and treatment, both pro and con; and your recommendations. You must also answer all the questions the patient asks during the discussion, so that he will have a good basic understanding of his condition, potential problems, and your proposals for treatment.

What if there is a language problem? You have the responsibility of making a more than reasonable effort to make sure the patient understands you. You undertake this responsibility when you accept for treatment a patient who does not speak your language. The patient must understand what you tell him about his condition, prognosis, and risks, and about your recommendations and instructions.

There are various ways to fulfill this responsibility. If someone in your office speaks the language of the patient, he or she can act as translator. You can request that the patient bring in a relative or friend to act as translator. You must question such a person carefully and be confident of his or her ability to translate. If the patient cannot provide a translator, or you are not satisfied with the proposed translator's ability, hire a professional translator and inform the patient that you will have to bill him for this expense. Make sure that the translator's name, address, qualifications, and relationship to the patient are carefully noted in the patient's chart when you record the substance of your discussion. In order to insure that you can prove you discussed these important matters with the patient and that the information was translated so that the patient could understand you, I recommend that important discussions (such as a recommendation for surgery or other treatment) and a discussion of the risks involved be recorded on a cassette, which can then be kept as part of the patient's records.

I will discuss informed consent in its entirety in Chapter 4, but I must recommend at this juncture that all such important discussions, especially those in which the risks of the proposed treatment are imparted to the patient, be tape-recorded, so as to have irrefutable proof that you discussed these matters with the patient. You must introduce the discussion on the tape by stating the date, the time, and the people present (there should be witnesses to these discussions), and by asking the patient whether he agrees to having the discussion recorded. The names, addresses, and relationship to the patient of all witnesses should also be recorded. The patient's consent to the taping, his questions, your answers, his answers to your questions about whether he understands what you are saying, and his consent to treatment must be recorded to prove that he was present, told you he understood (about risks and the like), and consented to the treatment—in other words, to show the tape was not made fraudulently, in the patient's absence. The consent to the proposed treatment must follow discussion of the treatment, risks, and related matters, and may come in a subsequently recorded discussion (after the patient has had a chance to think about it). Then, a brief review of what has occurred up to that point, including another question to the patient concerning his understanding of the risks previously described to him, should be taped by you and answered by the patient before his consent to the treatment is finally recorded.

Prescribing Treatment   After your discussion with the patient is completed, and the patient has agreed to the treatment you will either commence your treatment or take steps preliminary to the treatment. Invariably, this will involve instructing the patient. Physicians very often neglect this aspect of their care. The key is not to take the patient's intelligence for granted. As far as instructions are concerned, it is safest to treat each patient as if he were an infant. Make your instructions clear and unequivocal. If there is any special regimen you wish the patient to adhere to at home, you should give him written, dated instructions. A copy of these instructions remains in his chart. This way the patient has no excuse. He cannot claim that you did not tell him or make your instructions clear. This is especially important when the patient is supposed to take various medications on a certain schedule or maintain a certain diet. If translation is required, take the appropriate steps. All written instructions should also be translated. If you feel the circumstances merit it and you lack faith in the patient's ability to carry out your instructions, you should hospitalize him so that you can control the care he is receiving and be sure your instructions are being followed.

One extremely important area, about which physicians seem to be inexplicably careless, is medication. This aspect of your treatment merits caution and careful attention. The first area of concern is keeping up to date in regard to medication and its indications and contraindications. You must be aware of the current information in medical literature, manufacturers' inserts, and the *Physicians' Desk Reference.* There is nothing more difficult to defend than an action involving the contraindicated use of medication when the contraindication is noted in both the manufacturer's own insert and the *Physicians' Desk Reference.* Important discoveries concerning the use of medications reported in recognized medical journals, or in revised or new medical texts, can also present difficult defense problems.

If you disagree with the contraindications specified in either the manufacturer's insert or the *Physicians' Desk Reference,* you must be extremely careful to note your awareness of the contraindication and the reasons you feel the use of the medication is called for in the case in question. It is not overdoing it to record in your note the name of an article or study that supports your use of the drug. It is also a good idea to request a written consultation on the use of the drug.

You must be extremely careful about dosages and refills in prescribing medication. You cannot afford to be careless in evaluating weight, age, and the other factors that determine drug dosages. Make the dosage correct for the patient and the effect you desire. And, in this era of the overdose, you cannot permit unlimited refills. The maximum should be one refill. The patient should have to check back with you for more medication, and you should keep a careful record of what and how much you have prescribed. You should not prescribe medication or continue to renew prescriptions without seeing the patient. By keeping careful control over the medication you prescribe, you will prevent a patient from dragging you into a lawsuit because of *his* negligence or habit. You should not be sued for improperly prescribing medication, either overprescribing or negligently prescribing.

Before your new patient leaves your office after his initial visit, he must understand when he is to return and that he should call you immediately if any untoward or disturbing symptoms develop. This is part of prescribing your treatment. It is a good procedure to give the patient an appointment card indicating when he is to return. Appointment dates must be entered in the patient's chart, so you can show that you made an appointment for the patient to return and initiate your follow-up system if he misses an appointment.

Follow-Up Care

All office visits after the initial visit constitute follow-up care. Although these visits are usually less lengthy and involved than the initial visit, the concept of thoroughness must not be disregarded. Do not allow yourself to be loose or careless simply because you know the patient. For example, you should continue to keep track of the general health of the patient and from time to time make another general examination, especially if you suspect the development of a condition that may require the care of another physician.

Medication The above warnings about prescribing medication without seeing the patient and refilling prescriptions indiscriminately apply to follow-up care. If you have seen a patient very recently, are sure of the circumstances, feel confident in the patient, and know how much of the medication the patient received before, refilling a prescription over the telephone may be appropriate; however, extreme caution is merited. Prescribing over the telephone is dangerous and, generally speaking, inadvisable. The patient should be asked to come to the office. There are situations that call for an exception to this rule, but you must be careful. Only you can weigh such factors as the immediacy of the situation, the signs and symptoms demonstrated by the patient at the last visit, the date of the last visit, the type of medication, the honesty and reliability of the patient, and the testing required for the use of the drug. If you do not know the patient well, do not make any assumptions in his favor. Remember that if the patient incurs injury and sues you, prescribing over the telephone will be a liability to your defense. Whether or not the suit involves allegations that you prescribed medication improperly or failed to see the patient, it is particularly damaging from a juror's point of view if the plaintiff's lawyer can harp on the fact that you merely prescribed medication over the telephone and did not "bother" to call the patient in to examine and test him.

Testing a patient under medication at the required intervals cannot be overemphasized. Certain medications require blood testing to insure that the medication is not causing damage. Such precautions may be inconvenient, but they are important. They are usually well documented by the manufacturer of the medication; thus, should the patient develop a problem, it is invariably serious. When your patient develops a drug-caused complication and you have failed to heed the manufacturer's instructions concerning testing, you are in a hole. How can you defend a failure to test? If you did not know that the patient should have been tested, you are negligent. If you ignored the warnings and instructions in regard to testing, you are also negligent.

Such testing must also be scrupulously done in the hospital situation, when there is even less excuse for failure to test or infrequent testing. When a patient on anticoagulant therapy hemorrhages internally, the first thing his lawyer looks at will be the recorded clotting times. I watched a competent, highly qualified physician destroyed on the witness stand because he had not insisted that the requisite number of Lee-White clotting time tests be taken or checked to make sure that they were taken properly. The jury came in with a large verdict for the plaintiff.

Frequency In general, the frequency of follow-up examinations or testing depends entirely on the circumstances of the individual case. The point is that you must stay on top of any condition you are treating until you are satisfied the condition requires no further care or you transfer the patient to another physician's care. It is surprising how many physicians let their patients go after they have been discharged from the hospital. A post-discharge office visit may not be scheduled for months, if at all. If a patient was sick enough to be hospitalized, he should be followed carefully for the initial phase of recovery after discharge from the hospital to insure that no complications develop (and that, if they do, they are immediately recognized and treated) and that healing is proceeding according to plan. Such attention is also reassuring to the patient. I am not suggesting unnecessary checkups, but careful follow-up until the patient is totally out of danger.

Frequent follow-up care is a must in the treatment of potentially serious conditions. It never ceases to amaze me how many gynecologists are still sued for failure to follow up on a suspicious lump in the breast. They will note an abnormality or possible abnormality that bears watching, decide not to biopsy or order mammography, and then not have the patient back to the office for three months. This is pure insanity. Any suspicious signs that bear watching and could mean serious disease require more than the usual follow-up. Follow closely and take action as soon as it is appropriate. Do not allow something to develop between visits that later turns out to be the difference between life and death for the patient.

Consultation If you are stumped or not getting anywhere with your treatment, do not be afraid to use your colleagues in consultation. The best interests of your patient will be served—two, three, or more heads are better than one—and there is no harm in sharing your difficulty dealing with a problem. A request for the opinion of another physician does not reflect badly on your competence. On the contrary, it shows your honesty in dealing with the situation and your concern for the patient's welfare. Remember that you are not bound by the consultant's opinion. If you disagree with it, you can either ask for another consultation from a different physician or state in your note your reasons for disagreeing with the consultant and proceed. Either course shows that you have *considered* everything in exercising your best judgment. Calling in a consultant when you need another opinion will help you if you are sued.

Rehospitalizing When a patient can no longer be followed on an outpatient basis, due to complications or such unanticipated circumstances as a relapse, there should be no hesitancy about rehospitalizing him. You are not only insuring that the patient will get close observation and controlled care; you are also preventing the worsening of any condition because of your inability to treat the patient in your office or in his home. In making your decision about rehospitalization, you must take into consideration not only your ability to treat outside the hospital but also the ability of the patient or his family to handle the condition at home, including whatever treatment the patient or his family is supposed to render at home.

You cannot let the patient's desires or the family's protests alter your opinion. If you feel that the patient should be rehospitalized, *you* must prescribe that course of action. The patient or his family cannot be allowed to prescribe the treatment; if the patient suffers as a result of your acquiescence in their desires against your better judgment, you are put in a terrible position from a defense point of view. If the patient sues you for the injuries that developed, injuries the patient's expert will testify would never have occurred if you had rehospitalized the patient, you cannot defend yourself by saying that you wanted to rehospitalize him but that the patient did not want to go, or that his wife said she could take care of him. The plaintiff's attorney will be all over you. "Who is the doctor here?" "Who has all the training and expertise?" "How can the patient decide what the treatment is going to be?" Even if the jury believes that you wanted to rehospitalize the patient, it will find you negligent for letting him overrule your better judgment.

If the patient or his family *refuses* to accept your decision to rehospitalize, the situation is entirely different. As long as you have recorded your advice and the fact that you informed them of the possible consequences, they must take the responsibility for their actions. If such a situation arises, it is advisable to send them a registered letter stating your opinion and the possible consequences if it is not followed. Depending on the circumstances, you may continue to treat, provided you have taken the above precautions, or you may take the appropriate steps to have the patient put under the care of another physician, as described in Chapter 2. You must not allow the pigheadedness of the patient or his family to make you vulnerable to a claim of malpractice for a failure to hospitalize or rehospitalize, or for abandonment.

Office Procedures

There is no question that good office procedures will help you to practice carefully (defensively) and to render better care to your patients.

History and Physical Examination Forms At the initial visit some kind of history form should be used to insure that nothing is left out and that all the necessary information is elicited. As I have said, the filling out of such a form must not be left to the patient. Inquiries must be made by a qualified person, and you must make a check of the information obtained.

It may also be helpful to have a form on which to record the findings of the initial physical examination. This procedure insures that no aspect of the general examination will be overlooked and it allows for easy determination of the patient's initial situation.

The use of forms for both the initial history and the physical examination helps insure completeness and makes referral to the relevant data easier. Such forms can be especially helpful in such specialties as obstetrics and gynecology, in which initial information is so important.

Providing Authorizations When the history of a patient reveals prior treatment, you should have a procedure for obtaining relevant prior records, test results, and x-rays. Your staff should have blank authorizations for such material. The authorization and form letter requesting the material should be sent out immediately. If the patient is going to bring these materials to the initial visit, your staff should be able to advise him on how to obtain them. All of this can be done by your staff and need not take your time.

Consent Forms It is my opinion that the best way to prevent and, if necessary, defend a suit for lack of informed consent is to have the consent form signed and witnessed in the office after a full and frank discussion that is recorded on tape. There are many advantages to having the authorization or consent signed in your office, as opposed to waiting until the patient is hospitalized. Informed consent will be discussed at length in Chapter 4; suffice it to say here that if you are sued for lack of informed consent, it is vital to be able to prove that you did discuss the risks of the procedure involved and that the patient then agreed to it. If you can tape your discussion and the patient's consent, you have irrefutable evidence. In addition, to support such a tape or cover situations when you cannot make a tape recording, or if for your own reasons you do not want to tape-record these discussions, you must have the patient sign a properly worded consent form in your office in front of reliable witnesses, and you must document in your records the substance of what was said and the names, addresses, and relationship to the patient of the witnesses. This procedure creates the next best evidence to a tape recording of an informed consent. Even if you made a tape, you should never pass up the opportunity to create written evidence. What if the tape is lost or destroyed? What if the judge refuses to allow your lawyer to play it? What if the recording is defective? Your goal is to eliminate any possibility of a claim of lack of informed consent succeeding against you; therefore you should create both types of evidence in your favor. You can do this best *in your office.*

It is very difficult to make an acceptable tape recording or secure a meaningful signature on a consent form when the patient is in the hospital. You cannot control the environment; there is noise and the hustle-bustle of hospital activity. It is difficult both to have the reliable witnesses you want present and to maintain privacy without interruption for the amount of time you require. The patient may claim that at the time of the discussion and the signing he was under medication, or under mental and emotional duress because of the atmosphere in the hospital, and therefore that he did not understand and was unable to make an intelligent decision. By securing the consent in the quiet atmosphere of your office, which you control, you eliminate all these problems and prevent the patient from escaping the consequences of his consent.

Consider for a moment how a patient's signature on a consent form is ordinarily obtained. The patient is usually in the hospital; sometime before the procedure, a nurse gives the patient the form, asks him to sign it, and witnesses it herself. It is very rarely signed in the doctor's presence or immediately after the doctor's explanation of the risks involved. Whatever discussion there was may have taken place months earlier. The patient is probably alone and in bed. Under these circumstances it is easy for the patient, apprehensive about the upcoming surgery or under medication, to claim later that he did not know what he was signing, that he thought it was just another form, and that he did not read what he was signing. He can claim that he forgot what the doctor said months earlier about the risks of the procedure.

If the consent form is signed in your office, not only is it easier to make a tape of your discussion and the patient's consent but also the consent form can be signed immediately (or soon) after the discussion and it can be witnessed by a relative or friend of the patient and a member of your staff. (A witness from your staff would normally be easier to locate at the time of trial than a hospital nurse, who may by then have left the employ of the hospital.) These witnesses will be able to testify that you explained the risks of the procedure and answered the patient's questions, and that the patient read the consent form and knew what he was signing. The patient is not alone (he will be instructed to bring a witness for this visit), not under medication, not apprehensive about a procedure scheduled for the next morning. You have privacy. You control the environment. If the patient is not prepared to make his decision right away, he can take the consent form home and return within a short period. When he returns with his witness, you can again tape-record what is said and answer any questions he might have, and he can then sign the consent form. The form should definitely be signed *in your office*, so you and the witnesses are present and there can be no question that the patient knows what he is signing. Of course, this entire procedure must be documented in the patient's chart.

Obviously, following this procedure for the signing of the consent form is even more important if you do not tape-record the discussion and consent. The consent form is a powerful piece of evidence, and when you have followed this procedure and can produce your office records and possibly witnesses to verify your testimony, the patient will have a difficult time refuting you. He will not be able to prevail. (If there were no office visits prior to the procedure, do what you can to obtain the same conditions for consent in the hospital, using your own consent form in addition to the hospital's.)

The consent form you use should be clear, concise, and couched in simple language, so that a lay person will be able to understand that he or she is signing an agreement to be operated on by you notwithstanding the risks involved. It should state the name of the procedure to be performed and contain a short paragraph authorizing you to take whatever further steps you deem necessary to save life, limb, or organ in an emergency situation. The form should always contain certain important facts, such as anesthesia will be administered or a prosthesis is to be used. It should not contain any legal mumbo jumbo about "waiving all claims arising from the procedure" and the like. This can be left to the hospital form. In my opinion, furthermore, you cannot legally force a patient to waive any of his claims in regard to the procedure by including such language in the consent form.

Basically, a consent form is some evidence that the signer has been informed in writing that there are risks involved with the procedure and that, notwithstanding those risks, he agrees to have the procedure performed. It can be inferred that, before signing such a document, a reasonable person would ask about these risks if they had not been explained. Nevertheless, a consent form usually does not state what the risks are or what risks were discussed, and therefore is not conclusive evidence *by itself* of an *informed* consent.

Office Records It ought to be clear that one of the most important pieces of evidence that can be produced in your defense is your office records. They must be complete and clear. They must be unequivocal. The influence these records have in a court of law is terrific. They are ostensibly made for your own information, to assist in treatment. Since they are not made for legal purposes or to be read in court, they are usually honest and candid in what they reflect. They show the jury a great deal about the physician who wrote them. If they are thorough and well organized, they indicate that the physician and his treatment are also. If they are sloppy and incomplete, they say the same about the physician and his treatment.

I must add at this point that such reasoning by the jury is usually accurate. For the most part, physicians who keep good records are careful and thorough in their treatment. They may not be brilliant, but they are careful and thorough and for that reason easier to defend. You may be wondering why office records could not be made up or doctored after you receive the summons. Do you think you could make up a beautiful set of records after the fact? If so, you are already in deep trouble. Many desperate or foolhardy physicians have attempted either to make entirely new records or to embellish their existing records after learning of a claim. A skilled attorney can always recognize false entries or records. If we leave aside the criminal and ethical consequences of such a fraud, the immediate consequence is to destroy any chance you have of successfully defending the action instituted against you. There is no way to defend a physician who intentionally commits such a fraud. Remember that if your attorney becomes party to the fraud he exposes himself to criminal action and disbarment. If you lie on the witness stand about when you made your records, you add perjury to your fraud. Jurors rightfully resent any attempt to fool them, and they will punish you for it with their verdict.

I have succeeded in convincing a jury to accept an honest and sincere attempt by a physician to clarify his records, but such conduct is extremely dangerous and should not be undertaken. Never alter, clarify, or embellish your records after the fact. Make them clear and complete when you make them and make them immediately after the treatment. Every plaintiff's lawyer will seize any opportunities to assert that the defendant is attempting to cover up his guilt by altering, adding to, or making up new records after the fact. A plaintiff's lawyer does this because it is good strategy. If he can convince the jury that there is something suspect about your records, he discredits you and perhaps wins the case without the jury's actually considering the merits of the plaintiff's claims. The jury may reason that, since you are not being honest, what the plaintiff claims must be true.

Your only defense is the truth. There is no excuse for dishonesty in regard to your records or your testimony. One purpose of this book is to make the truth a strong provable defense to any action leveled against your treatment. (The other is to prevent the initiation of any action against you.) As an attorney I have occasionally encountered physicians who presented me with phony records or wanted advice on lying about an inadequacy, or both. This is sickening, and causes an attorney to lose respect for his client and all confidence in his client's treatment. Such feelings make defending that treatment extremely difficult. If the case cannot be settled, the defense problems at trial become insurmountable. Aside from the effect on the jury of phony records (which will inevitably be exposed), it is almost impossible to argue to a jury that a client's treatment was proper if one does not believe it. Every attorney expects to encounter problems in presenting any defense. Such problems can be dealt with, worked on, and solved when both lawyer and doctor believe in the treatment. When your attorney has confidence in you and believes in your treatment, he can work with deficiencies in your records and other problems; but if you try to "fix" things or cover them up, you destroy any chance for a successful defense. It goes without saying that the same principle applies to entries in hospital records.

When making entries in your office records (or hospital records), use a method that will not lead to confusion if the records are examined by others at a trial. Some physicians maintain that they do not record negative findings, and therefore that the absence of a notation on a given matter means that the physician found nothing abnormal. This method of recording can be misleading and injurious to your position if you are sued. It can also lead to pointless disputes as to what constitutes a negative finding. You should always list *all significant findings*, whether positive or negative. Anything of significance to you—a normal finding, a reduction of a prior finding, or whatever—should be noted. Be careful when there has been little or no change in the patient's condition between visits. You still must state the situation accurately in your note, indicating what has remained the same and what has not, even if your examination reveals only one or two changes. If you state that there has been "no change," you had better mean it. *All* exceptions to such a statement must be noted.

What do I mean by failure to note significant negative findings? Suppose that, when making your note concerning your examination of a man with a stab wound in his arm, you did not record that you listened for a bruit and heard none. Since you did not hear a bruit (which would indicate the presence of an arteriovenous fistula), you considered it a negative finding and recorded nothing. Unfortunately, this method of making notes provides for no written evidence that you did in fact listen for the bruit. This is significant because the absence of a bruit was the basis of your opinion that there was no fistula present at the time of your examination, which was in turn the basis for the treatment you rendered. When you are sued because the man later develops a fistula, the plaintiff's attorney will argue that the absence in your note of any indication that you listened for and did not hear a bruit shows that you never did listen for one, which is a deviation from accepted practice. He will cross-examine you with your record, asking why nothing is written down if you listened for a bruit. You can try to explain that because it was a negative finding you did not record it, but he will then come at you with the significance of the absence of the bruit. You will have to admit that you based your treatment of the arm on the absence of a bruit, which told you there was no fistula present. Now he has you:

Q You mean you based your treatment on a finding that you did not even bother to write down?

A Yes.

Q Doctor, isn't the real truth of the matter that you did not listen for a bruit and merely treated this injury as a simple wound without even considering the possibility of the presence of an arteriovenous fistula?

A No. That is not true.

Q But doctor, there is nothing in your note about listening for a bruit or stating "no bruit," is there?

A No. There isn't.

The plaintiff's lawyer will then confront you with the note of the physician who did hear a bruit and found a fistula and, of course, recorded his finding. The plaintiff's lawyer will argue that his client had the fistula when you saw him, and that the result achieved was prejudiced because your failure to listen for a bruit to detect the presence of the fistula caused the fistula to go untreated for three weeks, until the plaintiff went to another physician, who listened for the bruit, heard it right away, and immediately operated on the arm. He will claim that the plaintiff not only suffered for three weeks but because of the delay in treatment also incurred permanent injury to his arm (such as weakness) that prevents him from working and enjoying a normal life. The truth of the matter is that you did listen for the bruit, heard nothing, and wrote nothing in your note. You cleaned and bandaged the wound after stopping the bleeding. You took preventive action against tetanus and infection and adopted a policy of watchful waiting to see if a fistula might develop. Of course, you did not write down this plan in your note. You saw the patient twice more and everything appeared fine, so you changed the dressing, instructed the patient how to change the dressing, recorded that you changed the dressing and that the wound was healing, and told the patient to return in three weeks for a checkup and to call if there was any change. The patient became dissatisfied because his arm was still hurting. Meanwhile the fistula developed. (Apparently they can take time to develop under such circumstances.) The patient decided to go to another physician, who listened for the bruit, heard it, and operated to correct the problem. In fact, the bruit was in existence only a short time before it was discovered by the second physician, and there was absolutely no prejudice to the result. The truth is that if the patient had come back to you when he was supposed to, you also would have heard the bruit and operated. So you have become defendant in a malpractice suit not because you were negligent in your treatment but because you do not know how to document your treatment.

The case on which this example is based was even more painful to the defendant physician, whom I represented, because not only was there no real delay in operating on the fistula, but the injury involved a minor vessel, which was merely tied off. There was definitely no residual injury or weakness. Nevertheless, the plaintiff never worked after the incident and faked weakness. The plaintiff's attorney had a physician friend testify that the man did have permanent residual weakness. The plaintiff testified that he could not work and wanted compensation for loss of projected earnings for the rest of his life. The defense medical experts stated that there was no malpractice, and that injury to the vessel involved would not create the weakness claimed. The physician who examined the plaintiff for the defense said the man was a fake; there was no residual weakness. Despite what appears to be overwhelming evidence on behalf of the defense, the defendant physician became locked into a desperate struggle involving three separate trials and two appeals merely because of his poor notes.

Pretreatment Photos   In certain specialties pretreatment photos are a wise precaution and should be part of your office records. The most obvious specialty to call for pretreatment photos is plastic surgery. Many suits are instituted because the patient's image of what he will look like is unfulfilled after surgery. The patient becomes upset and claims that he looked better before the surgery. He claims that he has been disfigured. Very often he has forgotten what he looked like and why he came to the plastic surgeon in the first place. Accurate photographs, diagrams, drawings, and careful descriptions of the problem and your intentions will defeat such unfounded claims. You must always be careful to stress that you are not guaranteeing the result. Some hairdressers show their clients what they would look like with various hairdos by making a drawing from a Polaroid picture and placing overleaf drawings of the hairdos on the drawing of the client's face. In this way the client sees what he or she will look like before any hair is cut. The same technique should be used when possible in regard to proposed plastic surgery, as long as it is stressed that the drawing only represents what is intended and not a guarantee of what will in fact be achieved. A dated statement indicating the patient's understanding of this should be written on the picture chosen and signed by the patient. Such a statement should also be included in the consent form used. All the pictures and drawings, obviously, must be kept as part of the patient's chart, along with a note stating what was explained and which drawing was chosen.

Pretreatment photos are also useful for orthopedic surgeons in some cases. Visual aids that show and explain the proposed treatment are invaluable in proving informed consent, demonstrating the condition or deformity that occasioned the decision to perform surgery, and illustrating the severity of the problem you were faced with, as long as precautions such as those outlined are taken to prevent any claim of guarantee. Remember that visual aids do not eliminate the need for thorough notes.

Follow-Up Cards and Letters   As noted in Chapter 2, an efficient system of follow-up cards or letters sent to patients who miss visits is an essential office procedure. Remember that telephone calls noted in the chart are not in themselves sufficient as a follow-up system, since they are more difficult to prove, easily forgotten, and not so impressive to the patient or the jury.

The Hospital Situation

Prehospitalization Instructions

Arranging for your patient's admission to the hospital should be done carefully. If you are relying on the patient to fast or to take medication before admission in order for you to carry out your treatment after admission, this must be spelled out in writing along with your other instructions to the patient. Such precautions protect you if, for example, the patient vomits during the administration of anesthesia, aspirates the vomitus, and dies, and the next of kin sues you for wrongful death. This happened to a physician's wife who came in for her operation after eating breakfast, contrary to instructions. Certainly the patient should be asked by the anesthesiologist whether he or she ate, but if you are the surgeon it is your responsibility to make sure that important instructions are unequivocally and clearly given to the patient. It is not easy to prove that you did so after a tragedy results from failure to follow the instructions you claim you gave so clearly and unequivocally. However, if you can produce a copy of your instructions, clearly and unequivocally written, in conjunction with your office note that you gave the instructions to the patient, you will be better able to defend yourself. Remember that the anesthesiologist's failure to ask the crucial question only makes him another defendant with you and does not exculpate you from your responsibility to give the instructions properly. If you can prove you gave the instructions properly, he becomes the only defendant.

In view of the importance of clear and unequivocal instructions, the possible consequences of a failure by the patient to adhere to the instructions, the unreliability of patients, and the difficulty of proving the nature of the instructions you gave without a copy of them, I recommend that all important instructions (those that would produce serious consequences if not followed) and instructions that involve more than one step be written out for the patient, clearly and unequivocally, and translated if necessary. These instructions must be dated, and copies carefully kept in the patient's chart with a dated note indicating when they were given and what they related to. This procedure applies to all written instructions, prehospitalization or not. Whatever oral instructions you give must be carefully documented as to content, witnesses, and the place where you gave the instructions.

Initial Progress Notes and Orders

An area of hospital care that typically turns out to be a source of embarrassment for physicians when they are interrogated about the admission of one of their patients is the initial workup, including progress notes and orders. There are a number of reasons for this situation. In many hospitals the initial admitting histories and physicals are taken by interns and residents. Very often the resident will also put orders into the chart on admission. Since all this extensive notation is already in the chart, many attending physicians do not put anything in the chart for several days. Some physicians may put some orders on the order sheet. Some put nothing on the chart, not even their initials. This practice gives the plaintiff's lawyer something to work with on cross-examination. He will always start his questioning by asking when you first saw the patient after admission. Suppose you saw your patient on the day of admission and every day thereafter, but did not enter a note in the chart until two days after admission because of the extensive notes of the interns and residents. The plaintiff's lawyer knows this and wants to show that you did not bother to see your patient for two days after her admission and that you were generally lackadaisical about monitoring her condition. The questioning might go something like this:

Q Doctor, when did you first see Mrs. Jones after her admission?

A I saw her on the day of admission and every day thereafter.

Q What did you do when you saw her on that first day?

A I asked her some questions and performed a physical examination.

Q In your opinion, in a case like this would it be important for the attending physician to see the patient every day?

A Yes.

Q Is that because the patient had a serious neurological condition that could change at any time?

A Yes.

Q And if the attending saw any changes in the patient's condition, he would then be able to make decisions about treatment, correct?

A Yes.

Q In fact, for that reason, in a serious case such as this, a good attending neurosurgeon would see and examine the patient on more than one occasion during the day.

A Yes, and I did.

Q How many times did you see and examine the patient on the first two days of her admission?

A At least twice a day.

Q That was because of the seriousness of her condition and the necessity of the attending physician prescribing for the patient and keeping right on top of the situation in case of any change, correct?

A Yes.

Q A good, careful physician would never allow the resident or intern to follow the patient after admission and make the decisions as to the treatment by themselves, right?

A Right.

Q They are only in training and not as qualified as an attending such as yourself, right, doctor?

A Correct.

Q All right doctor, would you please read to the jury the note of your first visit on the day of admission, with the history you took and the results of your physical examination?

A Uh . . . there is no note . . . but the resident has a note . . .

Q Wait a minute, doctor. I am not asking about the resident. You said it was important for the attending neurosurgeon to be there and examine the patient, not just once but at least twice a day. You now tell us there is no note of your first visit. Then would you please read us your note of your second visit and examination, performed on the day of admission, when Mrs. Jones was admitted unconscious?

A I didn't make a note . . . but . . .

Q What? You mean to say that you have no note of that visit either?

A No.

Q Now doctor, it is good and accepted medical practice to make notes of one's visits to and examinations of the patient in the hospital, correct?

A Yes.

Q And one of the reasons for this—correct me if I am wrong, doctor—is that the hospital staff, including the residents and interns in training, who are seeing and treating the patient when the attending is not present, can read his note and know what the attending found on physical examination, what his impression or diagnosis is, and what his recommendations are, correct?

A Yes.

Q And yet you say you saw this patient *at least* twice on the first day of admission, examined her, et cetera, and there is no note to indicate this?

A Correct.

Q Well, surely you put your own orders on the order sheet when you visited Mrs. Jones to make sure that she received the medication, et cetera, that you wanted her to recieve?

A No.

Q You mean there is no order by you on the order sheet for that day either?

A The resident has an order . . .

Q No, doctor, I am not asking about the resident. You say that there is no order by you on the order sheet for that date either, is that correct?

A Yes.

Q Doctor, are you sure that you *did* see the patient on the day of admission?

Defense Counsel: Objection.

The Court: Overruled.

A (angrily) Of course!

Q And you say that you saw this seriously ill patient on the day after admission also, correct?

A Yes.

Q And that was in accordance with accepted standards of practice, right?

A Yes.

Q In fact, good and accepted practice required that you see the patient on these two days, correct?

A Yes.

Q And to not see the patient during these first two days of admission would be a deviation from accepted practice, right, doctor?

A I believe so.

Q Well then, doctor, will you read us, the court and the jury, your notes for your visits on the day after admission, please?

A I did not make any notes for that day.

Q You mean there are no notes in the chart by you for that day either?

A No.

Q None on the order sheet for that day either?

A No.

Q Yet you say that you visited and examined the patient at least twice on that day also?

A Yes.

Q And you told us that it was good practice to make notes of one's visit to the patient, correct, doctor?

A Well . . .

Q Well, didn't you say that, doctor?

A Yes.

Q Don't you follow good practice?

Defense Counsel: Objection.

The Court: Sustained.

Q Doctor, do you make progress notes of your visits to your patients, which you told us is good practice?

A Well . . . yes.

Q I see, doctor. You just didn't do it in this case, correct?

Defense Counsel: Objection.

The Court: Sustained.

Q Let me rephrase my question, doctor. Let me put it this way. You did not write any progress notes *or orders* in the chart for the first two days of this patient's admission during any of the four or more visits you *say* you made to the patient, did you?

A No.

Q That wasn't in accordance with accepted standards of practice concerning making notes in hospital records, was it?

A No. It wasn't.

You have been made to look foolish because you were too lazy to put your own progress notes and orders in the chart. Because of this cross-examination, the jury may believe that you are lying about seeing the patient on those first two important days after admission. It is possible that a nurse's note could save you by placing you there on one day, but you cannot count on this happening, and a nurse's note will not usually say whether you examined or just stopped to say hello. Even if the jurors still believe that you did see the patient, they now have the impression that you are sloppy. You have admitted your failure to adhere to accepted standards of practice in regard to making notes in the hospital record, which are important to the treatment rendered by others. This admission may cause the jury to believe that you have already carelessly endangered the patient and dispose them to believe you guilty of more serious deviations from accepted practice.

It is true that you may have an opportunity through your own lawyer's questioning to explain that you reviewed the resident's notes and orders, found them to be excellent, and therefore felt no need to add your own notes or orders for two days. It sounds logical, but if the remainder of the hospital record reflects that you made progress notes for each of your visits and most of the orders yourself, a seed of doubt about your presence and vigilance during the first two days after admission may be planted in the jury's mind. And the plaintiff's lawyer may then start picking at the resident's notes and orders, which you claim are excellent. There will almost always be something in these notes or orders with which you do not agree, and you will find yourself embarrassed again. Plaintiff's counsel will harp on whatever you disagree with in the resident's note or order, its importance, and your failure to indicate in the chart, for the benefit of others treating, your disagreement with the findings, impression, or recommendation, or to change the order.

As you can see, it simply looks bad not to have your own notes and orders in the chart. This practice is dangerous and can be easily avoided. Even your signature or initial on the resident's note or order, supposedly indicating your review, approval, and presence, is not really an out because either could have been added at any later date—perhaps when the plaintiff claims you came in, two days later. Your initials or countersignature on another's note or order does not prove you saw the patient on that date, since you could have initialed or signed the note or order at any time. This is not true of notes and orders in the chart in the proper chronological sequence between the notes and orders of other attending physicians. Your note in its chronological sequence is proof of when you saw the patient vis-à-vis the other recorded visits in the chart, since there would normally be no room for you to insert a complete note between the notes of other doctors at a later date. And if you attempt to squeeze your note in, enter it out of sequence, or add it on a separate sheet, your fraud will be detected. This is not quite so true for orders. As is true of *any record*, you must not make subsequent additions or alterations. Record your notes and date them (including the time of day) immediately after your treatment. To try to add anything later, even one day later, is a mistake. Making your notes immediately after treatment will also help insure completeness and eliminate any omission because of a faulty memory. Orders should indicate time and date entered.

You can eliminate any attack by the plaintiff in regard to the first days of your patient's hospital admission by entering a complete history, physical examination, diagnosis or impression, and recommendations—in your own hand or typed in by your staff and signed by you—as part of the admitting notes made the day of admission. Make sure that both the date and the time of the visit are clearly written at the top of the note, so as to eliminate speculation as to when you saw the patient on the day of admission. The same thing should be done on all your progress notes and orders. (Make sure that any orders prepared in advance of admission be so dated and put in the proper chronological sequence on the order sheet.) This procedure not only underlines your presence but also eliminates misunderstanding and error in regard to what is to be done for the patient. If the patient fails to receive what you ordered, it will clearly be the responsibility of the hospital. Otherwise, if the resident makes an error in ordering for the patient, especially on admission, the plaintiff or the hospital may try to shift some of the responsibility to you by alleging that you gave the resident the wrong order, were negligent in allowing the resident to give the orders, or failed to check the resident's orders.

You may feel that making your own complete admission note is repetitive and wasteful, but you are failing to realize that by doing so you unequivocally establish that you were aware of the patient's history, took your own expert physical examination, arrived at your own impression or diagnosis, and made your own recommendations for treatment. By making your own admission note and your own orders, you create powerful evidence of your conscientiousness. Such evidence shows you were on top of the situation and controlled treatment from the beginning of the hospitalization. It is wonderful when your attorney can have you read to the jurors your carefully and thoroughly written admission note and orders. This material will demonstrate that you are careful and thorough, and will plant seeds of doubt in the jurors' minds about the plaintiff's claims of your negligence.

One last point must be mentioned here. The fact that you are a senior attending, chairman or chief of the department or service, full professor or assistant professor, or famous author does not exclude you from being sued; nor does it excuse you from making your own notes or orders. The plaintiff and the jury do not care how many interns and residents follow you on rounds or are supposed to make notes on *your* patients. Only you can protect yourself.

The Workup

Many claims in medical malpractice suits involving hospitalization focus on the workup given to the patient in the hospital. Obviously, your workup must be thorough; but what does this mean? It means continuing your testing until you have obtained as much relevant information as you need to treat properly. It means taking further specialized studies to give you more specific information when the results of the routine tests are too general or equivocal. Therefore, if specialized x-ray studies can give you important information that can help you diagnose or treat, they should be taken. I am not advocating unnecessary x-rays; but if tomographs might tell you more about a fracture or the healing process, you should have the benefit of this information.

Claims attacking your workup should fail because they are totally unreasonable. No plaintiff should be able to allege that you merely used a broad-spectrum antibiotic to treat a wound infection rather than culturing the wound to identify the organism and determine the appropriate drug. If a blood culture will yield relevant information, it must be ordered, notwithstanding the fact that it is not done often. The plaintiff must not be able to ask why certain cultures were not made when they could easily have been ordered in time, would not have harmed the patient in any way, and would have yielded valuable information. Make the plaintiff allege that a crazy exotic test should have been taken if he wants to attack your workup. You will be able to defeat such an attack convincingly.

Consultations

Just as you must be thorough in your hospital workup, you must call in experts for consultation when indicated. (A claim of failure to call in adequate consultants should never succeed.) A consultant must be called in when you are stumped, when an area in which you are not so expert as someone else may be involved, when you need a test (such as a needle biopsy) performed by the expert consultant, when you want an opinion about an area outside your specialty (such as having your patient cleared for surgery by an internist), and other such situations. In other words, you should call in a consultant when his opinion is necessary for you to treat properly *with confidence.* Again, I am not suggesting that you run up the patient's bill unnecessarily to protect yourself. I am saying that the opinion of another physician in your specialty or another specialty will often yield valuable information or suggestions for treatment. This opportunity should be taken advantage of. It will help your treatment. If your treatment is prejudiced because you failed to call in a consultant when it is obvious that you should have done so, you are exposing yourself to a claim. Reviewing hospital records, I have always been baffled why some physicians are so recalcitrant about asking for the opinion of another physician when it is obvious that they are having problems in regard to diagnosis or treatment. Do not let your pride or hospital politics prejudice your treatment and expose you to a lawsuit.

Calling in a consultant will not normally hurt the patient, and does have a certain protective value when the consultant agrees with your opinion. It shows that another physician, evaluating the same information about the patient and anything else he can see or obtain, has applied his experience and training and come to the same conclusion you have. For this reason, all consultations must be in writing and made part of the hospital record. This practice is also important to insure that the consultant's opinion reaches you and is available to other consultants and personnel who may subsequently treat the patient. It is vital to you if you are the consultant. You will be able to show by your carefully dated (including time of day) consultation note the time when you received the request for consultation, the time when you examined the patient, the results of that examination, your opinion and suggestions, and the time when it was available to the treating physician. Obviously, if there is emergency or critical import to your opinion, you have an obligation to impart it to the treating physician immediately and not just wait for him to read your consultation note in the chart. If you feel that the patient should have an emergency laparotomy immediately because of a possible ruptured appendix and generalized peritonitis, do not wait for the treating physician to read your opinion; make every effort to contact him and impart your opinion, since any delay might mean the life of the patient.

Noting your opinion carefully and completely is especially important to you as the consultant when your opinion appears to be contrary to that of the treating physician. Should there be a lawsuit and should your opinion turn out to be the correct one in hindsight, your consultation report or note will prove what your opinion was and thwart any attempt by the plaintiff or the treating physician to claim that you agreed with the opinion and treatment that are under attack.

Do not misunderstand me. If you are the treating physician, you should not be afraid to call in a consultant because you fear an opinion contrary to yours. This is not necessarily unfavorable or damaging, as I have previously explained. Several options are open to you in this situation. If you feel that the recommendations of the consultant are correct, you should proceed with them notwithstanding your prior opinion. If you are not sure but feel that the recommendations cannot harm your patient, you may also carry them out. If you disagree with the consultant and feel that it would be dangerous to attempt what he suggests, you can request another consultation from another physician. You can also note that you have carefully considered the opinion of the consultant, and then document why you reject it and why you are proceeding according to your own plan of treatment. This is not negligence. On the contrary, it shows that you are making use of everything available to you, giving careful consideration to everything, and proceeding to exercise your best judgment for the benefit of the patient. Even if it develops that your judgment was incorrect, there is no indication of negligence on your part. An incorrect judgment is not malpractice if you can show that you took everything into consideration and that your judgment was within accepted standards of practice.

As a precaution, when there is a difference of opinion between you and your consultant you should make it your business to discuss the consultant's opinion with him, note that you have done so, and state your medical reasons for rejecting it. Even if you agree with the consultant, it is always impressive if your note states that you discussed his opinion with him.

For example, suppose a consultant suggests that surgery be performed to evacuate a small hematoma in the brain. You discuss his opinion with him and then reject it. Your note should state, for example, that you discussed the consultant's opinion with him and that in your opinion the patient's symptoms are not caused by the hematoma, because they are manifesting themselves on the side of the body controlled by the side of the brain opposite the location of the hematoma, and that the patient is not strong enough to withstand surgery on the hematoma, as shown by his inability to withstand a recent angiogram that caused a deterioration in his condition. This shows good, careful treatment, not negligent treatment.

Cosigning or Initialing

Just as physicians get into trouble by failing to make initial orders and progress notes, they also err by casually cosigning or initialing progress notes, orders, and discharge summaries. Your mark on someone else's work means that you approve it. It means that you agree with what that intern or resident has written. It is a dangerous thing to do because there will invariably be something in the summary, note, or order that you disagree with. The longer and more complicated the note, summary, or order, the greater the likelihood that you will disagree with something in it—something that just might be critical to your defense if a lawsuit develops. Suppose the resident's summary states that the patient was admitted with no significant neurological findings, and you initial it. Later, when you are claiming that you delayed surgery because the patient was admitted with a headache, facial weakness, and nuchal rigidity, which you considered significant neurological findings contraindicating surgery, you look stupid. If that is how you felt when the patient was admitted, how could you initial a discharge summary that says the opposite?

The same effect is created if you sign or initial a resident's note of his admitting physical examination that has omitted these neurological findings you considered so important. You can try to explain away your signature or initials by stating that you signed or initialed as a matter of routine without reading the summary or note. But isn't that foolish? What then is the purpose of signing or initialing it? Doesn't all this make you look lazy and incompetent? Doesn't it cast doubt on the actual existence of the neurological findings on which you based your decision to delay surgery? Doesn't it cast doubt on your credibility?

If there is something incorrect or missing in the summary or note that you are supposed to approve, isn't it obvious to anyone that you would correct it or make the necessary addition in your own note (or at least on the resident's note), so that no mistake in treatment will occur?

Consider what will happen on cross-examination. You will be forced to agree that the purpose of your signature or initial on a note or summary is to signify your agreement with its contents. Therefore, if you disagreed with the contents and did not make the necessary correction or addition, either you appear incompetent or the jury does not believe that the significant neurological findings on which you claim you based your decision to delay surgery were present. The latter belief may be supported if you did not make your own admission note, but merely cosigned or initialed various admission notes by residents and interns not including those findings. The jury may believe that the findings actually developed *after* admission, when you finally entered your own note, but not *on* admission, as you claim. Thus it may appear that you could have operated immediately on admission and saved the patient's life, because the neurological findings were not yet present to contraindicate the surgery. Furthermore, the plaintiff can argue that you sat on your hands and allowed the symptoms to develop instead of operating right away, which amounted to letting the patient die.

This whole problem can be avoided by writing your own notes indicating whatever disagreement you have with the residents' or interns' notes and stating what *you* found. You should not sign or initial their notes.

I frown on making corrections or additions in the margins of the intern's or resident's note, even if you add the time and date in addition to your initials or signature. An attorney can always argue that you added this marginal note at a later date. If you put your comments, corrections, additions, and findings in your own separate note, in chronological sequence, no such assertion of fraud can be made. The time and date of your presence, physical examination, and review of the notes of physicians in training will be unequivocally established. Even if you make no comments or corrections in regard to the notes of others but carefully record what you have found, you will be creating proof of the existence of those findings and indirectly demonstrating the errors and omissions in the notes of the interns and residents that do not agree with or contain all of your findings. Your note will be given more weight because you are not in training and you will not have approved any incorrect notes.

The same advice applies to summaries. You eliminate the problems created by signing or initialing incorrect summaries dictated by residents or interns by refraining from doing so and making your own summaries. This is important because the typical summary is lengthy and you are unlikely to take the time to examine it carefully to insure that it is accurate and complete. If your summary is not accurate or complete, you have no one to blame but yourself. If you remember that the summary is an outline of the treatment you rendered and ordered for your patient in the hospital that may be read and quoted to a jury, you will be more careful in making it.

If you do detect an error in a note, summary, or order, never cross anything out. Everything should be corrected in a separate writing. Otherwise if you are accused of covering up a damaging or erroneous entry you will never be able to prove when you discovered and corrected the error.

It is always wiser to do your own writing than to initial or sign the work of someone else. This is true even if you believe that the note, summary, or order of the intern or resident is accurate and complete. First of all, you eliminate any question as to when you signed or initialed the writing. Second, you create powerful evidence on your own behalf that will not only unequivocally establish your presence, actions, and findings but will also allow your treatment to be judged by what *you* describe in your writing. You cannot be effectively cross-examined with the writing of a less experienced intern or resident that you supposedly approved. Finally, your own writing in the chart establishes your involvement with the patient in the eyes of the jury.

This advice applies to orders as much as to summaries or notes. When you initial or cosign an incorrect or improper order, you approve the order. You join in any responsibility for injury to the patient caused by the carrying out of that order. You cannot escape that responsibility by claiming that you signed or initialed the order as a matter of routine and did not check it carefully because you were too busy or assumed that the resident knew what he was doing. In practicing carefully, you should always try to eliminate the possibility of error. This means relying on others as little as possible. If a resident or intern is competent enought to put orders in the the chart he (and his employer, the hospital) can take the responsibility for that order until your responsibility for checking on what your patient is receiving supersedes it.

Checking the Orders

Each time you see your patient, you as a treating physician have the responsibility of checking to see that he is receiving what you want him to receive, as ordered by you and others. This means checking not only the order sheet but also the medication sheets and any other portions of the hospital record (including nurses' notes, physical therapy notes, x-ray reports, and lab reports) that will reveal whether your orders and those of others treating the patient are being properly carried out. It also means examining what the interns or residents have ordered since your last visit and deciding whether you wish to make any changes in regard to what the patient is or is not receiving. You must be careful to insure that all changes in medication and discontinuances of medication are not only clearly ordered but also carried out *as ordered*. A jury will not hesitate to hold you responsible for failing to check the chart to make sure that a drug was discontinued or a new drug started, according to the orders in the chart, even if the orders are not yours.

In fact, I was involved in a case in which the jury seized on such a failure as a basis for holding a neurosurgeon liable for the wrongful death of a patient despite the fact that the failure was irrelevant to the death. A drug that had been ordered during the last phases of a terminal condition had not been given for three days prior to the patient's death. The thrust of the plaintiff's claim against the neurosurgeon was the failure to operate. The jurors had no trouble accepting the neurosurgeon's position that surgery was contraindicated, but they were upset about the patient's failure to receive the drug that was ordered. This drug had been ordered by the internist treating the patient. All the experts (including the plaintiff's experts) agreed that the administration of the drug would at that point have had little if any effect on the outcome. Notwithstanding this testimony and the fact that the order for the drug was made by the internist who was treating the patient, the jury found the neurosurgeon responsible, in addition to the internist and the hospital, for failing to discover this error. The jurors felt it was the neurosurgeon's responsibility to make sure that the orders were carried out properly when he came to see his patient.

You may be wondering about the hospital's obligation to make sure that orders are carried out. The hospital does have an obligation to carry out the orders, but this does not absolve you of your responsibility to see that it has done its job properly (through its personnel) when you see your patient. For example, when you put an order on the order sheet in the morning, you are entitled to assume, and rely on the assumption, that it will be carried out by the hospital staff until your next visit to the patient—but you cannot assume or rely on it for three days. If you do and the order has not been carried out properly for three days, or not at all, you are in a difficult situation from a defense point of view. It will be brought out that you saw the patient anywhere from three to ten times during the three days, but did not bother to check whether the order was being carried out properly. It will be shown that you could have prevented the administration of an improper dosage of medication, the improper discontinuance of a medication, or whatever happened, as early as the next time you saw the patient, which could have been the afternoon of the day your order was put in the chart. It is true that the hospital must assume responsibility for the failure of its staff during the time you are not with the patient (between your visits), but you have the responsibility of following your patient closely and making sure whenever you can that the treatment ordered for your patient is being given as ordered. You cannot be held responsible for the carrying out of orders from the time you saw the patient and either made the order or checked to see that everything was being given as ordered until your next visit; that responsibility belongs to the hospital. But you must check each time you see the patient that the orders are being carried out properly and that the orders entered by the resident or intern in your absence are correct. By doing so you again shift the full responsibility for the carrying out of the orders to the hospital. You can only correct the errors when you visit your patient.

One last point must be mentioned. When you check the order sheet at each visit, you must also check the orders written by other *attending* physicians treating the patient to make sure that you agree with them and that nothing ordered by another physician will have a deleterious effect on the aspect of the patient's care you are managing. If you disagree with an order of another attending physician, you must discuss the order with your colleague immediately and resolve the problem so that the patient's overall treatment is not compromised. The circumstances of each case will dictate exactly what action you must take in each case, but when you disagree with an order written by another treating physician your obligation is to act to safeguard the patient and resolve the disagreement with that physician as soon as possible. The well-being of the patient always comes first.

Telephone Orders

Telephone orders are another source of problems for physicians whose hospital care is being criticized. Telephone orders are always risky. If the person taking the telephone order misunderstands you or is simply careless, your order may not be put into the chart correctly and thus not be carried out as you intended. You also run the risk that you will not understand the situation correctly, because you are not present to examine the patient or because the person explaining the situation to you does not understand the situation, and thus will prescribe incorrectly.

Prescribing over the telephone may be appropriate in some emergency situations, but should in general be avoided. When a hospital record reveals several telephone orders in nonemergency situations, the jury wonders why you could not see the patient and prescribe in person. If you must order by telephone, make sure that you see the patient as soon as possible, examine him, and check to make sure that the order has been entered correctly and is being carried out as ordered. If the order is correct when you check it, you should note in the order sheet that the telephone order (identified by time, date, and physician who signed it) has been checked and should be continued, discontinued, or whatever, as you desire. Of course, your order will contain the date and time of its entry. You should also mention in your progress note for that visit what necessitated your telephone order and your opinion as to the patient's condition in light of your physical examination and the medication being given. If the order is incorrect when you check it, do not cross out the error or make changes in the note as written. Put on the order sheet your own order clearly and unequivocally stating that the telephone order is incorrect, canceling the telephone order, and stating the correct order. Make sure that the hospital personnel on the floor are aware of the error. Your order must include the date and time of its entry. Your progress note made after you examine the patient should contain the facts necessitating your telephone order, what you ordered by telephone, when you made the order, the person to whom you gave the order, when you arrived at the hospital, when you discovered the error, what steps you took to correct the error, the results of your physical examination, your opinion of the effect of the error on the patient, and any other pertinent information. You must not hedge or be protective in noting the mistake of the person taking the telephone order and any effects it caused. Be honest. In most instances your statement will not be important, but should there be a lawsuit it will help place the responsibility for the error on the proper doorstep.

Progress Notes

The progress notes that you enter in your patient's hospital record become your chronicle of the patient's complaints, the findings of your physical examinations, your impressions and diagnoses, your recommendations, your difficulties, your reasoning, crises, events that have affected the patient, relevant facts surrounding your treatment, discussions with the patient, and the like. A progress note should be entered immediately after every visit you make to the patient. It should always indicate not only the date and time of your visit, to establish when you saw the patient, but also what occurred and the results of your physical examination. In other words, your progress notes should reflect all occurrences relevant to your patient, from errors that you have discovered and their effects to important discussions with the patient.

By making complete progress notes you create a complete chronicle that can be introduced as written evidence to support your testimony. You can use it to refresh your recollection of past events. It can be used on cross-examination by your attorney to prevent others from lying about these events or conveniently forgetting what actually occurred. If you fail to make progress notes or make them infrequently or incompletely, you not only prejudice their use on your behalf but may also be creating negative inferences that can be used against you on cross-examination, as illustrated by the sample cross-examination on pages 65-68.

Reviewing the Hospital Chart

One question a defendant is always asked in regard to his visit to a patient in the hospital is whether he examined the hospital chart before examining the patient. You will be asked this question whether you saw the patient only once as a consultant or many times as the attending physician on the case. Invariably, the doctor asked this question will answer in the affirmative, although the opposite may be true. This answer often creates problems for the witness, since the questioning attorney can now point out to the jury that his treatment on that visit was rendered with full awareness of certain information contained in the chart, when that is not the case.

Suppose a nurse's note made at 2 A.M., during the night shift, from midnight to 8 A.M., states that your patient had an episode of seizures during which he had trouble breathing. The episode was over in fifteen minutes, and because the resident was not called there is no note in the progress notes concerning this episode. The only mention of it is in the nurses' notes. Knowledge of this episode would be extremely important to you in deciding whether you should continue the patient on the medication he has been receiving. You visit the patient at 8:15 A.M. the morning of the episode. You do not examine the hospital chart. You examine the patient, find no significant change in the patient's condition vis-à-vis your examination of the preceding morning, and decide to continue the patient on the medication you ordered for him the day before. That evening at 8 P.M., still on the same medication, your patient has another episode of seizures and dies. It is admitted that the immediate cause of death was a reaction to the medication, which is consistent with the results of the autopsy. There is no question that the drug you had prescribed was appropriate for the patient's condition. There is also no question that one of the possible deleterious side effects of the drug is seizures that can affect the patient's ability to breathe. You feel that the patient's death was just one of those events that could not have been foreseen or prevented. This is your defense position.

The plaintiff's attorney digs through the entire hospital record and finds the note in the nurses' notes about the episode of seizures that occurred at 2 A.M. Without mentioning the note, he asks you about contraindications to the medication, and, eventually, if an episode of seizures during which the patient had difficulty breathing would be a contraindication and would have affected the decision you made on the morning of the day the patient died to continue the medication. You state that knowledge of such an episode would have caused you to discontinue the medication. Keep in mind that you have already stated that you examined the hospital chart prior to examining the patient that morning. You can imagine the confrontation. A drama script writer could not do much better:

Q Doctor, you told us that you examined the patient's chart prior to examining him on the morning of July fifteenth?

A Yes.

Q And you told us that knowledge of an episode of seizures during which the patient had difficulty breathing would have caused you to discontinue the medication, correct?

A Yes.

Q Doctor, I now ask you to look at the nurses' notes for the night of the fourteenth and early morning of the fifteenth. Specifically, the note for 2 A.M. Have you found that note, doctor?

A Yes.

Q Would you read that note to the court and the jury please, doctor?

A "Patient resting comfortably until approximately 1:45 A.M. when suddenly developed violent seizures and experienced difficulty in breathing. Oxygen administered. Episode lasted 15 minutes, after which the patient calmed down and began to breathe normally. Oxygen discontinued at 2:30 A.M., at which time the patient appeared to be resting quietly. A. Roth, R.N."

Q Doctor, did you read this note by Nurse Roth when you examined the chart prior to your visit at 8:15 A.M. on July fifteenth, only six hours after your patient had suffered violent seizures impairing his ability to breathe?

A No. I didn't.

Q Actually, the fact of the matter is that you didn't review the chart at all on that morning, did you, doctor?

A Ah . . . no.

Q And you lied to us before when you said that you did?

A Yes.

Q And if you had read that note about the seizures, you would have discontinued the medication and Mr. Perez would still be alive today, correct, doctor?

A That's possible. Yes.

Q Doctor, it's more than possible, isn't it? It's true, right?

A Well . . .

Q Doctor, you did tell us, did you not, that the immediate cause of death was a reaction to the medication?

A Yes.

Q You did not consider the patient's condition as life-threatening at the time that you ordered the medication, did you, doctor?

A No.

Q So, it's not just "possible," doctor. It is probable with a reasonable degree of medical certainly that Mr. Perez would be alive today if he had not suffered a reaction to the medication, correct?

A Yes.

Q And, doctor, it was a deviation from good and accepted standards of practice not to review the hospital chart and apprise yourself of how your patient had fared during the night and early morning hours, was it not?

A Yes.

Q And that deviation was the proximate cause of the patient's death on July fifteenth at 8 P.M., since you told us that if you had known about the violent seizures you would have discontinued the medication, and you admit that the medication caused Mr. Perez's death, correct?

A Correct.

You may not break down and cry on the stand as witnesses do on television, but your attorney will cry inside. You have been had. The case is lost. Even if you had reviewed the progress notes and orders before you examined the patient, and so testified, you would appear incompetent and would not escape liability. You could never successfully argue that good practice required you to review only the progress notes and orders, and not the nurses' notes, when a review of the nurses' notes would have saved the patient's life. You would have to admit that the main reason for having nurses make notes is to allow a treating physician to learn what the nurses observed about his patient in his absence. You will also have to admit that if the resident on duty at the time of the occurrence was not called, he would not know what transpired and would not make any progress note concerning the occurrence (unless *he* happened to review the nurses' notes, which would be unlikely). You could never shift the blame to him by claiming he should have reviewed the nurses' notes and made a progress note about it that you would have seen when you reviewed the progress notes. (You can never blame a resident for failing to do what you should have done.) You could never claim that you relied on a verbal report of what happened from those on duty during the night, because they would probably have gone home before your visit to the patient (which could be at any time); to expect a verbal report to be passed on to the next shift to be reported to you would be unrealistic. This is why nurses' notes exist. All you have to do is read them. You can read them *any time* you come in. If the nurse on duty fails to record what occurred, she (with her employer, the hospital) becomes liable for the consequences of her negligence. You cannot learn about the occurrence if it is not recorded in the nurses' notes.

You could not escape liability by claiming that the amount of medication the patient received before your 8:15 visit would have killed him. No jury would buy such an argument under the circumstances of my example. Even if the jury considered it as a possibility, you would not be able to deny that the probability of the medication causing the death was greatly increased by the additional twelve hours that the patient received the drug because you failed to read the nurses' notes. You would never be able to state that it was *not* the additional twelve hours of medication that caused the reaction that killed him. The jury would not need more to find you liable.

You might try to claim that the nurse should have called you at 2 A.M., or called the resident on duty and had him call you. You might claim that the nurse was negligent in not calling the resident to examine the patient, and that if she had he might have discontinued the medication at 2 A.M. Even if these allegations were true, they would not excuse your negligence in failing to read the nurses' notes. If you could establish that the nurse deviated from accepted standards of hospital practice in not calling you or the resident, and that the deviation contributed to the death of the patient, you might have a partner in liability to the plaintiff. You must realize, however, that even if you proved the deviation and its contribution to the death, the jury decides who shall bear the responsibility, and jurors tend to look primarily to the attending physician to do everything possible for his patient. After all, they realize that the resident is still in training and that the nurse receives only limited training. You are the highly trained physician in control of treatment whose services come so dear.

I can imagine what you are thinking as you read this. How can I review the entire hospital record every time I see the patient? I will be spending all my time looking at records instead of treating. This is not true. You can review the entire hospital chart briefly every time you visit the patient if you devise a system for doing so and adhere to it. You only have to review that portion of the chart that was added since your last visit and review. It does not take so much time as you might expect if you do it *each time* you see the patient. This definitely takes a great deal less time than a lawsuit and all the reviewing of the hospital record it requires. A quick but careful look at each area of the chart will give you the information you need. You have to refer back to an earlier entry only if there is something specific you need to know, for reasons of comparison or whatever, and you do not remember it. How long does it take to look at the progress notes, orders, medication sheet, lab testing section, x-ray report section, nurses' notes, and the like for a twenty-four-hour period (or less)? Or even a forty-eight-hour period? Not very long. They can be read in anywhere from five to fifteen minutes, rarely more, depending on the patient. Whatever it takes, it is worth it. If fifteen minutes' worth of information has been put in the chart since your last visit, you *should* know it before you examine the patient. You could be cross-examined about any addition to the chart of which you were unaware because you did not take the time to learn that an improper drug was given, or that an important blood culture had come back from the lab, or that the patient's toes were blue, or that the pathology report revealed that the tissue you removed was not the appendix, or that the consultation you requested was or was not performed.

Correcting Prior Entries

If you discover an error in one of your own entries, you must never cross out or attempt to make corrections by writing in the margin or squeezing something in. This is poison. As I explained earlier in this chapter, any apparent alteration in the record will be attacked by the plaintiff's attorney as an attempt at fraud. Do exactly what you would do if you discovered someone else's error. Immediately take whatever steps are required to correct the error (including notifying the appropriate personnel). Make a separate note in the chart indicating what and where the error is; correcting it; if appropriate, stating the reason for the error (such as emergency); and stating your opinion of the effect of the error on the patient. Even if you find a mere recording error that had absolutely no effect on the patient, correct it in a separate note stating exactly that. This will then be the end of it. Your separate note will allow no inference of dishonesty, but will show that you are on top of everything and regularly review the chart.

For example, you might correct a recording error in a prior progress note by stating the following in your new note: "*N.B.* Please disregard my mention of reflexes on the *right* side in my note of 3 P.M., October 10. This was an inadvertent recording error. I obviously was referring to the *left* side, which is the side we have been treating all along. The right side was and continues to be normal." This looks much better than crossing out "right" and writing "left" over or above it. When you cross out words or numbers, it may be impossible to determine what those words or numbers were. This may allow the plaintiff's attorney to imply that the material crossed out was more damaging than it was. In addition, when you write over or on top of something that was crossed out it is impossible to prove when you made the correction. By making your corrections in a separate note in the chronological sequence of notes, you not only prevent dangerous speculation about the error but also establish when you corrected it, eliminating possible inferences of fraud.

Should you spot an error at the time you are reviewing the chart to make your summary, the same rules apply. It is best to make the correction in a final progress note stating your opinion of the effect of the error on treatment. You should also mention the error and correction in your summary, so that no one can allege that the summary constitutes a cover-up. You might state, for example, that although there was a written mistake in the progress note of a given date, the error was only a recording error and did not adversely affect the treatment rendered.

What if the error was serious and did adversely affect the treatment? It is still best to be honest; take the necessary steps to correct it, if possible; and make the correction in a separate note stating your honest opinion of the effect of the error. Never alter an incorrect entry. By stating the effect of the error honestly, you will have a better chance of being held responsible only for the real effects of the mistake (assuming it is yours), rather than the exaggerated effects. It is difficult to dispute the opinion of a physician honest enough to admit his mistake and to evaluate its effects as soon as he discovers it, before any claim is made. Hindsight analysis by physicians who were not there will usually not weigh as heavily.

If the serious error you discover is not yours, your honesty will prevent any accusations that you tried to cover it up and attempts to blame you for the error. You must understand that nothing will come of most errors you discover. Nevertheless, it is essential that you follow this procedure to show your honesty and to prevent any inferences to the contrary should there be a lawsuit.

Operating-Room Responsibility

In order to avoid unnecessary lawsuits involving surgery, you must be sure what you are responsible for in the operating room and what you rely on the operating-room staff for. For example, do you ask for a specific type of suture to be on the surgical tray prior to a certain procedure, or do you expect that type of suture to be a part of the operative set prepared by the operating-room staff without any request from you? Does anyone have the responsibility for counting instruments (including clamps)? What about lap pads? Are you supposed to keep track of these things in addition to operating?

If it is the policy in the hospital where you practice that a nurse will count sponges but no one is assigned to count instruments or lap pads, you should assign a resident or nurse to make a count of these items. This is important because, if an instrument is left behind, you will certainly be held responsible. In fact, you will be held responsible for any materials used in the operation that are not counted by hospital personnel according to hospital procedure. Surgeons have been sued and held responsible for everything from lap pads to clamps left behind in the patient. You must do everything you can to insure that this cannot happen. As the surgeon, you should insist that all materials used be counted and that the count be written in the chart as part of the operative record and signed by the person making the count. This procedure should shift some or all of the responsibility to the person who made the count if an instrument is left behind.

What do I mean? Suppose it is hospital policy where you practice to have a circulating nurse count sponges and nothing else. If she tells you the count is correct at the end of the procedure and you do not see or feel a sponge in the operative field during your inspection of the field prior to closure, you can proceed to close and rely on the nurse's count as correct. If it turns out that a sponge was left behind, the hospital will be responsible for the negligence of the nurse who counted incorrectly. In order to make sure that you are not held partially responsible, you must be able to testify that you made your manual and visual examination of the operative field and saw and felt nothing, and that you asked the nurse if the count was correct before closing and were told it was; in addition, you must be able to produce the written record on which the numbers in and out were recorded by the nurse.

As the surgeon, you should always insist that a sheet noting the numbers of all counts be filled out and signed by the person who made the count, and made part of the hospital record, *not* destroyed. Very often such sheets exist but are destroyed after the procedure. It is stupid and potentially harmful to throw away a valuable piece of evidence that can verify any testimony by you that the nurse told you the count was correct. Such a sheet will be available to you at the time of trial if the nurse dies, moves away, or disappears and thus cannot testify. It is evidence that your attorney can use if the nurse conveniently forgets what happened or contradicts your testimony that she told you the count was correct. It is invaluable in cross-examining a nurse who does not want to admit having made the error. The nurse will never be able to escape a written record, signed and dated, indicating the actual numbers of the count as correct.

I urge you to make it part of your procedure *always* to make a visual and manual examination of the operative field for retained matter before closing or ordering the resident to close. You should always state in your operative report that you performed both types of examination prior to closing. If it is not possible or advisable to make a manual examination, because of the type of surgery (such as delicate eye or ear surgery) or for some other reason (such as cardiac arrest), be sure to state this in your operative report. Such a statement may sound excessive, but it is invaluable if there is a lawsuit due to retained matter. You will be able to point to your operative report to show that you actually made the examination you testified you made or were prevented from doing so by the circumstances, and are not just saying so because of the nature of the lawsuit. Without such a statement in the operative report to support your testimony, it appears that you are only trying to protect yourself. What else would you be expected to say when you are accused of negligently leaving something behind? With such a statement in the operative report, made before discovery of any retained foreign body or any claim, you are able to show that you were careful and did all you could to prevent the retention of any foreign object.

All right, let us turn from sponges to all the other materials used in the operative field. Are you solely responsible for them, in addition to any complication of the surgery? Why shouldn't the protection you receive in regard to sponges apply to instruments, lap pads, and the like? It should, and in many cases it now does. In recent years many hospitals have instituted such counts. As with sponge counts, in order to guarantee the protection such counts afford you must make sure that the count is recorded on a sheet signed by the person who made the count and that it is made a permanent part of the hospital record.

If the hospital where you practice has not established this procedure for one or more members of the hospital staff to count all operative materials used in the operative field, you should arrange it. As the operating surgeon, see to it that a resident, intern, or nurse is present during surgery to count the operative materials used, record the counts on a sheet, sign the sheet, and make it part of the hospital record. If the hospital objects—which it might, since its responsibility is increased—join with your fellow surgeons to insist that such a procedure for counting all operative materials be established. After all, this procedure is important for your protection. How can you do any more than make a careful and thorough search of the operative area prior to closure? Why shouldn't the hospital also make counts to insure that nothing is left behind? This procedure will definitely reduce the number of retained foreign bodies and therefore result not only in protection for you but also in better treatment for the patient and a reduction in the number of malpractice suits based on retained foreign bodies.

The Anesthesiologist's Responsibility

What if you are the anesthesiologist? What are your responsibilities? Before the operative procedure the anesthesiologist is responsible for the pre-anesthetic visit and examination. In my opinion, the anesthesiologist is not responsible for informing the patient of the risks of the procedure or obtaining an informed consent. (I maintain that the *surgeon* must include the risks of anesthesia in his discussion with the patient about the risks of the procedure, so that the informed consent he obtains is for the entire procedure, including anesthesia.) Nevertheless, as the anesthesiologist, you should cover yourself by informing the patient of the risks of anesthesia and making a detailed record of having done so in your note in the hospital record. This is especially important if there are special anesthetic risks because of the particular type of anesthesia you are going to use or the condition of the patient. (A separate consent form for the administration of anesthesia is also a good idea.) Always answer the patient's questions about anesthesia honestly and refer questions outside the realm of anesthesia to the surgeon.

It is preferable that the pre-anesthetic visit be immediately prior to the surgery, so that you will be able to analyze the most current condition of the patient. This practice prevents any condition from developing between your visit and the surgery. No matter how imminent the surgery, it must be canceled if you, as the anesthesiologist, find a contraindication to the administration of anesthesia. You must not worry about fouling up the surgery schedule or the surgeon's schedule. If the patient reacts adversely to the administration of anesthesia because of a condition you should have discovered on your visit and examination, it will be your responsibility, not the surgeon's or the hospital's (assuming the hospital is not your employer).

Before visiting the patient you must check the patient's hospital chart in regard to history, physical findings, medication, and complaints, culling out what is relevant to the choice of anesthetic agents and the patient's ability to handle anesthesia. It is especially important to apprise yourself of the dates of all prior operations, the anesthetic agents used, and any adverse reactions the patient experienced. For example, if you learned that halothane had been administered to the patient two weeks earlier, you might want to avoid repeating the use of halothane within such a short period as a precaution against hepatitis. If the patient has an upper respiratory infection, you may not want to administer anesthesia until it has cleared.

After examining the patient's chart, you should question the patient about his medication history, reactions to medication, prior anesthesia, reactions to anesthesia, complaints, and anything else of importance that might be inaccurately noted or not noted at all in the patient's chart. For example, the patient's history as recorded in his chart may not identify the anesthetic agent used in an appendectomy performed one month earlier. By questioning the patient you will be able to learn that the patient received a spinal anesthetic, and why. If general anesthesia was used and the patient tells you that he experienced a terrible reaction to it, you should obtain the prior anesthetic record to see what agents were used and in what dosages. If you should know what agents were used in recent surgery in order to choose the proper and *safest* agents for you to use, you must make it your business to find out what the prior agents were.

Do not trust the hospital record alone. Make sure that you ask the patient the pertinent questions so as to learn everything you must know in order to administer anesthesia properly and safely. It never hurts to double-check the information recorded in the hospital record. Do not hesitate to obtain prior hospital records or call another hospital for information if the information is important to you. Doing so may save you a long and serious lawsuit.

After examining the patient's chart and questioning the patient, examine the patient. You should examine the mouth, teeth, and throat and listen to the patient's chest. In conjunction with your examination of the mouth, always inquire about the patient's dental work. Take whatever steps you can to prevent any suit for damage to such work. All removable dental work should be removed. If the surgery is elective and there is a possibility of damage to delicate dental work, it is advisable to obtain a letter from the patient's dentist indicating exactly what has been done and the dentist's opinion as to whether it can sustain intubation or other stresses. When there is a possibility of damage that cannot be avoided, you must discuss this situation with the patient and inform him of the risks involved. You must inform him that although you will do your utmost to safeguard his dental work, you cannot take the responsibility for any damage that cannot be avoided. The patient must agree to assume the responsibility for unavoidable damage before you agree to render anesthesia. If there is a possibility of serious damage, a written consent and assumption of the risk should be signed by the patient. The substance of your discussion with the patient should always be recorded in your note on your pre-anesthetic visit.

Your examination should also include the taking of vital signs so that you know what is normal for the patient. This could become extremely important to you if the patient develops any difficulty during the procedure. Your examination must include that which is necessary to assure you that the patient can accept anesthesia, to help you choose the proper anesthetic agents under the circumstances, to help you administer the anesthesia, to help you monitor the patient, and to maintain the patient should any difficulty arise during surgery.

If, after completing this entire procedure, you suspect that the patient may have a condition that you do not feel competent to diagnose but that could affect the patient's ability to withstand anesthesia, you should make a written request for a consultation with the appropriate specialist to obtain clearance for surgery and anesthesia. The fact that medical clearance may have been given prior to your pre-anesthetic visit should not prevent you from requesting another consultation on the basis of your more recent examination. Your request for consultation should state your suspicions. The condition you suspect may have developed since the earlier consultation and clearance or it may have been overlooked. Elective surgery must be postponed so that all suspicions and possible conditions that could cause problems can be checked out. There are enough unexpected developments that can occur once anesthesia begins; eliminating as many potential problems as possible reduces the number of such developments that occur in the operating room, and therefore the number of malpractice claims.

It goes without saying that every aspect of your pre-anesthesia visit, from reviewing the chart to examining the patient or requesting a consultation, must be documented in a carefully prepared note entered in the patient's chart (usually in the progress notes). As in any other note, the time and date must be stated, so that it can be unequivocally established when you made your visit. This note must be as inclusive as any progress note. It should include the substance of all important conversations with the patient, other efforts to obtain information (such as calling another hospital), the results of your examination of the patient, and your review of the patient's chart. Remember that your note constitutes evidence of what you did when you made your pre-anesthetic visit.

The importance of your pre-anesthetic visit and your note describing it cannot be overemphasized. For reasons that escape me, many anesthesiologists still do not make such a visit and briefly examine the patient for the first time only after he has been wheeled into the operating room and given pre-anesthetic medication. An examination under such circumstances is at best incomplete and is not preventive. Very few operations are canceled as a result of the anesthesiologist's quick examination of the patient in the operating room.

Even when a pre-anesthetic visit is made, it is very often cursory or incomplete and the note, if any, is shoddy. Sometimes such visits do not include any review of the patient's chart or any questioning of the patient. This is a mistake. Filtering out possible problems before they occur is vital and should be done conscientiously. A complete note of this process and the care being taken will enable you to prove it was done. If there is no note in the chart, you, as the anesthesiologist, will be attacked with the *absence* of the note. Can you hear the plaintiff's attorney? "You say, doctor, that you actually visited the patient the day before surgery, examined his chart, questioned the patient, and examined him, but you did not bother to make a note of all this?" The patient will not remember your visit, believe me. Most cases involving anesthesia are serious and involve significant injuries (and, therefore, damages). You can imagine the potential power and importance of a complete pre-anesthetic note.

When the patient arrives in the operating room, a new set of responsibilities arises for the anesthesiologist. You must examine the patient again to insure that his condition has not changed and that everything is as you expect it to be on the basis of your pre-anesthetic visit. If the patient has developed a huge mucous plug, it should be discovered during this examination and not when you are starting to intubate the patient. If the patient has, since the time of your pre-anesthetic examination, developed a condition that contraindicates the administration of anesthesia, you must inform the surgeon and cancel the surgery—if it is elective. If the surgeon objects, he can always try to obtain another anesthesiologist. Elective surgery can always be rescheduled when the condition has cleared up and anesthesia can be rendered safely. Do not endanger the patient's life (and risk a huge lawsuit) by proceeding because of the crowded surgical schedule, the loss of a fee, the surgeon's prestige, the surgeon's anger, or other pressures. The loss of one fee is much less expensive than a lawsuit; and, if we assume you are a private practitioner, neither the hospital nor the surgeon will be held liable if the patient dies or is injured as a result of inability to withstand anesthesia due to the condition you discovered but failed to act on. The liability will be yours.

If you discover a contraindication in your examination prior to emergency surgery, you must discuss all the relative risks and consequences with the surgeon. The decision to cancel or proceed must be made by him, with complete understanding of what you consider the risks of administering anesthesia under the circumstances. The entire discussion and the surgeon's decision must be carefully recorded by you in the hospital chart. (The surgeon should also make a note recording everything he took into consideration in making his decision.) In emergency circumstances only the surgeon can make such a decision. Unless you feel his decision cannot be supported as a matter of medical judgment, you should abide by it. Should the patient die or be injured, the responsibility will in my opinion lie with the surgeon. You can rely on his decision unless you know it cannot be supported as a matter of medical judgment. If this is the case, you must protect the patient. How to do so is difficult to say. You have great power, in that the surgeon cannot operate without anesthesia. You may request an emergency consultation or the approval of the hospital administrator after spelling out your objection. Whatever method you choose under such rare circumstances, you may not only be protecting the patient from the surgeon's improper medical judgment but also preventing a lawsuit that would include you as a defendant.

Once the patient has passed your examinations, your obligations in the operating room are clear. You must choose the proper anesthetic agents for the patient and the circumstances, administer them properly, and maintain the patient so that no injury occurs. This is a huge responsibility. Many things can occur that are beyond your control. Nevertheless, you must do everything you can to prevent injury to the patient caused by a failure to administer the agents properly, including negligently inflicted trauma. You must work hand in hand with the surgeon but remain cognizant of your area of responsibility. The "captain of the ship" doctrine is long dead and, because of your separate and distinct responsibility, you must assert yourself when necessary. You may have to delay surgery until the patient is successfully intubated or ask the surgeon to close as soon as possible because you can no longer maintain the patient. During any emergency situation that arises, you must work closely with the surgeon and institute whatever lifesaving procedures you can. If an emergency code is called, you should always remain with the patient and do what you can to help the emergency team unless you are in the way. (This sounds obvious, but I know of cases involving anesthesiologists who left everything to the emergency team when they could have rendered valuable assistance.)

When the patient goes to the recovery room, you should accompany him to insure that the transfer will be a smooth one. If the patient develops a problem on the way or when he arrives, you will be there to deal with it. You can check to see that no extremity is leaning against a bedrail, give special instructions to the recovery-room nurses as to medication and care, and the like. It is advisable to stay with, or check back frequently to see, the patient until he has reacted from the anesthesia. Consider him still under your care until he has come out from under the anesthesia. Always make a note of your findings concerning the patient in the recovery-room record. A note in the recovery-room record showing that you watched the patient to prevent any difficulty from occurring while he was still under anesthesia is proof of the high quality of your care. Should any untoward complication occur, your presence is all the more impressive. Once the patient has reacted from the anesthesia, your responsibility ends.[4] Until this time, do not rely solely on the surgeon or the recovery-room personnel to check the patient.

One of the most important parts of any hospital record is the anesthesia record. It is usually the basis for much of the testimony in any case involving an operative procedure. It is also put under intense scrutiny by many witnesses, from operating surgeons to experts, and, of course, by all the attorneys. It is the only real record of the condition of the patient during surgery, the length of time anesthesia was administered, the duration of actual surgery, the drugs administered during surgery, and the blood and other fluids administered during surgery. Unfortunately, these records are very often shoddy at best, and the system used to record the information is very often unclear and confusing. The medical profession must be able to come up with a universal standard anesthesia chart that is easy to use and read. The forms used in some hospitals are acceptable but others are difficult to read and allow for various symbols to be jammed together, making accurate interpretation impossible. This can be easily corrected.

You, as the anesthesiologist, must take care to make your anesthesia record accurate and complete. It is an important record of what you did and how the

4. However, it is a good idea to make a postanesthetic visit to examine the patient in his room for any complications related to your treatment.

patient reacted to the anesthesia and the surgery. The information it contains can sometimes determine whether the responsibility for a complication belongs to the anesthesiologist or the surgeon. It is an important piece of evidence and must be completed carefully. Sometimes it is difficult to record everything during the procedure, especially if a complication or emergency occurs; in such cases, be sure to complete your anesthesia record accurately at your first opportunity. The chances that your record will become evidence are always increased when anything untoward occurs in the operating room. You cannot afford an incomplete or vague record under such circumstances. To state that you were busy with the patient is never an excuse for a poor record. Record what you can during the procedure, in whatever fashion enables you to write down the most information, and complete the record when the patient is out of danger or in the recovery room while you are observing the patient. Do not wait! Trust your memory as little as possible. Make sure your anesthesia record is accurate and omits nothing by completing it as soon as you can.

Covering Up Your Mistakes

Throughout this chapter I have emphasized that one of the most serious mistakes a physician can make is to attempt to cover up an error. This phenomenon is most frequently in conjunction with operative error. The result can often be tragic. For example, consider the surgeon sued for malpractice after a patient on whom he had operated for a ruptured appendix dies. The surgeon claims that he had difficulty finding the appendix because of inflammation, adhesions, and peritonitis in the abdominal cavity. He removed some tissue, which he believed to be the appendix, and routinely submitted it to the pathologist. Despite his claims of difficulty in locating and identifying the appendix, he did not during the remaining nine days of the patient's admission check the pathology report, which identified the tissue as adipose tissue. The patient, surprisingly, improved during this time. Two days after the patient's discharge, the surgeon claimed, he was randomly looking at the patient's hospital record when he noticed the pathology report for the first time. The discharge summary had not yet been prepared. He was scheduled to see the patient in his office the following day. At this point he decided to cover up his mistake, and turned a salvageable situation into an unsalvageable tragedy.

The next day the surgeon saw the patient in his office. He did not tell the patient the truth about the operation, and prepared a phony office record in which he stated that he operated on the patient only to drain abscesses. He then signed a discharge summary in which he falsely stated that the appendix had been removed. The surgeon saw the patient in his office for six weeks and made false entries in his office records in regard to the patient's visits. In these records he stated that he told the patient he would have to be operated on again, despite the fact he recorded that the patient was supposedly asymptomatic for six weeks. The surgeon never put the patient back in the hospital to remove the rotten appendix. He told the patient to call him if he did not feel well and discharged him from his care. Somehow the patient managed to return to a relatively normal state after his hospitalization (perhaps the infection walled itself off temporarily). The surgeon hoped that the problem of the continued presence of the appendix would just disappear, but in case it did not he wanted the patient to call him so that no one else would discover his mistake. He was playing with the patient's life because he was worried about his reputation and the possibility that someone might find out about his mistake.

The patient managed to live relatively normally for six months before experiencing a severe attack of abdominal pain, abdominal distention, vomiting, and diarrhea. He went back to the emergency room of the same hospital he had gone to six months earlier when he had experienced the same symptoms. On admission to the hospital, he gave a history of having had his appendix removed six months earlier at the hospital. The physician treating him on this admission was puzzled by his symptoms and signs in view of this history of a removed appendix. This confusion delayed diagnosis and an emergency laparotomy for 26 hours. (The delay was also caused by the failure of this physician to obtain the patient's prior hospital record from the record room as soon as possible. The prior record was finally obtained by a consultant on the day after admission; although the summary and operative report stated that the appendix had been removed, the pathology report revealed that it had not. By this time the patient had been in shock for some time and was being operated on.) The patient died. He was 42 years old, with two families and a total of six children.

The tragedy in this case is that the surgeon who initially operated on the patient did not commit malpractice in missing the appendix. This apparently can occur in an abdomen distorted by peritonitis, adhesions, and inflammation. His negligence began with his failure to check the pathology report of the tissue he removed, but that error could easily have been corrected by a second procedure without adverse effect on the patient and probably without a lawsuit (if there were a suit, the damages would be minimal, such as the cost of the second procedure). The die was cast when the surgeon failed to admit and correct his operative error. His attempt to cover it up killed the patient and created an indefensible case.

Sounds incredible? Such cover-ups take place. Surgeons have done some unbelievable things to cover up their errors at the patient's expense. I was once involved in a case in which the defendant surgeon had inadvertently cut the patient's ureter in a pelvis full of adhesions and tried to cover it up by burying it. The patient lost her kidney. Both the surgeon and the urologist involved ended up settling the case for a large amount of money.

The moral of these examples is: Do not try to cover up your errors. Such attempts either create lawsuits that would never have existed or aggravate a situation that is already dangerous from a defense point of view. Remember that, once an attempt to cover up is discovered, whatever defense or bargaining point you had vanishes. If the case must be tried, you run the risk of angry jurors rendering a very high verdict against you as a punishment for trying to deceive them. Whatever chance you had of settling your case for a reasonable amount also dies when your attempt at fraud is revealed. The plaintiff's attorney knows what the jury's reaction to your attempted cover-up will be. He has your attorney over a barrel, and the price of settlement rises dramatically. Face up to your error immediately, make an honest evaluation of its effect, do everything you can to correct or lessen the effect and mitigate damages, and you will be doing yourself and the patient a service.

Products Liability

What if an instrument breaks or a piece of equipment fails or malfunctions during use? What should you do? The actions you take as the user of the instrument or piece of equipment will become very important should a lawsuit develop as a result of failure or breakage. If you want to claim that the product you were using failed or broke because of faulty manufacture, maintenance, storage, or design, rather than as a result of your negligence, you must take responsible action regarding the failure or breakage. In writing, notify the operating-room supervisor, department head, hospital administrator, and anyone else involved in acquiring or regulating the use of the product about the defect. Send a letter of complaint to the manufacturer or, when appropriate, request that the hospital do so. The point is that you do not want to be held responsible for the damages (injuries) caused by the imperfect manufacture, faulty maintenance, or the like, of an instrument or piece of equipment. If you are to allege successfully that the patient's injuries were caused not by your negligence but by the negligence of the manufacturer, distributor, and others, you must show that you took actions consistent with that belief *at the time of the failure or breakage.* The precise actions you take will depend on the circumstances. If the failure occurs in your office, you will have to notify the manufacturer about it yourself. Your actions must be consistent with your belief that the product you used was defective: for example, not using it again, arranging to use a different product, arranging for a safety check of the product by the manufacturer (when appropriate), and the like. If the failure occurs in a hospital, you must notify the appropriate personnel in writing to prevent further failures or breakages that could harm patients. Consider the following sample cases.

Some years ago I was involved in the defense of a case involving a broken or sheared intravenous catheter. A section of catheter had broken or sheared off in the patient, traveled through the circulatory system, and lodged in the patient's heart. Open-heart surgery was required to remove it. The patient sued for a tremendous amount of money, alleging that the anesthesiologist, whom I represented, had been negligent in using the catheter to monitor central venous pressure. The anesthesiologist, as well as the chief of anesthesiology at the hospital, informed me that the design of the catheter used was inherently dangerous and that the catheter could easily shear without negligence on the part of its user. In speaking with other anesthesiologists whose opinions I respected, I found that they shared the same opinion concerning the dangerous design of this particular catheter. They explained that the catheter tubing passed through the insertion needle and that there was no locking mechanism to prevent the catheter tubing from moving against the sharp edge of the needle and shearing. This could take place as a result of movement by the patient. They pointed out that inside-the-needle catheters manufactured by other companies had locking mechanisms, and that catheters made with the needle within the tubing were much more unlikely to shear. These experts added that the so-called needle guard on the catheter in question was ineffective and that the manufacturer's instructions in regard to taping the catheter tubing to the patient's arm did not prevent shearing.

The chief of anesthesiology at the hospital in question (which was also a defendant) took the witness stand and testified that the catheter was inherently dangerous in design, giving the same reasons as had the experts to whom I spoke. On cross-examination by the attorneys for the manufacturer and distributor of the catheter, he was torn to shreds. Despite the incident in question and his belief that the catheter was inherently dangerous, he had taken absolutely no steps limiting or forbidding the use of this particular catheter at the hospital. He did not promulgate any rules, regulations, or warnings concerning the use of the catheter by personnel in his department. He made no written complaint to the manufacturer. He made no complaint to the hospital administration. In sum, he did nothing consistent with his belief that the catheter was dangerous in design. In fact, he continued to buy the catheter in question and other catheters of similar design manufactured by the same company. The cross-examining attorneys pointed this out through their questions, completely discrediting his opinion. If this catheter was inherently dangerous, why didn't he make a complaint to anyone? Why didn't he take steps to prevent or qualify its use? Why didn't he at least issue warnings to the anesthesiologists in his department? The jury did not believe his opinion that the catheter was inherently dangerous because of his failure to substantiate that belief by acting on it.

I was also involved in the defense of a case in which a suture needle broke during a tonsillectomy. The patient sued the surgeon, claiming that he had used undue force and caused it to break. The surgeon maintained that he had not used undue force and that the suture must have been defective. The manufacturer was brought into the case (impleaded) by the surgeon on that basis, but it was difficult to assert the surgeon's claim against the manufacturer due to his failure to take simple steps after the needle broke.

After the incident the surgeon should have searched for and preserved the wrapper the suture needle came in, any remnant of the needle, and any other evidence of its type, number, model, and manufacturer. You cannot claim that a manufacturer has made a defective product unless you can specifically identify the product that failed or broke as having been made by the manufacturer. In this case the doctor had to show that the suture needle that broke was indeed manufactured by the company he sued (impleaded). You must also positively identify the model of the product you are claiming was defective, so that the manufacturer has an opportunity to defend itself by presenting evidence on the manufacture, quality control, shipping, and other handling of that model. In this case the surgeon had to positively identify the specific model of suture needle that broke, from among the hundreds of models manufactured by the company sued. Both of these requirements were problems for the surgeon because he failed to search for and preserve evidence identifying the specific manufacturer and model of needle that broke.

What else should the surgeon have done to protect other patients and himself? He should have checked with the operating-room nurses to affirm what needle was put on the tray and subsequently handed to him. He should have checked the supply room in the operating suite to learn what suture needles were present and available for use at the time of the surgery. He should have taken a suture needle of the same model from the supply room and preserved it as evidence. He should have complained in writing about the defective needle to the operating-room supervisor, the chief of surgery, the purchasing director, the distributor, and the manufacturer (one letter with copies is satisfactory), identifying the needle by every method possible (manufacturer, model number, and any other data). He should have carefully described the occurrence in his operative report, identifying the needle and describing the amount of force he used and the amount of resistance he encountered when he inserted the needle and it broke. Obviously, all efforts to retrieve the broken segment of the needle in the patient should have been noted in the report. The surgeon did none of these things.

You must remember that if you want to assert the claim (defense) that the product you were using was defective, *you* must take these steps. You cannot rely on anyone else. You cannot rely on the hospital to preserve evidence. Because it is your defense, nobody will keep the evidence as carefully as you. If you search the garbage can in the operating room and find the wrapper the suture needle came in, you have positive identification of the manufacturer and model of the needle that broke. Why let this piece of evidence be destroyed? Why let it be retained by anyone but you? Imagine the advantage of being able to testify that immediately after the incident you searched the garbage for the wrapper the suture needle came in, since you were sure the needle was defective, and that it has been in your possession ever since.

Taking the steps I suggest requires a minimum of effort when you consider the importance of the evidence they create and the fact that no amount of effort at the time of the trial can either make up for the failure to have such evidence or have comparable impact. In fact, as the catheter case illustrates, your failure to take some of these steps will be used to discredit you and your claim against the manufacturer at the time of trial. Since there is a good chance the patient will be adversely affected and a lawsuit will develop if an instrument or piece of equipment breaks or fails, doesn't it make sense to take the steps that will help protect you and subsequent patients?

Again, I am not for a moment suggesting that you manufacture *false* evidence. I am advising that as soon as possible you find and preserve all the evidence you can, notify all the appropriate parties in writing concerning the defective product, and make detailed and honest notes of what occurred and what you did (carefully identifying the defective product), so that you will have this evidence as proof of your actions, the defect of the product, and your freedom from negligence, assuming that is the case.

If the failure or breakage occurred as a result of both a defect and your negligence, you should take the same steps despite your own admission of negligence. Doing so will mitigate your negligence and help your attorney settle the case reasonably or obtain a fair verdict from the jury. By showing the steps you took after the incident, such as making complaints and warning against the use of the product, your attorney will be able to demonstrate that, notwithstanding your own negligence, you are honest and concerned, and that the manufacturer (or whoever is responsible for the defect) must also be held liable for the plaintiff's damages. It goes without saying that a dishonest attempt to claim a defect in a product as a method of escaping liability is usually discovered and results in the consequences described in the prior section, "Covering Up Your Mistakes," on pages 89-91.

The Operative Report

Like the anesthesia record, the operative report is almost always a vital piece of evidence in any suit involving allegations about surgery. Like the anesthesia record, it is often neglected. It must be complete and detailed. When something unusual takes place in the operating room, great care must be taken to describe in detail everything seen and felt and everything that occurred. If the assistant incorrectly places a clamp and you are the operating surgeon, you must state what occurred in your report, whether you were directly supervising him or relying on his ability to do it correctly. You should also state your opinion of the effect of the misplacement, if any, and the corrective steps taken. If untoward results develop, you will have covered the bases. By noting the incident in your report, you have made sure that the only claim that can be made against you involves either your decision to allow the assistant to place the clamp or your supervision of him. There can be no claim that you attempted to cover up the negligence. There can be no dispute as to who placed the clamp. Also, your on-the-spot evaluation of the effect of the misplacement of the clamp is in the record.

By making a complete operative record you have drastically reduced the chances of being held liable for your assistant's error. If you had not mentioned the misplacement of the clamp in your operative report, you, as the operating surgeon, would probably be held responsible for any adverse effect. As a result of the operative report, any adverse effect attributable to the misplacement of the clamp will probably be the responsibility of the assistant or his employer (the hospital is responsible for the assistant's acts if he is a resident). Any claim that you failed to supervise the assistant properly or should not have allowed him to place the clamp you should be able to defeat. Such claims are rarely prosecuted successfully.

If *you* make a mistake during surgery your operative report should describe what you encountered, what happened, what you did to correct or ameliorate the situation, and your opinion of the effect of your error on the patient. This evidence will permit an expert to know exactly what occurred and to make a fair judgment concerning your treatment. He will be able to formulate an intelligent opinion as to whether your error was unavoidable under the circumstances or a result of your negligence. The completeness and honesty of such an operative report eliminates the possibility that an adverse expert can make negative inferences based on omissions or vagueness. By making such a report you permit your attorney to obtain an intelligent opinion from the defense experts and to decide whether he should attempt to settle the case or defend your treatment. Should the case go to trial, the experts for each side will have to argue opinion over a clear statement of what occurred and the jury will have to decide which opinion it believes. It will be a clean dispute. There will be no question as to what happened, and no negative inferences or innuendo based on an incomplete operative note, which can only help the plaintiff and hurt you.

Your operative report must not be a standardized dictation and must not be left to a resident or intern. As with progress notes, orders, and discharge summaries, I am a firm believer in the surgeon's making his own operative report. You are responsible for your operation, and should there be a lawsuit any decision in regard to your surgery will be decided largely on the basis of the operative report. It is a vital piece of evidence and should not, I feel, be made by the resident or the assistant. If you performed the operation, you know best what took place and thus should dictate the report. (If you insist on allowing someone else to dictate the report, you must make sure that it is complete and accurate before you sign it. As is true of anything you sign or initial, your mark is your imprimatur. The report you sign becomes yours and you will be judged on its contents. If the report submitted to you for signature is unacceptable, have it redictated or, preferably, dictate a new report yourself.)

In deciding what should be included in your operative report, a good rule of thumb is that another surgeon must be able to decide from reading your report, without any other knowledge of the case, whether what you did was proper under the circumstances. Any anomalies encountered must be carefully and specifically described, stating size, shape, and location. If the operative field is distorted by adhesions that made it difficult for you to locate the appendix, this circumstance should be noted in your operative report. If the operation is a team effort, each physician should dictate a description of the surgery he performed and sign that portion of the report.

All operative reports must be dictated immediately after the surgery. They should be completed and *in the chart* no later than 24 hours after completion of the surgery. It is also good practice to put into the hospital chart immediately after the surgery a brief handwritten operative note that can be referred to while the more complete dictated report is being typed.

I was recently involved in a case that concerned three separate operative procedures performed during three separate admissions. Two of the original hospital records contained no typed operative reports. For one of these procedures there was a brief and incomplete handwritten operative report in the progress notes. During the examinations before trial (depositions), the attorney for one of the surgeons being sued produced a copy of a typed operative report, the original of which was not contained in the original hospital record. Such occurrences are more common than you would believe and are inexcusable. A typed operative report that is detailed, complete, clear, and easily read is essential to the postoperative care of the patient. Anyone who needs to know what was done or found at surgery should be able to do so quickly and easily by referring to the operative report. Anything less could prejudice the care received by the patient.

In terms of defending yourself, putting your typed operative report in the hospital chart as soon as possible is vital. Testimony by other physicians or hospital personnel that your report was not in the chart when they saw the patient two or three days after the procedure is damaging. The information in your report could be important to their treatment. When the jurors hear such testimony, they begin to wonder why the report was not there. If the date of transcription on the report is days after the surgery, questions may arise in the jurors' minds. Why the delay? Did you destroy your original report because it was damaging? Did you make a new report to hide something? And in practical terms, the longer you wait to dictate your report the greater the likelihood of forgetting something. Your mind will already be occupied with the surgery on another patient. Do not risk confusing patients or forgetting important details by allowing yourself to get behind in dictating operative reports. Make it a practice to dictate your operative report immediately after your surgery; then make sure it is typed and put directly into the hospital chart. Do not let it stay on a belt, tape, or secretary's pad, where it could inadvertently be lost, erased, or destroyed. You cannot dictate a complete operative report a week after the procedure, when you have performed intervening operations and are preoccupied with upcoming operations. Do not allow your staff to put you in this position.

Postoperative Care

Once your procedure is terminated, the period of postoperative care begins. It starts in the recovery room. You should check on the patient there. Make sure that no complications have arisen. By examining the patient in the recovery room, you may nip a complication in the bud. If a complication has arisen, it is very impressive when you can show that you examined your patient in the recovery room, discovered the developing complication, and immediately initiated the appropriate corrective measures, perhaps even taking the patient back to the operating room. Even the anesthesiologist, who may be with the patient in the recovery room, may not have the expertise to pick up what you can. Thus you should check on your patient notwithstanding the presence of the anesthesiologist in the recovery room.

Note all your visits to the recovery room in the hospital record. Your careful observation and examination must be documented. It is to your credit. You cannot rely on the recovery-room nurse to note your visit or examination, although she should. If you discover a complication in the recovery room, it is important that you stay with the patient as much as you can until the situation is well in hand. Especially when the patient must be returned to the operating room, it helps if you can show that you were concerned, stayed with the patient as much as possible, arranged for the return to the operating room, and performed the corrective surgery without delay. After such an incident, you should return with the patient to the recovery room and stay with him for a sufficient period of time to insure that the complication has been corrected and no further complication has developed. After you have satisfied yourself that everything is under control and have left the recovery room, you should make it your business to check back frequently during the day to insure that no new complications have developed.

Your immediate reaction to this advice is probably, "This guy is nuts. How can I hang around the recovery room all day? I may have to perform another operation immediately after the first one. We have recovery-room nurses to watch the patients. I am a surgeon. I won't be able to operate. I won't be able to make a living." My answer is that it is precisely such an attitude that has caused a depersonalization of care, a lack of thorough care, and an increase in medical malpractice suits. The model I have outlined represents what would be best under the circumstances and can probably be done in most instances. Some modification may be required, depending on the individual circumstances. You may have another operation scheduled or become involved with an emergency, but the basic spirit and concept of what I have outlined should be adhered to. You should not overschedule yourself. You should not schedule procedure after procedure without allowing for a break or a chance to check your patient in the recovery room. If after surgery you must go immediately to another patient, either to operate or for another reason, you can still return to check on the patient in the recovery room when you become free. You can always call the recovery room and ask the nurse for a report on your patient. You can also tell her what to be on the lookout for. Once you have fulfilled your other obligation, you can go back and check on the patient in person. In fact, if you were forced to perform a second procedure immediately after the first, you could check on both patients in the recovery room at the conclusion of the second procedure. The point is that you, the operating surgeon, must keep an extra-close check on your patient during the first 48 hours postop (or more, depending on the surgery and condition of the patient), when complications are most likely to manifest themselves. It is during the immediate postoperative period, when the patient is in the recovery room recovering from anesthesia and the trauma of surgery, that he is most likely to manifest complications such as excessive bleeding, high fever, shock, heart failure, and seizures. The sooner your expertise is brought to bear on any complication, the better it will be handled and the greater the likelihood that any damage will be reduced to a minimum or corrected. You cannot rely on the recovery-room nurses, the anesthesiologist, the residents, or other staff members to pick up all complications, treat them properly, or notify you when something does occur. They may or may not do the correct thing. It may be enlightening to evaluate the recovery-room situation in the following way: If the anesthesiologist goes to the recovery room at all, he will stay only until the patient comes out from under the anesthesia. He cannot be counted on to pick up symptoms unrelated to the anesthesia. The recovery-room personnel are there to observe the patient in your absence and to render the minute-to-minute care that you order and that is required by the circumstances. Thus it is clear that you must make at least one appearance in the recovery room to examine your patient, and also check periodically with the recovery-room personnel on your patient's condition, if you are to stay on top of the situation.

After the patient has left the recovery room your postoperative care continues. The patient should be seen and examined at least once a day, and you should write a note stating what occurred during your visit and your findings. Obviously, some exceptions to this general rule are allowable once the patient has stabilized and is not in danger. It is permissable to miss a day or two on a weekend when your patient is in good condition, but as a general rule you should try to see the patient at least once a day, especially in the initial postoperative period. As I emphasized earlier in this chapter, the patient's hospital chart should be reviewed for data added since your last visit. I cannot stress enough the importance of following the patient closely by means of frequent examination and chart review. Never rely on hospital personnel to notify you of anything. By keeping yourself aware of everything going on in regard to your patient, you will be able to render timely treatment and reduce the likelihood of being sued.

When complications do develop, obviously, your postoperative care must be more intense. You should visit the patient more frequently and carefully document your visits. Keep in mind that complications increase the likelihood of a lawsuit, which means that your treatment and your progress notes will be subjected to close scrutiny.

Whenever you operate and remove tissue, it should be submitted to the pathologist for examination in order to verify the identity and condition of the tissue. Part of your postoperative care must be to ascertain the results of the pathologist's examination. This should be done as soon as possible; it is best to call the pathologist to obtain the results, rather than waiting for his report to be put in the patient's chart. Be sure to contact the pathologist if his report is not in the chart within two days. As the case of the missed appendix illustrates, you can put yourself in an indefensible position by failing to learn the results of the pathologist's examination.

Discharge

Once your patient has been guided through the postoperative period in the hospital, the time will come for his discharge. The patient will be leaving your complete control and will to a large extent be caring for himself. It is important, therefore, that you take nothing for granted; make sure that all your instructions are explicit and clear; written, if they are not extremely simple or involve more than two instructions; translated when necessary; and well documented in the hospital chart. Copies of all written instructions should be made part of the hospital record, and another copy should be kept in the patient's office record. All prescriptions must also be recorded in the hospital chart. It is advisable to record in your final note the date on which the patient is to return for his first post-discharge office (or clinic) visit. There must be no opportunity for the patient to claim he was left in the lurch once the hospitalization was over. In other words, all medications that must be continued, therapy that must be arranged, diet, instructions you wish the patient to follow at home, the date when you want to see the patient again, and the like must be unequivocally communicated to the patient, written when appropriate, translated when necessary, and carefully documented in the hospital chart. You must make a more than conscientious effort to eliminate the possibility of misunderstanding.

Autopsies

If your patient dies, the question of autopsy arises. This is a delicate situation. A consent must be obtained. It must be written and properly witnessed. Occasionally, unauthorized autopsies are performed and give rise to lawsuits for damages for interference with and prevention of the right of sepulcher. The damages in such an action are for the wounded feelings and mental distress suffered by the next of kin due to mutilation or dissection of the decedent's body or prevention of the right to bury his entire remains. Such a suit should never occur.

Death Certificates and Medical Examiner's Cases

In some states any death occurring in the operating room is considered a medical examiner's case. The cause of death will be determined by the medical examiner and will be part of his report. Those deaths that will be investigated by the medical examiner's office are determined by the rules of the locality where you practice. Whatever those rules, you will probably be required to fill out death certificates in certain cases.

Like any other record, a death certificate can become extremely important should there be a lawsuit. The cause of death you list must reflect your honest opinion and not be a source of potential embarrassment for you at a later date. If there is no reasonable basis for reaching a definitive conclusion as to the cause of death, or if you are not sure and do not wish to venture an opinion, do not guess on the death certificate. State that you have no opinion. However, do not purposely avoid stating the cause of death or list an erroneous cause of death (or any other information) *in an attempt to be evasive or protective*. It makes no sense to be evasive or protective in filling out the death certificate. You will not prevent an action for wrongful death by failing to list the correct cause of death or by inaccurately recording the time of death or some other detail. On the contrary, if the information on your death certificate seems evasive or inconsistent with the information that must have been available to you, it will arouse suspicion and cause someone in the patient's family to see an attorney. If a lawsuit is commenced, the inaccurate information you put on the death certificate can be extremely damaging at the time of trial. Remember that the death certificate is another piece of evidence by which the jury will be judging your honesty and competence.

Summaries

Hospitals frequently employ or permit the practice of having discharge summaries dictated weeks or even months after the patient has left the hospital, and often transcribed even later. The procedure requires that the chart be completed before it is sent to the attending physician for him to prepare his discharge summary. Since the patient has been discharged, the completion of the chart is not immediately attended to, and it often takes some time before all the test results, x-ray reports, and other data are put in the chart. Sometimes the procedure is for the entire chart to be completed and the summary to be dictated and transcribed by the resident before the whole package is sent to the attending physician for his signature of approval. Neither procedure makes any sense from a defense point of view.

Any procedure that allows more than a few days to elapse between the discharge of the patient and the attending's dictation of his summary or approval of the resident's summary (if the resident *must* make the summary, which I shall discuss later) is bad. Time erodes your memory and adversely affects your ability to dictate a complete and detailed summary or to review the resident's summary carefully to insure that it is complete and accurate. Weeks or months after the patient has been discharged and you are otherwise involved, you will not have the patience to refresh your recollection of the details from the chart in order to dictate a proper summary or review the resident's summary adequately. By that time, reviewing the patient's hospital record in order to insure a proper discharge summary will constitute a boring administrative requirement and it will not be done properly.

To make matters worse, after allowing the chart to languish in each department while it is being completed, many physicians allow completed charts that finally do reach them to sit on their desks for weeks while they pursue "more important" matters. Dictating a summary or checking the resident's summary for completeness and accuracy is seen as mere paperwork that can wait. This practice allows more time for the memory to erode and for the physician to become even further removed from the case.

In fact, some physicians feel that summaries are merely exercises for their residents and do not even bother to review them. They simply sign or initial the summary and send the chart back to the record room. How sorry they are when they are confronted on cross-examination with all the embarrassing errors and omissions they approved.

Imagine the difficulty an inaccurate or incomplete summary creates at the time of trial. How do you lessen its impact on the jury's opinion of your competence? Dictation and transcription dated weeks or months after the patient's discharge allow for additional unfavorable inferences. The plaintiff's attorney will always be anxious to show that you are dishonest or trying to hide something. When the date on your dictated summary is weeks after the date of discharge, it looks suspicious. The plaintiff's attorney will try to suggest to the jury that the original summary was destroyed because it contained damaging information and that you made up a new one to hide your errors, accounting for the late date on your summary. If the summary is not dictated by the time a request is made for the hospital chart or a summons is served, it looks especially bad.

It must be clear by now that if you are to practice carefully (defensively) you cannot have a loose attitude about any record you make. If you do not want to be sued often, and want to be able to win when you are sued, you must abandon careless procedures that create liabilities, rather than assets, from a defense point of view. Consider what an asset your discharge summary could be. It represents an opportunity to tie the case together and describe in writing everything relevant to understanding the treatment you rendered, including the situation you faced, your reasoning, and special considerations, in addition to the treatment itself. Don't waste this opportunity.

As you will have gathered, I am not in favor of allowing the resident to dictate your summary. As I noted in discussing the operative report, you know best what should be in the summary and thus should make this important piece of evidence. For example, does your resident know your reasoning in ordering a specific drug? Does he know what your considerations were in delaying surgery? Again, if you insist on allowing someone else to make your summary, you must make sure it is complete and accurate before you sign it. This may be more of a burden than making your own summary. You must not approve a summary that is faulty. If the summary submitted to you for signature is unacceptable, have it redictated or, preferably, dictate a new summary yourself.

The summary must be dictated (and transcribed) or approved as soon after the discharge as possible. Certainly it should be dictated no more than three days after the patient leaves the hospital. The hospital chart should be complete within one day; if you require material that is not in the chart in order to make your summary, you can easily acquire it.

One of the advantages of dictating your summary immediately after discharge is that you can do most of it from memory, with a minimum of referral to the hospital record. Your memory is still fresh and there have not been a large number of intervening cases. The amount of effort required to dictate a proper summary under these circumstances is considerably less than if even a small amount of time has been allowed to pass. If you are reviewing the resident's summary, it will be easier to spot errors and omissions.

Your discharge summary should be *in the patient's chart* within one week of discharge. If the summary is dictated by someone other than yourself, the same rule applies; however, the summary should not be put into the hospital record until it has been carefully reviewed and approved by you. It should be understood that you will be responsible for the accuracy and completeness of the summary put in the chart.

Since you cannot depend on the hospital to adopt the requirements I have described, you must adopt them for yourself. Dictate your discharge summary at the time of discharge, or as soon thereafter as you can. Do not wait for the hospital chart to reach you before dictating; obtain the chart for yourself. Obtain from the source data you need that are not yet in the chart. Do not allow the hospital chart to sit on your desk waiting for your summary, or your review and approval of the resident's summary. Do not permit your dictation to remain on a belt, tape, or secretary's pad for days before it is typed, checked, and put in the chart. If you discipline yourself to acquire good habits, you will not only find it easier to make good records but you will also be protecting yourself.

4   Informed Consent

In recent years the claim of lack of informed consent has become more and more prevalent as part of many medical malpractice suits. In Chapter 3, I discussed what you should do to help protect yourself against this claim. A better understanding of informed consent will make those recommendations more meaningful.

Theory

Operating on a patient without consent is technically an assault and battery. Legally it is also a trespass, an unauthorized invasion of the patient's body. Thus operating without consent is in the same category as stabbing someone in an alley. An informed consent is in effect the patient's permission for you to invade his body, so that it can no longer be considered a trespass or an assault and battery. The question that next arises is the effect of an uninformed consent: a consent given by a patient who did not have sufficient information to make an intelligent decision.

It has been held that an operation performed without an *informed* consent is the same as an operation performed with no consent.[1] However, the overwhelming weight of authority holds that failure to obtain informed consent constitutes malpractice, not assault (and is thus governed by the malpractice statute of limitations).

Unfortunately, determining when a consent is informed can be a difficult task. There are many questions that could be relevant, depending on the individual circumstances and the applicable law where you practice. For example, what constitutes "sufficient" information to make an intelligent decision? Was the risk not disclosed too slight to warrant disclosure? Was consent by or on behalf of the patient reasonably possible? Did the patient give the physician a "blanket" consent, stating that he would undergo the treatment regardless of the risk involved? Did the patient request not to be informed of

---

1. *Darrah* v. *Kite*, 32 App. Div. 2d 208 (3d Dep't 1969).

matters about which he was entitled to be informed? Under the circumstances, did the physician use reasonable discretion in regard to the manner and extent of his disclosure in the belief that it could reasonably be expected to affect the patient's condition adversely?

Probably the most important issue in regard to informed consent is what constitutes "sufficient" information to allow for an intelligent decision. Many physicians argue that a conservative degree of disclosure should be sufficient because one does not want to scare the patient out of consenting to a procedure that he needs. A patient might argue that the disclosure must be very broad and complete before it is sufficient to allow for an intelligent decision, asking, "How can you make an intelligent decision if you do not know everything?" The New York legislature dealt with this question by enacting Section 2805-d of the New York Public Health Law which states:

1. Lack of informed consent means the failure of the person providing the professional treatment or diagnosis to disclose to the patient such alternatives thereto and the reasonably foreseeable risks and benefits involved as a reasonable medical practitioner under similar circumstances would have disclosed, in a manner permitting the patient to make a knowledgeable evaluation.

Thus this statute defines sufficient information as the amount of information any reasonable physician would disclose to his patient under the same circumstances. Whatever the rule in your state, in the final analysis the jury will decide whether your disclosure was sufficient to allow the patient to make an informed consent.

What does all this mean to you? It means that in order to be sure of securing an informed consent your disclosure must be broad. You should outline every realistic alternative of treatment and all the generally known risks of the procedure *and anesthesia*. You should explain the chances of success of the various modes of treatment that could be rendered, the consequences if the treatment you recommend is not rendered, and the relative frequency of the risks involved. The more complete this discussion, the less chance there is of a successful claim of lack of informed consent. If you do *not* mention an extremely rare risk of the treatment, or a risk not normally associated with the treatment or the anesthesia to be rendered, and such a complication occurs, you still may be sued for lack of informed consent; however, it will be difficult for the plaintiff to prove that you should have informed the patient of this possibility. You will be able to call witnesses to testify that the complication is not usually associated with the treatment, or is extremely rare and therefore not usually discussed with the patient.

If the patient has told you that he will undergo the proposed treatment regardless of the risks involved, or that he does not want to be informed of the risks, I believe that the plaintiff would not have a valid cause of action for lack of informed consent. In order to recover for lack of informed consent, the patient would usually have to establish that he would not have undergone the treatment that caused the injuries for which recovery is sought if he had been fully informed. The rule could also be that a *reasonably prudent person* in the patient's position would not have undergone the treatment if he had been fully informed.[2] In my opinion, neither rule can apply if the patient tells you he wants the treatment no matter what the risks or that he does not want to be informed of the risks. Notwithstanding my opinion, you should carry out the procedures for fully informing the patient outlined in Chapter 3 unless the patient absolutely refuses to be informed. When this occurs, you must carefully document this refusal in the same manner that you would normal disclosure. If you are not tape-recording the refusal, I would suggest that you write a release stating that the patient refuses to be informed and wishes the treatment no matter what the risks, and have the patient sign it before a witness in your office. Doing so creates a document releasing you from any liability for lack of informed consent because the patient refuses to be informed.

If the circumstances are such that obtaining an informed consent is not reasonably possible, a claim for lack of informed consent cannot exist. For example, when immediate surgery is required by the condition of an unconscious patient who has no identification on his person, obtaining an informed consent is not reasonably possible. Under such circumstances, the surgery must be performed without any consent.

Although it may in some states[3] be a defense to a claim of lack of informed consent to allege that you did not disclose the risks of the proposed treatment because of the possible adverse effect of such disclosure on the patient's condition, this contention is difficult to prove and dangerous from a defense point of view. Your discretion in this regard should not be judged by a jury if it can be avoided. Your disclosure should never be abbreviated or omitted unless there is absolutely no doubt that your disclosure will damage the patient's condition. Such circumstances occur very rarely. Patients should almost always receive full disclosure. Apprehension that your disclosure of the risks involved will cause the patient to refuse treatment you feel is essential is not grounds for failing to disclose the risks. Unless you have *very* strong grounds for your opinion that your disclosure will have a serious adverse effect on the patient's *condition*, you must make full disclosure to your patient. Anything less will not hold up as a defense against a claim of lack of informed consent. Should this situation actually arise, it goes without saying that your reasons for not making full disclosure to your patient must be carefully and explicitly spelled out in your records.

No matter what the rules in your state, you should as a general rule give the patient all the pertinent information and let him make the decision about the treatment to be rendered. If you are uncertain whether a given complication should be discussed, due to its rareness or complexity, it is best to err on the side of disclosure. You can always note the rareness of the complication and explain it simply enough so that it can be understood. Should the complication actually occur, you are covered. Extremely rare complications are not usually alluded to

2. New York Public Health Law § 2805-d.
3. *Ibid.*

in normal disclosure unless there is some reason to believe one may occur to your patient. It is proper that the patient make his own decision about treatment, no matter how difficult that might be, since it is his life and health that are at issue.

The Proof

It might appear that lack of informed consent would be a difficult claim for a patient to prove, and that most physicians would stand a better than average chance of defending themselves. In reality, the claim of lack of informed consent is one of the most difficult to defend against. The only sure defense is full, complete, and provable disclosure to the patient. The other possible defenses involve special circumstances and are usually more difficult to prove and to succeed with.

Consider what the plaintiff must prove. He must prove that he received insufficient information from his physician to allow him to make an intelligent decision about the proposed treatment, and that he (or a reasonably prudent person) would not have agreed to the treatment that resulted in his injuries if sufficient information had been disclosed to him. These claims are, of course, at issue only after the patient has suffered some complication—after a risk about which he claims he was not informed has actually occurred. His testimony that he would not have agreed to the proposed surgery—let us say an ankle arthrodesis—if he knew that he ran the risk of losing his leg will be very convincing if he in fact lost the leg. It is difficult to question such testimony, and the one-legged plaintiff will have no difficulty proving this element of his cause of action (claim) for lack of informed consent.

The fact that the risk actually occurred will lend a great deal of weight to testimony that it is not that rare, is reasonably foreseeable, and should have been disclosed to the patient. Only overwhelming proof that the complication is extremely rare or unknown will escape such a presumption. Thus the plaintiff will usually be able to elicit credible testimony that the risk that occurred should have been disclosed to him. You, as the defendant physician, will be under the burden of proving otherwise unless you can prove that you did disclose the risk to the plaintiff.

The key to understanding what must be done to defeat a claim for lack of informed consent, and why the procedures I outlined in Chapter 3 are necessary, is this: The injured plaintiff need only testify that you did not tell him about the risk of the terrible complication that happened to him and that, if you had done so, he never would have agreed to the treatment; in order to defeat the claim, you cannot merely take the stand and assert the contrary. It will merely be your word against his—and he has the injuries, not you. You must produce corroboration of your testimony that you disclosed the risk, or that special circumstances made it proper not to disclose the risk. Your evidence must be as strong as possible, since the plaintiff is saying that the injuries from which he is suffering would never have occurred if you had disclosed everything to him, because he would never have agreed to the treatment. When you produce a tape recording of your explanation of the risk to the patient and the patient's statement that he understands all the risks you have explained and agrees to the treatment, you destroy the plaintiff's claim of lack of informed consent and go a long way toward destroying any other claims of malpractice he may be making.

The tape recording is the most dramatic and effective evidence you can employ to destroy this claim. Nevertheless, other evidence produced by the procedures I have outlined is also effective. When you produce office records specifying the complication that occurred as one of the risks you discussed with the patient, the witnesses to the discussion, the clear and carefully worded consent the patient signed in your office, and whatever other evidence you created following the procedures I outlined, you will be able to overcome the testimony of the injured plaintiff, notwithstanding the added weight his injuries give that testimony. By following the outlined procedures and creating such evidence, you also defeat any attempt by the plaintiff to circumvent your testimony of disclosure by claiming coercion or inability to understand due to anxiety, medication, or language difficulty.

What Treatment Requires Informed Consent?

A cause of action for lack of informed consent does not exist for all treatment. The doctrine of informed consent generally applies only to elective (nonemergency) treatment, including diagnostic procedures, involving invasion or disruption of the integrity of the body. In my opinion this definition includes x-ray for diagnosis and treatment, although some states may limit it to only x-ray treatment. In an emergency situation, when time can mean the difference between life and death or serious injury, an informed consent is not required. In effect, informed consent is presumed because of the dire consequences of not treating. This exception applies only to true emergencies, when in your judgment it would be impractical and possibly detrimental to attempt to obtain an informed consent. Examples are an emergency appendicitis situation or sudden complication requiring further surgery that arises during or immediately after a consented-to procedure.

5   Suit-Producing Activity and Special Situations

Situations to Avoid

Certain situations are fraught with danger from a malpractice point of view and should be avoided.

Treating Outside Your Specialty

Due to greed, friendship, unrealistic evaluation of their own ability, or fear of losing a patient, some physicians treat ailments that are outside their specialty or expertise. This is a mistake.

When you treat outside your specialty or expertise, you multiply the chances that something will go wrong. Though you may have a good idea how to treat the ailment involved, someone trained in the appropriate specialty is better able to treat it. He will have more experience at treating the ailment, and will be more aware of relevant new developments, new medications, and associated problems. He is in a better position to defend himself should a complication arise.

If a complication arises, a physician treating within his specialty can defend his treatment on the basis of his training and expertise in treating the ailment. The patient cannot claim that the physician was unqualified to treat the ailment or that a specialist trained to treat the ailment should have been called in. If you treat outside your specialty and problems develop, you leave yourself open to charges of lacking the qualifications to treat and failing to refer the patient, in addition to charges of negligent treatment. It is difficult to assert the defense that complications can occur even with the best care when you must admit that on the basis of training you are not the most qualified to treat the problem. Even if you can show that your treatment is within the accepted standards of practice and that the complication that occurred is a recognized one, you have created an obstacle to the jury's believing you.

When you treat outside your specialty, you permit the plaintiff to produce an expert in the appropriate specialty who will testify that you are not qualified to treat the ailment, that you should have referred the patient to someone in his specialty, and that your failure to refer the patient is itself a deviation from accepted practice, as is your treatment. In addition, the law will probably hold you to the standards of the specialty that deals with the ailment involved. For example, if you, as an internist, treat a fracture, you will be held to the standards that apply to orthopedists. This situation gives the expert (and the plaintiff) a distinct advantage. He has more to criticize, and his credibility and the power of his opinions are enhanced. Even if you call an expert in the appropriate specialty, he will not be able to deny that you are not best qualified to treat the ailment and that it would have been better to refer the patient to a specialist. He can only try to convince the jury that your treatment was nevertheless *within* accepted practice.

Since treating outside your specialty increases the chances of complications and therefore the chances of being sued, and also creates problems in defending your treatment, you should not do it. Treat within your realm of expertise and refer the patient to the appropriate specialist for ailments outside that realm.

Treating as a Favor

Whenever a physician tells me that he has treated or is treating a patient "as a favor" I become wary, since this usually means there will be problems in defending his treatment. I once defended a dermatologist who not only took Pap smears for his neighbor "as a favor" and acted as her "local" gynecologist, but even went so far as to send her cat's feces to the lab for analysis. His friendship did not prevent her husband from suing him after she died of cervical cancer.

Whether you are treating "as a favor" within or outside your specialty, doing so creates defense problems if you are sued because it invariably involves loose, unprofessional procedures. Such unprofessionalism also increases the chances of complications developing, and therefore the chances of being sued. Treating as a favor does not give you any immunity from being sued if a complication develops. The fact that you are not being paid for your services does not mean that you need not take any precautions, make records, or otherwise conform to procedure, or that you can treat outside your specialty. If you examine a friend and do not, for example, make a record of what you did, you will have difficulty defending yourself when you are sued. Suppose that the friend you examined develops a serious complication two days after you examined him and gave him a clean bill of health. Your friend tells his lawyer that he thought he was fine because you told him so, and did not seek further medical attention although he did not feel good. The lawyer will allege that you missed important signs and symptoms that should have alerted you to the impending complication and that you should have hospitalized the patient. He will further allege that if you had done so you would have prevented the serious permanent injuries that developed. You will have no records to substantiate your claim that at the time of your examination the signs and symptoms were not present and that there was no indication for hospitalizing the patient. If you have treated your friend for an ailment outside your specialty, you will be in a worse position. Can you imagine trying to defend a dermatologist who is treating his neighbor as a gynecologist? Remember that, if something untoward develops subsequent to your treatment rendered as a favor, the possibility of recovering a money award for injuries suffered will outweigh the friendship or whatever else caused you to render the treatment.

The key to the friendship or favor situation is to remain thoroughly professional as far as treatment and its concomitants are concerned. If you do not wish to charge your friend for your services, that is your business; but you had better stay within your specialty, make good records, keep test results, write follow-up cards, and the like to avoid being sued and to be able to defend yourself if you are sued. Conduct your treatment as if the person were one of your regular patients. You are still treating, despite the fact that you are doing it for something other than money. The patient is relying on your treatment as does any other patient. If he suffers because of what he believes to be your negligence in treating him, he will sue you as readily as any other patient.

Treating under the Plan or Influence of Another Physician

Once I met with a physician to review his treatment prior to his examination before trial (deposition). I had reviewed the file before our meeting and could not understand certain decisions he had made in regard to the care given. When I asked him why he did not order certain tests and a consultation before agreeing to the surgery that was performed, he said that he wanted to do so but he did not because he was following the treatment plan of the physician who sent him the case. He explained that the other physician was a friend of the patient's who did not have privileges to treat at the hospital; thus he agreed to treat the patient under the plan of that physician. He consulted daily with the other physician, who actually visited the patient in the hospital but made no notes or orders since he was not on the staff. When I asked my client why he agreed to the surgery, he stated that the other physician wanted it and had even chosen the surgeon and arranged for him to perform the procedure. My client had put himself on the line by adopting a treatment plan he disagreed with as a "favor" to his colleague.

In addition to the probable violation of hospital rules and regulations, such behavior is disastrous in terms of defending your treatment in a malpractice suit. You cannot defend your documented treatment by stating that you were only carrying out the plan of the family physician. The family physician will deny it; he will assert that although he made a few suggestions he was relying on your judgment, and that you had complete control. Even if the jury believes you, it will clobber you with its verdict. You will still be liable for implementing the negligent treatment of another physician. In fact, it will anger the jury that you acted against your better judgment and carried out the wishes of your colleague at the expense of the patient.

When a physician refers a patient to you, you must insist on complete control. (I am not referring here to a consultation, which is a request for your opinion and recommendations.) You must treat in accordance with *your* best judgment, based on your training and experience, because *you* are responsible for that treatment.

A similar dangerous practice is allowing a physician member of your patient's family to influence your treatment. Sometimes such a physician will visit his relative in the hospital and then seek you out to volunteer his opinion and recommendations. He may be pushy because of his relationship with your patient. In such a situation it is best if you can be tactful; but even if tact is unavailing, you must remain firm concerning your treatment. You must judge all medical opinions offered to you on their merits; never alter or change your plan of treatment because of the influence or pressure of another physician. If the patient or his family wishes to replace you because of your refusal to yield to the influence of a family member in the profession, that is their business and should not be your concern. I was involved in a case in which a physician relative of the patient pressured the treating physician to adopt a certain mode of treatment, encouraged the patient to sue when a complication developed, sought out experts to testify against the defendant physician who had yielded to his pressure, and denied all his interference.

Treating to Please the Patient or His Family

Just as you must not allow a physician in the patient's family to influence your treatment, you must not treat to please the patient or patient's family. The patient or his family may be convinced that surgery should be performed and actively campaign for it. You cannot permit yourself to succumb to such pressure. Again, you must follow what in *your* judgment is best for the patient. Recent studies reveal that there is a great deal of unnecessary surgery in the United States.[1] One of the reasons for this situation is that too many physicians accede to the patient's desire for surgery when it is not absolutely indicated. When death or some untoward result occurs, the physician is sued for performing unnecessary surgery. It is no defense that the patient wanted it. You are in charge of deciding what is the proper treatment.

When the Patient Refuses Treatment

The Emergency Situation

If your patient refuses treatment, you are put in an awkward situation that requires extra caution. Each situation must be individually evaluated, and you must keep in mind the patient's welfare and your own protection. When the patient is in critical condition and he or a family member refuses lifesaving treatment, such as a blood transfusion, you should in my opinion proceed to render the lifesaving treatment if you can, notwithstanding the fact that you can still be sued for assault and battery. If you are successful, the patient must sue you for saving his life. Even if the reason for refusing the treatment (such as religious conviction) is legitimate, such a claim will not succeed. If you permit the patient to die without rendering treatment, you are in a much worse position from a

1. Boyce Rensberger, "Unfit Doctors Create Worry in Profession," *New York Times*, 26 January 1976, p. 1; Jane E. Brody, "Incompetent Surgery Is Found Not Isolated," *New York Times*, 27 January 1976, p. 1.

defense point of view, as I noted in Chapter 3, pages 48-49. It is difficult to prove that a patient refused to be saved. If the patient dies or is injured, I believe you must be able to prove that you rendered emergency treatment and tried every proper emergency procedure possible. Generally speaking, our society still believes in maintaining life.

Euthanasia

A related question is that of a patient or his family who refuse the medical maintenance that is keeping the patient alive. The subject of euthanasia lies outside the scope of this book, but I would make a few general comments. In situations involving the possible withdrawal of life-supporting treatment, there is time to consult your attorney, the attorney for the hospital, attorneys for the insurance companies involved, and the district attorney before any decision is made. Public policy still favors maintaining life whenever possible, and the effect of the wishes of the patient or his family is only now being tested in the courts.

The request of a terminally ill patient that no life-sustaining apparatus be utilized to keep him alive when his time comes creates a delicate situation for any physician. When this occurs, you must seek out legal advice on your state's policy on this situation. If you intend to honor such a request, you must take all the steps described earlier in reference to obtain an informed consent. Under such circumstances I believe that a tape recording of the patient stating his desires and his understanding of the consequences of his request is mandatory, *in addition to* a carefully worded consent containing the same information, signed by the patient, and witnessed. Your note in the hospital record or office record should cover your conversation with the patient and his family. There must be no question that the patient is mentally capable of making such a request and understanding its consequences. I would suggest that you ask for legal opinions in writing, so that they can be kept in your records.

Generally speaking, keeping the patient alive until all the legal ramifications have been explored and resolved is the only course of action. This could take a long time and be very difficult if the patient is suffering terribly. Nevertheless, in addition to the possible criminal ramifications, there always remains the possibility of a malpractice suit if you take any action to end the patient's suffering. The patient's family may claim that as long as there is life there is hope, and that the patient was entitled to be kept alive as long as possible. If such a claim is compensable under the law of your state, the next of kin may assert that the patient was not suffering so badly and that you arbitrarily deprived him or her of the patient's company for whatever time he would have lived with the life support systems (even if it was only two weeks).

Nonemergency Treatment

What if the patient refuses nonemergency treatment? This can present a problem. If there is an alternative mode of treatment for the condition, you must note that the patient refused your first choice of treatment and then render the alternative treatment if it is acceptable to you as appropriate and within accepted standards of practice. It is advisable to have the patient sign your note, a letter, or a separate document stating that he refuses your first choice of treatment and wishes another form of treatment for his condition.

If you feel that any alternative to your first choice of treatment would be unacceptable, the problem becomes more complex. I would suggest explaining to the patient that in your judgment the treatment you have chosen is the best and there is no acceptable alternative treatment, so that if he refuses to accept your judgment you cannot continue to treat him. In other words, force the patient to accept your judgment or leave your care, instead of administering what you consider inferior treatment. Obviously, you must guard against any claim of abandonment. If the patient's condition can in any way be prejudiced by an immediate discontinuance of your care, you must make reasonable efforts to be sure that the patient is under the care of another physician before you stop treating, as outlined in Chapter 2, pages 37-40. If the treatment is purely elective and not important to the patient's welfare, abandonment is not a factor. If you have not actually started to treat (other than taking a history, performing a physical examination, and related preliminaries), you must carefully document the discussion of treatment with the patient, including the patient's refusal to accept your judgment and your offer of the names and addresses of several other physicians who might be able to treat the patient.

The principle you must remember under these circumstances is that the patient must not dictate your choice of treatment. You should not render inferior care because of the patient's refusal to accept your judgment as to the proper treatment. To do so would make you extremely vulnerable should a lawsuit develop. Even if you decide that an alternative mode of treatment is acceptable and continue to treat, you must take the steps outlined to be able to prove the patient's refusal to accept your first choice. You must not be penalized for the patient's refusal should any question be raised concerning your treatment.

A Claimant as Your Patient

If a patient comes to you because he was unhappy with the care rendered by his former physician, you may be thrust into a difficult situation. There is no reason to dwell on the treatment of your predecessor. What is more important is the treatment you render. Because an unhappy patient is liable to be suit-prone, your treatment must not be sloppy.

There is a possibility that such a patient might include you in any lawsuit he brings against his prior physician, or that he may want you to come to court to testify about his condition or to criticize the treatment of a prior treating physician. (I shall not discuss the patient who is suing a nonmedical person or entity, since the situation is clear. You may go to court voluntarily to testify about the patient's condition or you may be subpoenaed to do so if you refuse.) You should know your rights in this regard. In some instances you may be able to determine that the patient is seeing you to obtain such testimony, and either reach an understanding prior to commencing your treatment or decline to accept the patient.

Generally speaking, you cannot be forced to be your patient's expert against your will by subpoena or any other means. You can, therefore, always decline to render *expert* testimony. If you agree to testify as an expert—that is, to testify as to your expert opinion—you are entitled to be compensated for your time.

The rule in regard to your treatment is different. Once you have commenced treating a patient, you can always be subpoenaed to court to testify about your treatment. The exact scope of what you can be compelled to testify about may vary, depending on the evidentiary rules in your state. The trend has been to compel broad disclosure. The usual rule is that the physician can be compelled to testify about his treatment and anything relevant to it, including the patient's history, his condition, your treatment, and your prognosis, including your opinion as to permanency as of the last date of treatment. Your prognosis may seem to you to qualify as expert opinion, but an argument can be made that your prognosis during your treatment was essential to your treatment, and therefore that it is information about which you as the treating physician can be compelled to testify. If you are asked to give your prognosis as of a time *after* your last date of treatment, such as the time of trial, you could decline to offer such an opinion on two grounds: It calls for expert testimony, and it would require you to have examined the patient as of that time, which you have not done. (It is expert opinion because the interrogator is asking you to render an opinion involving something other than your treatment and based on your speculation, or whatever information he provides you, concerning what has occurred since your last date of treatment. If your last date of treatment was close to the time of trial, or if you are still treating, you will not be able to object.)

If you have been subpoenaed to testify about your treatment, you are not entitled to be compensated. If you come to court voluntarily to testify about these matters, you can, of course, arrange for compensation. Voluntary witnesses are usually paid for their time.

Strangely enough, a patient who has sued you will sometimes try to continue to, or return to, see you as a patient. As a general principle, the continuation of the relationship is unwise. It only creates the possibility of further problems, and in most cases extends the running of the statute of limitations.

Once a patient has commenced the prosecution of a claim against you, he usually will not continue to see you or return to your care.

Complication, Error, or Unanticipated Result

If an error, complication, or unanticipated result occurs during your treatment, you are in a special situation that requires special care. The first rule is that you must never try to conceal or minimize what has occurred. You must immediately make it your business to have an uninterrupted calm conversation with the patient, or the person who is controlling treatment (as in the case of an infant or incompetent patient), concerning what happened. It may take place in your office or in the hospital, but it must not be hurried or interrupted. It should not take place in a hallway. You should be able to sit down and talk in privacy immediately after the occurrence. Do not delay.

Once you have found an appropriate setting for this discussion, use your discretion as to those who should be present. Depending on the circumstances, it may be appropriate for one or more members of the patient's family to be present. If it is obvious that a particular person plays a major role in deciding what treatment the patient receives, that person should be present. If the presence of a given person would be disruptive, whether or not he is a family member, he should be excluded from this discussion. It is advisable to have your nurse, a hospital nurse, or another physician present as a witness to your discussion, if possible. If this is not feasible under the circumstances, or if in your judgment it would be disruptive, such a witness may be omitted. However, you must not fail to make a thorough note of what was said as evidence that you informed the patient of the complication, error, or unanticipated result after it occurred.

The first item of discussion must be full disclosure of what occurred and, if appropriate, an explanation. Caution is required when discussing the "why." If you are discussing a complication or unanticipated result, not an error, and there is no question of negligence, you should explain what occurred as explicitly as possible. If the patient can be made to understand the "why," he will be less prone to assume negligence and consider suing. If you do not know the reason for a complication or unanticipated result, perhaps because it is a phenomenon not yet understood by medical science, simply be as honest as you can; your frankness will be perceived and appreciated by the patient and his family. If, for example, the patient has suffered an unexpected idiosyncratic reaction to a drug for which there is no sensitivity test, you would explain that medical science does not yet know why a small percentage of people have such reactions and that there is no way to learn in advance whether any particular patient will do so. You would also explain that the drug is used because the percentage of people who react thus is very small and the benefits of using the drug are great. If you then describe a few of the benefits for the patient, he will understand that the drug was given with his best interests in mind and that what occurred was beyond your control.

If the complication, error, or unanticipated result occurred because of pure unequivocal negligence, such as leaving behind an instrument, this must also be fully disclosed. In this situation you need only explain what occurred, since the cause is clear. If you are asked the reason for the occurrence, admit that it should not have happened without using the word *negligence* or *malpractice*. Do not discuss responsibility. Any attempt to absolve yourself or blame someone else is a mistake. If you are questioned about responsibility, you should decline to render your opinion and inform the inquirer that you must concentrate on remedying the situation. Responsibility will be determined by lawyers, or by a jury if necessary. The important thing after such an occurrence is to mitigate damages, to ameliorate or correct the condition with a minimum of discomfort and anxiety on the part of the patient. Since the effect of what occurred is extremely important to both you and the patient, make sure your discussion of it is clear and honest. There must be no claim by the patient that you attempted to mislead him.

In cases of clear negligence, you must assume that someone will have to pay for what occurred. There are exceptions to this rule, but they are rare. The goal, then, is to keep the damages as small as possible. The most common mistake is to think that liability can be escaped completely. Subterfuge and lying to the patient invariably aggravate the situation and drive the cost of settlement or the amount of the verdict sky-high. Attempts at hiding negligence are almost never successful. They are easily discovered and are extremely inflammatory. The value of the case to the plaintiff increases dramatically, because he knows that the jury will punish for anything less than complete honesty. If the plaintiff cannot obtain his price during settlement negotiations, he will leave it to the jury to render a high verdict against you.

If the cause of the complication, error, or unanticipated result is open to question—that is, if negligence is a possibility—your discussion must not include your opinion as to the reason for the occurrence. Under the circumstances, you are in no position to discuss this issue. Confine the first part of your discussion to what occurred. Being involved in the treatment, fresh from the occurrence, and sympathetic with the patient, you cannot and must not make a judgment on the question of negligence. Rather than risk making unintentional damaging admissions that you will regret later, and that could easily be misunderstood in such an emotional atmosphere, it is best not to discuss the cause of the occurrence at all in your first discussion immediately after the occurrence.

Do not invent excuses or fabrications to protect yourself, your operating team, or the hospital, or to make the patient and his family feel better. Avoid the issue as tactfully as possible. Never be rude; merely decline to discuss the cause of the incident and tell the patient that you will discuss it with him at a later date. Complications, errors in judgment, and unanticipated results can of course occur without any deviation from accepted standards of practice, especially during difficult surgery. The questions of negligence and causation are often difficult (close) questions that are sometimes decided only after days of hearing conflicting expert opinions. How can you possibly discuss these matters with the patient or his family in the agitated emotional state you share immediately after the occurrence? There is a great danger of misunderstanding, inaccuracy, damaging statements, and bad feeling at such moments.

Certainly the patient is entitled to an explanation of the occurrence at some point. My advice is that your explanation be deferred until the air has cleared. You need time to reflect on what has happened and to discuss your treatment with your lawyer. The patient and his family need time to absorb the shock of what has happened, to accept it as reality, and to calm down. A calm, rational explanation at a later date will greatly reduce the chances of damaging statements, misunderstanding, or bad feeling. At that time you will be able to take the same precautions you would when obtaining an informed consent: to have reliable witnesses present, to tape-record the conversation, and to make a complete note in the patient's chart so that you can produce irrefutable evidence of what you said should a lawsuit develop.

To return to the conversation with the patient immediately after the occurrence, once you have explained what occurred and as much of the "why" as is appropriate under the circumstances, you should carefully outline what you have done to alleviate and correct the condition created and the options that lie ahead. Make sure that the patient knows you are doing everything possible to achieve the best result. This is important to the patient, even if the outlook is bleak. He must know that you are going to see him through this untoward development.

Your discussion of the alternatives that are available to correct or ameliorate the condition should be coupled with complete disclosure of the risks and chances for success of each one. When the time comes to obtain the informed consent for any additional treatment required, you should follow as many as possible of the procedures outlined earlier. You must not allow a cause of action for lack of informed consent to arise here. The danger when discussing additional treatment required by a complication, error, or unanticipated result is downplaying the problem and embellishing the proposed remedy in order to make the patient feel better. It is important that you be realistic so that the consent can be informed.

Because of this danger and the anxiety created when a patient is informed of an untoward development, it is advisable to obtain the patient's consent for additional required treatment at a second meeting and discussion, if possible. This approach allows the patient time to think about the information you have imparted during the first discussion; thus he cannot claim that he was rushed. I recommend it when time is not a factor. Thus the full discussion of the proposed treatment is held, witnessed, and recorded in the notes, but the patient's final consent is deferred to a second conference, when the shock of what has occurred has lessened; the treatment, risks, and chances of success can be reviewed; and final questions can be answered. This conversation should be tape-recorded. (When appropriate, it may also be the occasion for your deferred explanation of the cause of what occurred.) This procedure will prevent the patient from claiming that the shock of learning what occurred made it impossible for him to give an informed consent.

Questions may arise about the cost of the additional treatment required. This subject should not be discussed immediately after an untoward development occurs. Remember that you cannot forego or reduce your fee without running the risk of its being construed as an admission of liability.

In order to be prepared for an untoward development occurring to an infant or incompetent patient, you should always know whom to notify to discuss what has occurred and from whom to obtain an informed consent for further treatment when it is required (assuming there is time to do so).

Allowing a Resident to Operate on Your Private Patient

When a patient retains you as his private physician and agrees to be operated on after discussing it with you, he expects *you* to perform the operation. When you intend to allow a resident to perform the operation, under your supervision, the patient is entitled to be so informed. If you do not inform the patient, you are committing a fraud. Even if the consent form the patient must sign states that you, *or someone you designate*, will perform the operation, the patient is entitled to be informed by you that you are not actually going to perform the procedure. Of course, the drawback to such a revelation is that most patients will not agree to the operation. This situation would drastically cut the number of teaching operations and set back the teaching of surgery.

There is no easy solution to this problem. Before offering several suggestions for possible solutions, I shall describe certain precautions you should be aware of if this fraud is a part of your practice. Before every procedure you should examine the consent form signed by the patient to insure that it is filled out and signed properly. Doing so is especially important if you plan to allow a resident to perform the procedure. Make sure that the patient has not crossed out any language permitting you to designate another person to perform the procedure or written the word "only" by your name. If the patient has made it clear on the consent form that he is aware that a resident might be allowed to perform the procedure and that he is giving permission only for *you* to operate, do not permit anyone else to do so. If you do and something goes wrong, you can be sure that the patient will investigate whether you actually performed the operation; when he discovers you did not, he will produce the form, consenting only for *you* to operate. An assault and battery or trespass has been performed on him with your knowledge, and he should be able to recover without having to prove malpractice.[2]

When you do permit a resident to perform surgery on your private patient, do not aggravate your fraud by misrepresenting the truth in the hospital record. This is a mistake. The patient will never see the hospital record unless something goes wrong, in which case it is better to have the truth in the record. Record that the operation was performed by the resident under your supervision. Aside from the moral preferability of being truthful, there are distinct defense advantages.

First of all, hiding the truth under these circumstances does not prevent malpractice suits. What it does is insure that only *you* will be held responsible for what occurred, since the record says that you performed the procedure. If you record the truth, the responsibility for the negligence of the resident can be shared with his employer, the hospital. You are putting yourself on the line in terms of responsibility by allowing a resident to operate on your private patient under your supervision in order to carry out the hospital's teaching program. Why should you bear the responsibility for his acts alone? Why falsify the records so that it appears that *you* were negligent and that you alone are responsible for the consequences of that negligence? When you record the truth,

2. In Chapter 4, see "Theory," p. 103.

you do not absolve yourself. You will be held partly responsible for the negligence of the resident, perhaps because you were directly supervising him[3] and more certainly because of your fraud. However, the hospital will share responsibility because it employs the resident.

Second, you eliminate the possibility of having your cover-up exposed, with disastrous consequences. The jury can be upset with you for failing to tell the patient that the resident was going to perform the operation, but it cannot punish you for trying to cover up by falsifying the hospital record.

If the resident you are supervising does make an error, do not hesitate to take over. Obviously, you are more qualified to perform whatever corrective measures are possible to remedy or ameliorate the error. If you are able to correct the problem created by the resident's error, you may prevent a lawsuit. No matter how successful you are, always record that you took over and what you did. Such a statement will show that you were on top of the situation and took whatever measures were possible to remedy the situation. Should a lawsuit develop, you will have mitigated damages.

I have no definitive answer to the teaching dilemma. Disclosure *should* be made to the patient, and when it is not you take a tremendous risk. Since this risk is assumed on behalf of the hospital's teaching program, perhaps the hospital should insure you against any suit occurring as a result of the act of a resident you are teaching. Certainly as much teaching as possible should be done on cadavers. This would be especially advantageous in reducing the risk of a mistake by the resident when it is impossible for the supervising surgeon to see what the resident is doing until after he has done it and removed his hands because the operative field is so small.

One possible solution to this problem is to offer to operate at considerably lower rates if the patient consents to the resident's performing the operation under your supervision. Perhaps the hospital could also share in making this option attractive to the patient by lowering its rate for certain services it renders if the patient agrees to be a teaching case. This option might eliminate the reason for misrepresentation to the patient and permit full disclosure. Everything possible should be done to eliminate deception in treatment. This cannot help but reduce the number of malpractice suits and the size of malpractice settlements and awards.

3. In Chapter 2, see "Direct Supervision," p. 37.

6   Minimizing the Chance of a Suit

Personalizing Your Treatment

One of the reasons for the increased number of medical malpractice suits against physicians is, as I have said, the depersonalization of treatment. This phenomenon, though in part due to increased specialization, can also be attributed to the assembly-line method of treatment, overscheduling, and the failure of many physicians to allot a few minutes of time to each patient to discuss his problem and treatment. The last three factors are obviously interrelated and can certainly be prevented. In order to do so you must develop your sensitivity to your patient's needs and relate personally to each patient. This requires understanding how the patient feels.

The most important element in personalizing your treatment is time. Every patient wants and is entitled to a few minutes of your undivided attention to discuss what is on his mind in regard to his condition and treatment. Providing for such a conversation makes him feel that you care and that you have invested time and consideration in deciding the proper course of treatment for him. By giving him your undivided attention for a short time, you create a personal bond and relationship with the patient. If you make him feel that he is important, not just another number, he will not be so quick to consider suing you. If your patient never has a moment with you when you are not on the phone or running to see someone else, he will have no positive feelings about you to discourage him from suing. Why shouldn't he sue you if you will not spend five uninterrupted minutes with him but you will charge him a nice fee for your services? Creating a relationship with your patients will improve your treatment and will help protect you from being sued.

Scheduling Your Patients

Personalized treatment must be accompanied by realistic and fair scheduling. Many physicians forget what a hardship it can be for patients to come to their offices in the middle of the day, and think nothing of keeping their patients waiting for hours. It is usually the same physicians who complain if they have to wait five minutes in their lawyers' offices and who object to coming to court because of the loss of their valuable time. A patient's time is valuable too, and you as a physician must make a reasonable schedule that allows you to spend enough time with each patient and does not keep other patients waiting inordinately. This consideration helps build good relationships with your patients and is another way of showing that you care. Though unanticipated circumstances will occasionally throw you off schedule, your patients will recognize and appreciate your efforts to see them at their appointed times.

Office Atmosphere and Personnel

The atmosphere of your office and the attitude of your personnel can also play a role in keeping your relationships with patients healthy. An unpleasant atmosphere created by unfriendly personnel reflects badly on you and makes the patient feel uncomfortable and unwelcome. The attitude that a patient is a nuisance to be tolerated by your busy personnel cannot be allowed. This attitude on the part of your personnel drives patients away and creates the kind of ill feeling that encourages the decision to sue if anything goes wrong. Your personnel can be efficient without sacrificing friendliness and concern for your patients.

Hospital Demeanor

Personalizing your treatment is also important in the hospital. Physicians who are seeing their patients on rounds or who simply have many patients to see in the hospital often seem rushed, brusque, and impersonal with their patients. Patients in the hospital are usually more anxious than office patients. They have a special need for several moments of your undivided attention to be reassured, to know that you care and are watching out for their welfare. Taking an extra minute to ask how the patient feels in general or if the patient has any questions or complaints may not mean a great deal to your treatment, but it will mean a great deal to your patient.

This means taking the time to be alone with your patient, away from interns, residents, and the patient's family when necessary. It means speaking to the nurse on duty about your patient's comfort or nonmedical problem. The hospitalized patient feels alone and helpless in a foreign world, and he has to know that you are aware of everything going on and are protecting his interests. Confidence in your care not only benefits his health in general but also strengthens your relationship and his feelings toward you, discouraging the bringing of a lawsuit against you should a complication arise. It will also make him more likely to believe your explanation of any problem that develops. If you make the patient feel that you are on his side while he is in the hospital, he will be on your side should any untoward development occur.

Your Follow-Up System

The system of follow-up cards or letters described in Chapter 2 is another means of showing your concern for your patient's welfare and personalizing your treatment, as well as protecting against claims of abandonment and premature discharge. The wording you use should be firm but show concern.

Your follow-up system should take possible complications into account when possible. For example, if a known complication after a certain type of surgery usually takes two to three weeks to develop, you should use your follow-up system to insure a follow-up office visit no later than three weeks after the surgery. Remember that phone calls may be used to supplement your system, but they cannot take the place of cards or letters because they have less impact and are harder to prove.

Responsiveness to Your Patient

Personalizing your treatment means being honest with your patients and answering their questions candidly. Doing so creates trust and credibility, and expresses a genuine responsiveness to patients that you must try to develop and maintain. Personalized treatment costs you a little more time but creates a climate in which it is difficult for your patient to sue you.

7   Prelawsuit and Pretrial Activity

Contact from Another Physician

When inquiries are made about your treatment, there is always the possibility that they are in regard to a possible lawsuit. An inquiry from a fellow physician is likely to concern further treatment for the patient, but on certain occasions it may be made to gather information for a lawsuit. In order to safeguard against unnecessary or improper dissemination of information, certain precautions should be taken.

As a general rule, you should not release information about a patient without receipt of a signed authorization. If an inquiry is made without such an authorization, you should request one. Information about your patient is privileged, and you cannot release it without an authorization or knowledge that the patient has waived the privilege by putting his physical condition in issue in a lawsuit (or in some other legal manner). Therefore, except when the patient has waived his privilege, you must require an authorization signed by the patient before releasing any information concerning your treatment of him. This principle applies to the patient's medical history and other data.

Never send original records or documents; keep your records intact and send copies when you determine that records must be provided. The same rule applies to x-rays. If possible, they should be copied and the originals kept in your office. If this is not feasible because of the number of films and the expense involved, your films should be carefully counted, numbered, and delivered by messenger directly to the physician requesting them; a receipt listing the identifying numbers of the films lent must be prepared by your office, signed by the physician receiving them, and returned to your office by the messenger; and a date must be agreed on for the return of the films. In order to insure the return of your x-rays, your secretary should call prior to the agreed-on date to arrange for their return by messenger. This agreement should be diaried so that it will not be forgotten. A record of the numbers and quality of the films lent should be made in the patient's chart in case the messenger loses or damages the films. This record, along with the signed receipt, will allow the secretary to check that all the films have been returned in good condition. Returned film should always be examined by someone in the office who can recognize whether they are copies or have been damaged. If any films have been damaged or are missing, or if copies have been returned in place of the originals, this occurrence must be recorded in the patient's chart and called to your attention. You should do what you can to correct the situation. The borrowing physician should definitely be notified.

These precautions may seem elaborate, but too often physicians are caught short when they are sued by their failure to have in their possession the x-rays on which they based their entire treatment. When asked on the witness stand where the x-rays are, they can only reply that they were lent to another physician and never returned. How can you defend your treatment without the x-rays you based it on? Without the x-rays in court, your interpretation of the films cannot be verified by an expert. The jury might not believe your testimony about the x-rays. In sum, you must take every precaution to preserve your x-rays because you cannot defend yourself properly without them.

What about x-rays that are taken at the hospital? When you can retain the films taken at the hospital as part of your own records, you should do so. If this is not possible and such films are considered part of the hospital's records, you can only urge that the hospital keep them on file and not destroy or lend them out without consulting you. You should do everything you can to make it hospital policy to preserve all records, including x-rays, for the period required by the applicable statute of limitations, or, to be safe, a period of three years beyond the statute. It is advisable to record your patient's chart numbers and film numbers in your file on the patient so that you can readily locate his chart or x-rays. This practice also helps eliminate any possibility of disputed identification of the x-rays belonging to your patient.

When an inquiry from another physician is received and an authorization obtained, it is best to supply the information to the inquiring physician orally (in person or over the telephone), if possible. You will thus be able to ask him precisely what he wishes to know and provide him your best answer, explaining anything he does not understand, without worrying that the language you choose may be picked apart or attacked as meaning something other than what you intended. Should there be a lawsuit, there will be no written document for a lawyer to pore over and attack you with because it is written unclearly or ambiguously.

If the inquiry is solely for the purpose of further treatment, a phone call or conversation at the hospital should usually suffice. If the inquiring physician requests the information in writing, it may be grounds for suspecting his motive.

If the inquiry concerns test results, you should provide the results or copies of the laboratory data and nothing more. Your policy should be to provide the data requested as accurately and concisely as possible, and to put as little as possible in writing. This principle minimizes carelessly written or incomplete writings that can be used against you.

I am not advising that you be evasive or prevent the gathering of relevant information by a subsequent treating physician. I am advising that the dissemination of information concerning your patient be undertaken in a fashion that will present the fewest problems if you are sued, and will facilitate your defense, not aid in the prosecution of a suit against you. If information is imparted by means of a summary that can be produced at the time of trial, any ambiguous wording or omission can be used against you to impeach your testimony and to attack the opinion of your expert or the validity of other evidence introduced in your behalf. If possible, your *only* writing in response to the request should be a brief note in your office record or in the hospital chart indicating when the conversation took place and summarizing what it covered. This note will establish that you answered the inquiry and identify the subject matter covered in the discussion; it cannot be attacked, since it does not profess to document all the details of what was discussed.

If you impart the information orally, the only thing that can usually be introduced against you is the testimony of the inquiring physician concerning his recollection of what you said. It is doubtful that he will have recorded the substance of the conversation. If the inquiring physician can be produced in court, his recollection can be attacked on cross-examination and you can deny his version of what you said if it is faulty. In addition to your brief note on the subject matter of the conversation, you will have all the information in your records or the hospital record to substantiate what you say you imparted to him.

You cannot deny an incomplete document written by you and produced by the opposition. All you can do is attempt to explain away any ambiguity or omission and produce any evidence you can that tends to correct the negative inference created by the incomplete document. This may not be effective. Such a document inevitably creates questions in the minds of the jury about what the truth is. The jury may believe that you are trying to alter the truth to fit your defense. Unless the evidence to the contrary is very strong, the jury will tend to lean toward the negative interpretation of what you wrote or failed to write. Why not avoid this possibility if you can? In fact, you should always assume that a jury will favor an interpretation of written evidence beneficial to the plaintiff and contrary to your interest when there is any question as to its meaning. This is the main reason why you should answer inquiries about your treatment orally, if possible, and why you must be careful to make all your writings concerning your treatment clear and complete.

If the inquiring physician requests copies of your office records, you should ask him for what purpose the request is being made and offer to provide orally the information he seeks. If you are suspicious of the inquiry, seek the advice of your attorney and insurance carrier.

If the request is legitimate (that is, if it makes sense to you), ask the inquiring physician what period of time he is interested in and provide copies of your records only for that period. Do not add any other records, explanations, or summaries.

In general, you should be suspicious of continued requests for copies of your records made despite your offer to discuss your treatment orally. Most physicians with innocent inquiries will prefer discussing your prior treatment with you to deciphering your records. Obviously, requests to see copies of certain tests that are subject to interpretation, such as x-rays and electrocardiograms, are logical and should be honored.

When a legitimate request for your findings cannot be fulfilled orally because it is made for such purposes as insurance, compensation, or school absence, send a short letter listing your findings and keep a copy for your records. Do not include information that is not requested. Do not offer long summaries, interpretations, or opinions on paper if they can be avoided. If your diagnosis is required, it must be stated clearly. If you have not reached a definitive diagnosis and are still entertaining several possibilities, this should be made clear. By stating that such and such will be only your working impression until you have completed further testing or observed the patient's course for a longer period, you can avoid being embarrassed by this letter if the definitive diagnosis you later reach differs from the working impression you were entertaining at the time of the request. In sum, what you write should fulfill the request without volunteering additional information, and it should always accurately reflect your findings or thinking at the time. It is not an indication of incompetence if you cannot state a diagnosis with certainty at the time of a request. Do not reach for a conclusion or guess merely because your diagnosis is requested. State what your thinking really is. Remember that you may be confronted with anything you write if at a later time your treatment is being questioned.

Physicians have a tendency, in fulfilling requests for information, to include statements of justification for their treatment or opinions. You do not have to justify your actions to anyone in a report, and such statements should be avoided.

Suggestions for treatment should also be avoided unless the request is a consultation request soliciting your recommendations. Highly relevant information, such as the patient's refusal to accept certain proposed treatment, should *always* be included when appropriate. Such information in a letter constitutes further evidence that the patient *did* refuse the treatment. It goes without saying that copies of all your writings and those you receive must be kept as part of the patient's records.

The most dangerous request is a request for a written summary. As I have said, you should be suspicious of such requests and offer to provide the information orally if the request seems legitimate. It is almost impossible to write a summary that will be detailed enough to cover everything. To write a complete summary requires a great deal more time and effort than to deliver it orally. Consider the difficulty of including important conversations, negative findings, and other relevant data. You can be sure that whatever you omit from a written summary will become an important issue at the time of trial. Furthermore, the practical advantage of discussing your treatment with the inquiring physician is that he can question you about specific items that interest him.

If your offer to provide the requested information orally is rejected and no adequate reason is given for the necessity of a written summary, you should decline the request and contact your attorney and insurance company. Any correspondence declining a request for written information should be cleared by your attorney.

If an adequate reason is given for the necessity of a written summary, you must take care to make it accurate and complete. If a copy of your discharge summary of the patient's hospitalization will fulfill the request, it should be sent. I am assuming, of course, that your discharge summary is complete and accurate. If the written summary need cover only a specific period of treatment, so much the better. If a mere rough outline of your care is required—in order, for example, that the patient be allowed to collect compensation—you should indicate that your outline is not meant to be all-inclusive. This precaution may afford you some protection from being attacked for omissions. Nevertheless, you should always strive for accuracy and completeness, even if certain details can be omitted because only an outline is requested. There is never any excuse for inaccuracy.

Keep in mind that under normal circumstances the only compulsion to fulfill requests for information from a physician (or anyone else) is moral; therefore, you can and should choose the mode of communication that protects you most without prejudicing the treatment or benefits the patient will receive.

Contact from the Patient

Sometimes it is the patient, rather than another physician, who requests information about your treatment. Such requests are made for various reasons. For example, apparently innocent forms requesting such information as your findings, your diagnosis, your treatment, and your prognosis can hurt you at trial if you are not careful. A good attorney will learn about these forms and will subpoena them to court. If the information on these forms is inconsistent with your position at the time of trial, they can be used as effective tools to impeach your testimony.

As defense counsel, I once had to deal with the problem of workman compensation forms that had been filled out inaccurately by the secretary of the orthopedist whom I was representing and signed by him. The diagnosis that she wrote down negated the orthopedist's defense position. Thus it was necessary for him to explain to the jury that the diagnosis on the form was incorrect and had been written by his secretary, who did not understand the true condition. He had to admit that he signed the forms without reading what was written on them. This made a terrible impression. It appeared that he was either lying or very careless. This helped the plaintiff immensely, since the diagnosis on the forms was consistent with the plaintiff's allegations. The entire problem could have been avoided if the physician had been careful and realized that all writings are possible pieces of evidence.

I would remind you that, if the forms you have been requested to fill out do not contain an authorization for the release of medical information signed by the patient, you should have the patient sign a separate authorization. There is no reason to be sued for the unauthorized release of privileged information.

Patients may also request information ostensibly for the benefit of subsequent treating physicians. The best and, in my opinion, only method for handling such requests is to ask the patient to have the physician contact you directly. This, though not foolproof, will help insure that the information is indeed for further treatment, and will allow you to take the precautions outlined in the previous section when dealing with the requesting physician. It is especially helpful when the patient states that his physician would like a summary of your treatment. Deal directly with the physician. A physician will not usually gather information for his patient to sue another physician. Find out what the physician is interested in learning about your care and discuss it with him. If the patient insists that the information be provided directly to *him*, refuse. You should always be able to deal with the organization or physician requesting the information. The same principle applies to forms that you complete: They should always be sent directly to the party for whom they are being completed, not given to the patient.

When you are requested to write a summary on a form or on your own stationery for an insurance company, school, employer, or other institution, always be as complete and accurate as possible. Do not provide more than is requested; when only a general outline is required, as I have said, indicate that the information provided is not all-inclusive, and that details will be provided on request. Remember to insist on having your staff mail such information directly to the requesting party, and always keep copies of all forms or letters sent out. The patient is not entitled to summaries prepared by you merely for his own use (especially in an attempt to entrap you). This procedure should prevent illegitimate requests for information.

This same rule applies to original documents in your records or x-rays: They are never to be given or sent directly to the patient. Such materials do not belong to the patient. They belong to you. They are your records of treatment that substantiate your fee, help you to treat properly in the future (by documenting what took place in the past), and allow you to defend yourself. If the patient takes your x-rays and loses them, destroys them, or keeps them to prepare his case against you, your defense suffers. I have been involved in the defense of cases in which the patient asked for the x-rays on false pretexts and then would not return them. The patient then used the films extensively in prepraing his case against the physician who "lent" him the films. The physician did not have an opportunity to see the films again until the examination before trial, when he was questioned about them. After the examination before trial, the patient's attorney kept them. Thus the physician and his attorney did not have access to the x-rays in preparing the defense. The defense expert had to come to court to see the films for the first time; he could not examine them at his leisure in his office. The defense was burdened by the inability of the defendant physician, his attorney, and his expert to work with the films at their convenience. Even if your attorney can arrange for copies of the films to be made, you as the defendant should have the originals to work with.

If the patient loses or destroys the films, the consequences to your defense could be worse. If the patient denies that he ever received the films, it will appear that you lost or destroyed them. Furthermore, you will not have the films in court to use in explaining your treatment.

When originals *must* be lent to a subsequent treating physician, always deal directly with the physician and use the procedure outlined on pages 125-126. Originals should never leave your possession. If they must, under very special circumstances, take every precaution to insure their safe return.

Copies of materials in your records should not be given or sent directly to a patient. Always deal directly with the party requesting the copies so that you can employ the procedures and precautions previously described.

If your patient reveals that his attorney wants the information requested, you should request that his attorney contact you or your attorney directly.

Contact from an Attorney

You may be contacted by an attorney under any of a variety of circumstances. The most common such situation comes up when you have been treating a patient who was injured and who is making a claim against someone for causing the injuries. The patient's attorney contacts you ostensibly to arrange for you to testify about the patient's injuries, the treatment you rendered, and your prognosis. Although this situation is harmless enough, you should always be alert to any attempt to bring you into the suit as a defendant, and you should routinely employ certain self-protective procedures in dealing with your patient's attorney.

The first contact from an attorney is usually by letter. Your first step should be to call the attorney and inquire exactly what it is he seeks and why. You must always insist on a duly executed authorization from the patient before any discussion of the patient's condition or your treatment takes place. If the patient's attorney is prosecuting an action for the injuries you are treating and wants you to testify concerning those injuries, your treatment, and prognosis, ask him to come to your office and discuss the subject with you. There is no need for written summaries or copies of your records to be transferred to him at first contact. The disadvantage of passing such information in writing is that it creates evidence that may be used to manufacture a claim against you, or that may be used against you on cross-examination in the patient's case against another party.

There are advantages to meeting with the attorney in person. It gives you an opportunity to evaluate the attorney and his motives firsthand. If a report is necessary for legal reasons, he can advise you as to the type of report you should make in order to minimize the ability of the opposing attorney to use it against you on cross-examination. If the attorney is planning to include you in the lawsuit and you do not give him anything in writing, you have not provided him with written evidence to use in his prosecution of a claim against you. Even if you prepare a brief report of your findings for him, you will have provided him with a great deal less written evidence for use against you than if you had prepared an extensive summary in lieu of meeting him and discussing your treatment.

When you are treating a claimant, there is always a possibility that the party your patient is suing or your patient himself will sue you for aggravating the patient's injuries by your treatment. There is no reason to provide written evidence that may be used against you when it is not necessary.

Once you have discussed the case with your patient's attorney, assured yourself that the request for your testimony is legitimate, and agreed to testify, you may be asked to provide copies of your records for the attorney to study. If your treatment is not extensive, this is not necessary; if it is extensive, this is an appropriate request. The attorney will want to study your treatment to prepare the questions he will put to you. Never lend or give the originals to the attorney. They are your protection. Have them copied and provide him with copies. If he must look at the x-rays, let him do so in your office. Do not give him your records for copying. Attorneys are notorious for losing records, and if you are sued you are defenseless without your records.

If you receive a request to testify concerning the condition of a patient you have not treated for some time, or a patient you know has been treated more recently by another physician, inquire why your testimony is required, why the other physician is not testifying, and who the other physician is, if you do not know. Contact the other physician and discuss the case with him before agreeing to anything. If you are suspicious, contact your attorney and let him discuss the matter with the patient's attorney before the decision to be a witness is reached.

If you receive from an attorney an authorization for the release of medical information and a request for a summary of your treatment or other information when, as far as you know, your patient is not prosecuting a claim for the condition or injuries you are treating, you should be circumspect. Your first step is to contact your own attorney and insurance company. Do not deal with the patient's attorney without the guidance of your own attorney. It is my position that you are under no obligation to help your patient decide to sue you or make out his claim against you.

Under these circumstances your attorney's intervention is invaluable. He can and should contact the inquiring attorney to find out the purpose of the request for information. Your attorney will do what he can to keep you out of a lawsuit and will advise you as to what action to take. He may allow you to provide information to the attorney in exchange for the attorney's promise that he has no intention of suing you. There is no guarantee that such an agreement will be honored, but it is worth a try, since the plaintiff can sue you and obtain the information through discovery procedures. Once he goes to the trouble of suing you to obtain this information, he may be reluctant to let you out of the suit. This is especially true if he finds something to criticize in your answers to the intensive questioning that is part of discovery, and if he wants you to contribute toward a possible settlement. If your attorney does advise you to provide information to the patient's attorney, you should provide as little as possible in writing as a precaution in the event you are sued. Take all the precautions in regard to the use of your records described on pages 125-129.

If your attorney determines that the attorney who requested information is planning to sue you, he will advise you to refuse the request and force the patient's attorney to go to the trouble of suing you to obtain the information he seeks. This response obligates the attorney to invest a little time and money to obtain the information he needs to evaluate the merits of his case, and affords you the protection of legal counsel throughout the discovery process.

You should never provide an attorney information about a patient on your own unless you are convinced that the attorney wishes your testimony to prosecute an action that does not involve medical malpractice. Do not operate under the delusion that you will be able to persuade the attorney not to sue you, another physician, or a hospital once you have given him "the whole story." Do not be naive. When medicine is the basis for the lawsuit, you must have your attorney do the dealing. He has expertise and will be able to decide what level of cooperation, if any, is advisable. If you are insured, your insurance company will provide you with counsel. In most cases this attorney will have more expertise in regard to medical malpractice than a private attorney you retain for other matters.

Contact from the Codefendant's Attorney or Insurance Company

Sometimes, after a lawsuit has been commenced against you, you will be contacted by a representative of the insurance company representing a codefendant or by the codefendant's attorney himself. If, for example, you have been sued along with another physician and a hospital, the company insuring the hospital or the other physician, or perhaps one of the attorneys representing either, may send an investigator to speak to you and obtain copies of your records. This is dangerous, and you must not act on your own. First of all, the interests of another treating physician or even of the hospital where you treated are not necessarily the same as yours. Very often your codefendants will want to lay the blame for the patient's injuries at your doorstep. They are seeking whatever information they can to achieve this end and to protect themselves. Since a codefendant can be just as dangerous as the plaintiff, you must not discuss the case with, sign written statements for, make summaries for, or give copies of your records to, any representative of a codefendant, whether he is an investigator or an attorney. When you are contacted by such a representative, refer him to your attorney and immediately tell your attorney what occurred.

Your attorney should handle *all* contact with representatives of codefendants. He must decide what you should provide to the codefendant's attorney. He may not want you to provide anything, or may secure an exchange of information that will benefit your defense.

If an investigator or attorney comes to your office in person without advance warning, therefore, you must not discuss the case with him; refer him to your attorney. Do not be goaded or cajoled into making statements about the case, your treatment, the treatment of another party, or the patient. Remember that whoever hears you can testify to what you said. Furthermore, any statement you sign can be used against you at the time of trial. Do not create defense problems for yourself by failing to use your legal representation.

Contact from Your Own Insurance Company or Attorney

For obvious reasons, you must verify the identity of the person with whom you discuss your care. This is especially important when someone who identifies himself as a representative of your insurance company or attorney's office comes to your office for information or to take a statement. You should receive advance communication informing you that such an individual is coming, and providing his name and title. No one should be just dropping in on you.

When you receive a phone call concerning the case, you should require the person calling to give you his name and title and your policy number. If you have any doubts about the person's identity, hang up and call your carrier or attorney to confirm his identity. Never discuss your case with someone unless you are sure of his identity. Thus you should also require identification and knowledge of your policy number from an individual who arrives at your office. If he cannot produce adequate identification or tell you your policy number, you should decline the interview and send him away. Your insurance company or attorney can make new arrangements with you for such an interview if the person is legitimate. If he is merely an enterprising investigator affiliated with the plaintiff or a codefendant, you will have thwarted his attempt to obtain information from you.

8 The Lawsuit before Trial

The Pleadings

Before the actual trial of any malpractice suit, the lawsuit must go through various stages. The first stage, the portion of the suit that sets out the issues between the parties, is the pleading stage. Because the pleadings have a large influence on the lawsuit, you should have a basic understanding of what the pleadings are.

The Summons

No lawsuit for medical malpractice, or any other lawsuit, can start without service of a summons. It is the proper service of the summons that puts you under the jurisdiction of the court. If the service is not proper, the court has no jurisdiction over you. If you successfully challenge the jurisdiction of the court by successfully challenging the propriety of service, the lawsuit must be dismissed.

The summons served may or may not be accompanied by a complaint setting out the allegations of the plaintiff against you, depending of the procedural rules of the jurisdiction involved. Service of the summons can be made in several ways, again depending on the procedural rules of the jurisdiction and the individual circumstances (such as inability to find the defendant). The most common method of service is personal service, or personal delivery of the summons to you by a sheriff or process server. (A summons can be served by anyone over 18 years of age who is not a party to the suit.) The lawsuit does not officially begin (or the statute of limitations stop running) until service of the summons is completed. (Nonpersonal service can involve several steps; service is not completed until the last step is performed.)

The summons usually contains the following information: the court in which the lawsuit is being brought, the county or district in which the suit is being brought, the basis for bringing the suit in that county or district, the names and addresses of the parties in the lawsuit, the name and address of the attorney who issued the summons, and the date. The summons may or may not have to be filed in court, and it may or may not indicate the nature of the lawsuit and the amount of money being sued for. The complete contents will depend on the procedural requirements of the jurisdiction, and the wishes of the attorney issuing the summons for service when the rules allow some choice.

Venue

The county or district where the lawsuit is being brought and where it will be tried is known as the *venue* of the action. Venue means the location of the lawsuit. There are various rules that apply to venue, and the question of venue can be disputed and litigated. The plaintiff usually selects the venue because his attorney prepares the summons. Venue is usually based on the residence of one of the parties to the action, and the plaintiff obviously chooses the venue that is most convenient or advantageous to him. This is usually the county of his residence. If this venue is unfair or works an injustice on the defendant, the defendant may object to the venue selected by the plaintiff.

For example, if the plaintiff has sued several physicians and a hospital in regard to an incident that occurred in the hospital, and if the physicians' residences and the hospital are located in a county other than that the plaintiff has chosen as the venue of the action, the defendants can object to venue and apply to the court to have the venue changed on the grounds of undue inconvenience and in the interests of justice. Under such circumstances the court will usually change the venue.

The Notice of Appearance

When a summons is served without a complaint, your attorney can send a notice of appearance to the attorney for the plaintiff. This document indicates that he is appearing on your behalf and requires that a complaint be served by mail on your attorney within a specific time period. A notice of appearance usually submits you to the jurisdiction of the court; therefore, if there are questions of improper service, your attorney will use another method to advise the plaintiff's attorney that he is representing you and to demand a complaint that does not submit you to the jurisdiction of the court. This is especially important when the statute of limitations has expired since the alleged service, because the plaintiff's attorney will have no further opportunity to serve you again if the first service is held to be invalid. Your attorney will be able to handle these procedural matters correctly if he obtains the necessary information from you subsequent to your receipt of any legal papers.

What to Do When Served

When you receive any legal paper, you should immediately write down the circumstances and the exact method by which it was served on you. A good practice is to dictate a letter to your attorney or insurance company stating this information immediately after you receive the paper or papers. Whatever method you choose, you should record the date you received the paper, the time of day, the method of service (by mail, by a person who handed the paper to you, by a person who left the paper on your secretary's desk, or whatever), the names and addresses of the persons who witnessed the service, the name and a description of the person who served you, and any other data on your receipt of the legal paper. It is important for your attorney to know whether the paper was attached to your door when you arrived at your office or whether a process server handed it to you. You should also always retain, copy, and forward the envelope in which a summons or any other legal paper was received, especially if it was received by mail.

Once you have recorded this information, contact your attorney or insurance company to find out where the legal paper and the information concerning service should be sent. Always keep a copy of the paper and the recorded information concerning service in your file on the patient involved. It is a good idea to send the original legal paper served on you, along with the information on service, to your attorney or insurance carrier by registered mail.

I always ask a physician served with a summons, or a summons and complaint, to include a very brief summary of his care, including the first and last date of treatment, when he sends the summons to me. Such a summary, which need only be one paragraph long at this point, helps your attorney deal with the legal paper procedurally. It tells him whether there is a statute of limitations question and gives him a general idea of your involvement. For example, if the service of the summons on you was improper but the plaintiff still has a year left before the statute of limitations expires, and therefore a year within which to serve you again properly, your attorney may advise that you accept the improper service instead of challenging it and forcing the plaintiff to serve you again. If, however, there is a question of improper service and the running of the statute of limitations is a factor, he will not allow you to submit to the court's jurisdiction by accepting the service and serving a notice of appearance. He will challenge the improper service.

By providing your attorney with the details of service and a brief summary of your treatment, you help your attorney to avoid procedural mistakes and to afford you the best protection. By doing so, you allow him to capitalize on any procedural error made by the patient's attorney. For example, I was involved in a case in which the plaintiff claimed that he had personally served the physician whom I represented two days before the expiration of the statute of limitations. By the time my office received the summons and complaint from the physician, the statute had expired. My client denied that he was personally served but had made no notes about the details of his receipt of the summons and complaint. I challenged the service in my papers, and a date was set for a hearing to decide the question of whether the service on the physician was proper. This was a mini-trial on the question of the propriety of the service of the summons and complaint.

Prior to the hearing the attorney for the plaintiff sent me the affidavit of service of the process server, who swore that he had served my client. I discovered that this man had previously been found to have falsely sworn to such affidavits. The process server swore in his affidavit that he had served my client at the hospital where he practiced. My client had been in the hospital on the day in question, but swore at the hearing that he had not been served there at any time. Fortunately, I was able to trip up the process server when I questioned him concerning the description of the hospital, the manner in which he allegedly served my client, and his description of my client. The deficiencies in the process server's answer caused the referee to decide that service had not been made.

Though we prevailed, my client was extensively questioned as to his receipt of the summons and complaint. Because he had no notes of the details and could not recall them accurately, he began to improvise (contrary to advice) and almost inadvertently admitted *proper* service *at his office*, where the papers had been improperly left. Because this physician failed to make notes concerning his receipt of the summons and complaint, he almost lost the opportunity to bar the patient from suing him because of the patient's failure to properly serve him within the statute of limitations.

You can imagine how effective it is, in a dispute concerning service of a legal paper, when you can testify from notes taken immediately after the service. If your notes reveal that you were served by a tall, slim, dark-haired man in a suit on August 15 at 10 A.M. at your office, you will have strong evidence with which to oppose the affidavit and testimony of a small, fat, red-haired process server who claims that he served you at your office on August 8 at 2 P.M. while in his shirtsleeves. If you record what you were wearing when served, your attorney may be able to impeach the process server's testimony about serving you personally. In some instances the actual method by which service on you is attempted can make it improper under the applicable procedural rules; thus recording how you receive the legal paper can make the difference. Do this for *any* legal paper you receive, whether it be a summons, summons and complaint, notice, or subpoena.

The Complaint

If a complaint is not served with the summons, it will eventually be served by mail on your attorney (the attorney who responds to the summons). When this occurs, a copy of the complaint will usually be sent to you for your examination and records. Thus you will be able to read either the original complaint served with the summons or a copy of the complaint sent to you by your attorney. The complaint specifies the allegations against you, couched in general language, and the amount for which the plaintiff is suing you. The clause containing the amount sued for is called the "ad damnum clause."

When a physician reads the ad damnum clause in the complaint against him and discovers that he is being sued for a very large amount of money, he usually tends to panic. This reaction is understandable, but there are certain factors you should keep in mind when considering the amount in the ad damnum clause of any complaint. For several reasons, plaintiffs invariably sue for a great deal more than they feel the case is worth.

First, it is always better to overestimate the amount of damages (money) the injuries seem to be worth because, if there is a development that increases the actual value of the case, no amendment of the ad damnum clause will be required. If, for example, before the trial is reached the plaintiff has to undergo additional surgery or his condition deteriorates, a sufficiently large amount demanded will cover the increased damages created by such developments.

Second, the plaintiff always keeps in mind that he can never recover more than he demands. He is afraid that if he demands a realistic figure he may miscalculate. The jury may want to punish you or may feel the case is worth more than previous cases of the same type, and the plaintiff wants to be able to receive a verdict for the largest amount the jury could possibly come up with.

Third, by suing for a large amount of money the plaintiff scares you, the defendant physician, and convinces you of the seriousness of his belief in his case. If your insurance coverage is low, doing so may arouse in you the additional fear that a verdict could exceed your policy limits and invade your personal assets. There is no penalty for overestimating the amount put in the ad damnum clause; therefore, considering the possible advantages, there is very little reason for the plaintiff not to overestimate it.

There are other factors you should keep in mind when reading a complaint against you that contains a large amount in the ad damnum clause. Medical malpractice cases are very often cases in which the plaintiff either loses or wins a substantial amount of money. Injuries that are associated with claims of negligent treatment tend to be serious. If the jurors believe that the plaintiff's injuries were not caused by a deviation from accepted practice, they are compelled to find for you, as unfortunate as the injuries may be. However, if they believe that the injuries were caused by your deviation from accepted practice, they will award substantial damages for the serious injuries. You must keep in mind, therefore, that the amount demanded in no way reflects on the merits of the case or insures that the plaintiff is guaranteed to win at least a lesser amount.

Many plaintiffs have sued for millions in cases involving grievous injuries, such as brain damage and quadriplegia, and have left the courtroom without a cent. Sympathy or compromise verdicts sometimes occur, but they are not the rule. Presenting a strong, honest defense definitely minimizes them. It may surprise you to learn that honest lay people *will* render a verdict in your behalf, notwithstanding the involvement of horrible, heartrending injuries, if they believe that you rendered good, careful treatment. They realize that such injuries sometimes cannot be prevented.

A case early in my training as a medical malpractice defense attorney drove this point home to me in dramatic fashion. I went to court to argue a motion and, after completing my argument, stopped in to watch the trial of a medical malpractice case being defended by one of the senior members of the firm I was with. I admired his proficiency and hoped to learn from watching him in action. When I entered the courtroom I could feel the tenseness and emotion in the room. It was an electric scene.

The plaintiff, a policeman, was suing on behalf of his brain-damaged daughter, who was thirteen years old and blind. She was sitting in court flanked by her mother and father, who appeared to be simple, good people. The couple's other children, well-scrubbed and well-behaved, were also in court. The basic claim was that the infant plaintiff—the retarded, blind daughter—had been brain-damaged thirteen years earlier at birth due to negligent delivery by the defendant obstetrician. The infant had presented in a double footling breech position and the complaint alleged a failure to perform a cesarean section and improper use of forceps.

The defendant obstetrician was a young resident in obstetrics and gynecology at the time of the delivery; by the time of trial he had become a well-respected obstetrician-gynecologist with excellent qualifications.

The little girl was pathetic and had required a great deal of special care. She had obviously disrupted the lives of the members of her family. The plaintiffs were suing for approximately three million dollars.

I watched the impressive-looking defendant physician take the stand. My associate questioned him about the delivery thirteen years earlier. As the doctor began to explain what had happened, he became so involved in what he was saying that one could see he was reliving the entire episode. The lawyer let him continue without interruption. Everyone in the room was watching and listening without a sound. The doctor explained how he had come to his decision about the mother's ability to deliver from below. The birth canal by measurement had been more than adequate for the size of the infant. The delivery had gone normally up to the point when one shoulder was delivered. The doctor became more and more intense as he continued with his description. This delivery was obviously etched in his memory. He directed himself to the jurors.

After one shoulder had been delivered, he had encountered difficulty because the baby's head had become extended and was preventing passage through the pelvis. The doctor was sweating. He explained to the jurors that he had had approximately three minutes to bring the baby's head down and deliver the child or it would die. He said that he had had the option of attempting to bring the head down with various manual techniques or with forceps. All of a sudden he went down on his knees to show the jury the position he took when trying to bring down the head with his hands. He had had to go on his knees to position himself properly in respect to the mother. He could not bring the head down with his hands. It *had* to come down. He brought it down with forceps and delivered the remainder of the infant. The doctor stated that he had used as little force as possible in bringing the head down with the forceps. He looked at the jury and stood up. He was exhausted from recounting what had occurred. There was no question in my mind that he was competent and sincere and had done the best he could in a difficult situation.

Testimony went on. Yes, the baby experienced convulsions after the delivery. Yes, the baby had brain damage. You can imagine the remainder of the testimony. Expert opinions on both sides about the delivery and the cause of the brain damage were elicited, not to mention the emotional testimony about the effect of this brain-damaged child on her family.

There was a great deal of speculation about what the result of the case would be. If there were a verdict for the plaintiffs (the infant and father), it would be a very high one. There was no dispute about the extensive damages, and the family had made a good impression. The plaintiffs lost. They received nothing. The jury came in with a verdict for the defendant physician. Why? I am sure that, after observing the defendant explain what had happened, they felt he was a dedicated physician who had done everything he could, properly and with sound medical reasons, in a problematic situation. As unfortunate as the outcome of treatment was, the jury did not find the treatment negligent and therefore could not hold the doctor responsible.

The Answer

Once the complaint has been received, it must be answered by your attorney within a period of time specified by law. This period can be extended by stipulation between attorneys. In order for the allegations to be answered properly, your attorney must have in his possession an extensive statement of your treatment or must conduct a preliminary interview with you from which he can obtain the necessary information.

Certain principles that are used in answering a complaint often confuse physicians. Sometimes a physician will call his attorney, agitated and upset after reading the answer prepared on his behalf because he does not understand the reasons why some allegations are denied or the manner in which they are denied. This book does not purport to teach pleading; therefore, should you have a question concerning the answer served on your behalf, you should discuss it with your attorney so that you can understand the answer. Keep in mind, however, that in order to put any fact alleged in the complaint *in issue* to be resolved by the jury, that fact must be denied in some form by you in your answer.

Verification

If a pleading is verified, it means that the party doing the alleging has sworn to the truth of the pleading based on his own knowledge of facts or on information and belief (facts within his knowledge that lead him to believe in the truth of the allegations). This is done by signing such a statement in front of a notary public.

If the party pleading is not within the county (or district or whatever) in which his attorney is located, the procedural rules may allow his attorney to sign the verification on his behalf. This means that the attorney is swearing to the truth of the allegations on behalf of his client, on the basis of the information he has obtained from the client.

If the complaint is verified, the answer and the other pleadings must usually also be verified. A pleading that is verified by the party making it can be used more effectively on cross-examination to impeach that party if it can be shown the party had no knowledge of the veracity of the allegations or knew them to be untrue despite his signature.

Counterclaims and Cross-claims

An answer on your behalf may contain affirmative defenses, such as contributory negligence, and may also assert a claim on your behalf in addition to your responses to the allegations of the plaintiff. A claim you assert against the plaintiff based on the same facts on which he is basing a claim against you, such as a claim for your bill for the services the plaintiff claims were negligently rendered, is called a counterclaim. If your claim is against another defendant, it is called a cross-claim.

A medical malpractice defense attorney is usually asked by the physician he is representing if a claim can be asserted against the plaintiff for wrongfully suing him. Generally speaking, the system in the United States gives anyone the right to sue if he believes in good faith that he has been negligently wronged and injured by that negligence. The only limitation on this right is that it cannot be used falsely and maliciously to harass. Thus, notwithstanding certain rare cases of physicians' successfully recovering against their patients for improperly suing them,[1] you cannot normally counterclaim against your patient for suing you, despite your belief that the suit has absolutely no basis and despite the great cost to you in terms of inconvenience and dollars, unless you can *prove* that you are being sued maliciously and that the plaintiff is bringing the suit not in good faith because of his belief in the merits of his claim but to harass you.

The fact that you ultimately win the suit your patient has brought against you does not prove malice. It is an extremely difficult element to prove, and the effort required and the poor chances of success usually make such a claim against a patient unrealistic. One way to prove malicious intent would be to show a series of acts and pattern of behavior that could have no purpose other than to harass you. Without such evidence, though, it is almost impossible to prove the malicious intent of the patient.

Notwithstanding the existence of a comparative negligence system, your claims against other parties should always be pleaded by means of counterclaim or cross-claim, so that you can introduce evidence against these parties to prove your claims.

The Third-Party Complaint (Impleader)

When you wish to assert a claim, based on the same facts surrounding the claims in the plaintiff's case, against a party who has not been sued by the plaintiff and is therefore not in the action, you may do so by adding a third-party complaint to your answer. Thus, in addition to answering the plaintiff's allegations against you and asserting whatever affirmative defenses, counterclaims, and cross-claims you have, you would also include a separate section asserting your claims against the third party. This answer, along with copies of the other pleadings already served in the case, would then be served with a summons on the third-party defendant as if it were a normal complaint.

The third-party defendant has all the rights of any party to the lawsuit, and he will serve a third-party answer responding to the third-party complaint and

1. See *New York Times*, 3 June 1976, p. 20.

asserting any defenses he has against the third-party plaintiff and any claims he has against *any* party in the action. Bringing a third party into the lawsuit in this manner is also called impleader.

A good example of the use of impleader is the situation in which a defendant wishes to assert that the plaintiff's injuries were caused not by his negligence but by the defective instrument or machine he used. If the plaintiff has not sued the manufacturer of the instrument or machine, the attorney for the defendant may bring in the manufacturer by serving a third-party complaint.

The Bill of Particulars

Once the complaint and answer have been served, the defendant will serve a demand for a bill of particulars, which is exactly what its name says: Based on the complaint, the defendant makes up a list of particulars he wishes to know about the claims of the plaintiff. The purpose of the demand is to make the plaintiff be more specific about his claims, giving details, and narrow down the issues between the parties. Very often there are disputes between the plaintiff and the defendant as to how particular the plaintiff should be and as to the adequacy of the responses to the defendant's demands. (The document called the "demand for a bill of particulars" actually contains numbered demands.) These disputes are resolved by the court after considering the arguments made by both sides.

The document that contains the responses to the numbered demands is the "bill of particulars." If the other pleadings are verified, the bill of particulars must also be verified.

Your Legal Representation

Conflict of Interest

Your attorney is your modern-day knight, your champion. He must fight your battle for you in court. He will decide strategy, tactics, and means to destroy the plaintiff's claims. He must endeavor to tear down the plaintiff's witnesses on cross-examination. Obviously, he must be dedicated to your interest; thus he cannot represent a party whose interest may be adverse to, or conflict with, yours. This is often a subtle distinction, because it can benefit your defense for your lawyer to represent other codefendants who are united in interest. When two parties are united in interest, sharing a lawyer avoids incompatible philosophies of defense and prevents unnecessary and damaging conflicts between parties who must stand or fall together. Such conflicts can only benefit the plaintiff.

Usually the question of conflict of interest will be decided by your attorney as a matter of ethics. If, however, you question your attorney's representation of another party whose interest you feel conflicts with yours, you should discuss this matter with him. Do not be shy. Ask him to explain why his representation of that party will not be harmful to your defense, and point out those areas in which you feel your position conflicts with that of the other defendant he is representing. Your attorney may not fully understand your position, the position of the other party, or the facts, and thus he may not have been aware of the conflict.

If you are satisfied with his explanation that there is no conflict and that you are united in interest with the other party, you should not object to joint representation. If, however, you are not satisfied and feel that your defense will be compromised, you should ask your attorney to refer the representation of his other client (or your own representation) to another attorney. If you retained him, you can discharge him and seek other counsel. If your insurance company retained him, you can arrange for the company to do so. It is absolutely vital that you trust and respect your attorney. You must feel confident that you are receiving uncompromised representation. You can be sure that both your attorney and your insurance company will be sensitive to this issue and anxious to avoid any possible conflict of interest.

Your Own Personal Attorney

Is the attorney retained by the insurance company to represent you competent? Is his representation sufficient? Should you retain your own personal attorney? These are all questions that may come to your mind when you are sued. In general, it is my experience that hiring your own personal attorney is unnecessary and possibly even harmful to your interest. This is true for several reasons. Most personal attorneys whom you would normally hire at your own expense are not medical malpractice defense experts. Medical malpractice is a very narrow specialty within negligence trial law. The number of attorneys who specialize in defending medical malpractice cases is quite small. The attorney who handles your other legal affairs may know wills or mortgages, or even automobile accident cases, backward and forward, but it is doubtful that he has any expertise in medical malpractice. If you retain him and he interferes with the expert attorney retained by your insurance company, you are paying an attorney to disrupt the application of the expertise of a medical malpractice specialist. This invariably occurs when you bring your own personal attorney into the case because the personal attorney wants to earn his fee, so he feels compelled to participate, notwithstanding his lack of experience. You cannot have two chiefs running the defense. On occasion the personal attorney recognizes his lack of expertise and does nothing, and so you end up paying for exactly that, nothing.

If you do not retain your own personal attorney but seek out a medical malpractice defense specialist of your own to be your own personal attorney in addition to insurance counsel, you will pay handsomely for his expertise. You will also be faced with conflict between the two malpractice attorneys and their egos, which can prejudice the presentation of your defense. It seems wasteful to me to hire a malpractice specialist when your insurance company has already done so. The adequacy of your defense does not increase with the number of attorneys hired to represent you. Your defense must be consistent, clear, strong, honest, and smoothly presented. You cannot afford ill feeling and fighting between members of the defense team. There can be only one chief—one attorney who will take the responsibility for and make the decisions, often on the spur of the moment, that will constitute your defense.

I am assuming that your insurance company is a good one and that it will retain competent expert counsel to defend you. Usually this is the case. Most insurance companies have their own medical malpractice defense specialists or know such attorneys. It is also in their best interest to retain such attorneys.

Nevertheless, if you feel (on the basis of research, your own impression, or other information) that your insurance company has selected inferior counsel to represent you, in order to save money or for political or other reasons, if the company will not retain new counsel for you, and if you can afford a medical malpractice defense lawyer in whom you have more confidence, hire him. Under such circumstances the lawyer retained by the insurance company often yields to the superior expertise of the personal attorney (if that is the case) and does not interfere with his running of the defense. He simply makes his presence known and lets the personal attorney do the work. However, this is not always the case; sometimes even a less experienced lawyer retained by the insurance company will resent the presence of the personal attorney and fight him every step of the way. The same thing can also occur in reverse, if the less experienced personal attorney fails to yield to the more experienced insurance attorney. Both situations are intolerable.

It is my considered opinion that you should not be forced to retain your own attorney to defend you when you are insured. Legal defense is part of what you are paying premiums for. A quality insurance company should retain quality counsel to represent its assureds. If you have evidence to the contrary concerning the attorney assigned to represent you, you should make it known to your company and request new counsel. Your insurance company should then either grant your request or convince you that your information is incorrect. I am not suggesting that you have the right to insist on being represented by the malpractice defense attorney with the biggest reputation. You are entitled to be represented by a firm that has a respectable reputation for integrity and expertise in medical malpractice defense. Such a firm will give you good representation. The attorney who will actually try your case will depend on the circumstances (such as availability and the complexity of the case). You cannot insist on the biggest gun. You can insist on good, honest, competent representation. You should protest being represented by hack counsel who lack integrity or expertise in medical malpractice defense.

The amount for which you are being sued should not be a factor in the decision to retain personal counsel. A good attorney will give you the same quality of representation whether you are being sued for $500 or $5 million. Your insurance company must inform you of the amount of any uninsured exposure—that is, the amount sued for that exceeds your insurance coverage, which is called your uninsured interest. For example, if you are being sued for $5 million and your coverage extends only up to $3 million, you have an uninsured interest of $2 million. The insurance company must inform you of this amount and of your right to retain your own attorney to represent your uninsured interest. This is a legal technicality and should not be the basis for retaining a lawyer if you are satisfied with the one retained for you. Remember that the existence of any uninsured interest is solely determined by the amount demanded by the plaintiff, which may be wholly unrealistic and highly inflated. The representation that the attorney retained by the insurance company will give you on behalf of the first $3 million covered under the policy is the same representation you would receive if the coverage were for the entire $5 million demanded in the complaint. He will give you the best defense representation possible, no matter what the extent of the coverage. The insurance company does not want to lose any of its money or yours.

Do not misunderstand. In evaluating the case and the advisability of settlement, a good lawyer will always take into consideration the risk of a verdict in excess of your coverage; but the overall quality of defense representation will not change when there is uninsured exposure. This being so, notification of uninsured interest is not a reason to retain your own personal attorney.

House Counsel

As I have said, your insurance company may have its own legal defense staff. Attorneys from the insurance company's legal department, called house counsel, should be evaluated by the same standards as any outside counsel retained by the company to represent you.

Judging the Quality of Your Attorney

You may be saying to yourself at this point, "Fine, but how the hell do I know if I have a competent malpractice attorney or not?" You make this judgment in the same manner in which one of your patients decides whether he is being treated by a competent physician. Of foremost importance are the feelings you have when you are in personal contact with your attorney. This is one reason why you should ask for and have an early interview with your attorney. Like a patient, you will get a feeling about his competence from the way he handles things and deals with you.

Second, there will be the matter of reputation. A competent firm or attorney will often have a reputation for defending medical malpractice cases well. If your impression accords with the reputation, you are probably in good hands.

Finally, notwithstanding reputation, you can make specific inquiries about your attorney. You can ask your personal attorney to inquire about the attorney's competence. If you know another physician who has been represented by your attorney, you may be able to speak to that physician. You should compile as much information from these various sources as you need to satisfy yourself about the integrity and competence of your attorney.

Judging an attorney is as difficult as judging a physician. A great many intangibles are involved. I can only suggest that you explore any feelings you have that you are not being represented properly.

Investigation and Preparation of Your Defense

Once you have been sued, you must do everything you can to assist your insurance company and your attorney to put together your defense. Copy relevant office records for your attorney. (Remember, nothing should be altered as a result of your being sued.) If you can obtain hospital records, autopsy reports, texts, or articles relevant to the case, provide them to your attorney. Do not make it difficult for your attorney to have an early meeting with you. If you know physicians in your field who would be good choices to perform a physical examination of the plaintiff or to review the case as experts on your behalf (and who could not be impeached as witnesses because they are personal friends or on the same staff), you can assist your attorney by preparing a list of such physicians.

Once you are aware that a claim is being asserted against you, you must be careful not to discuss your treatment with others. You will be asked about such discussions. You must not be forced to admit that you made a damaging admission. You must not be quoted by the person you spoke to as making such an admission. Obviously, you may check the hospital records, make copies, and do whatever else is necessary, but it looks bad if the operating-room supervisor testifies that *after the summons was served* you asked her what type of suture you used during the procedure in question.

Your assistance consists of helping to gather information, making suggestions, working with your attorney, and avoiding unnecessary mistakes. This means being careful to preserve your original records, not to give information to representatives of another party, and not to make damaging admissions.

Examinations Before Trial (Depositions)

The Purpose

An examination before trial (sometimes called an EBT, or deposition) is part of what is called *discovery*. This is the process by which each side "discovers" as much of the evidence the other side possesses as possible. For example, your attorney may serve a notice on the attorney for the plaintiff to produce a certain prescription that the plaintiff claims you improperly prescribed. If the plaintiff or his attorney possesses this document, it will then have to be produced for examination by your attorney. The plaintiff's attorney can also use this method of discovery to obtain for examination documentary evidence that you possess.

Though there are numerous procedures involved in the discovery process, such as the notice to produce, by far the most important is the examination before trial. By serving a notice of examination before trial, an attorney can demand that a party be produced for questioning with his records, x-rays, or other evidence in his possession. Such a notice can be served by either side, and if the examinations before trial cannot be arranged by notice, either side can apply to the court to order that they be held. Examinations before trial are usually confined to parties to the lawsuit, but under special circumstances (such as impending death) important nonparty witnesses can also be examined before trial to preserve their testimony or obtain vital information.

You are examined before trial under oath, so as to pin you down to a story, let the other side know what your position is, and allow the party questioning you to learn new facts to investigate. The questioning party also attempts to elicit damaging statements from you under oath.

It is extremely difficult later to change the testimony you give at your examination before trial. An attempt to change your testimony at the trial resembles perjury and can destroy you. The examinations before trial are usually taken well in advance of trial, and therefore closer in time to the events in question (sometimes years closer). If you try to correct or change your testimony at the time of the trial—a time further removed from the events—it looks as if you were coached or are lying to protect yourself. Your memory should be fresher at the examination before trial, and therefore you must be accurate when you testify at it.

Preparation

Many malpractice suits are in effect decided at the examination before trial, because of the importance of the sworn testimony elicited. It is obvious, therefore, that careful preparation is merited before you testify at your examination before trial. Nevertheless, many physicians are unprepared to testify at their examinations and make mistakes that cost them the lawsuits.

It is easy for a physician to be lulled into underestimating the importance of his testimony at the examination before trial. Very often the testimony is taken before a certified shorthand reporter at a lawyer's office. The atmosphere may be friendly, and often there is joking between the attorneys. Even if the testimony is taken in a room in the courthouse (it is not taken before a judge, although a judge may settle disputes about the propriety of certain questions), the atmosphere may be relaxed, with friendly banter between the attorneys. No matter what the atmosphere at the examination before trial, you must remember that your testimony is of the utmost importance.

Preparing for your examination before trial is a great deal like preparing to testify at your trial (which will be covered in detail in Chapter 10). You must not only know your treatment but also familiarize yourself with all the pertinent medical records, x-rays, test results, and data so that you can refer to this material with ease. You should obtain all the additional data you can from your attorney, possibly including materials that he has obtained through discovery or investigation that were not previously available to you. Such material may involve the treatment of other physicians or the actions of the plaintiff.

You should also review any areas of your specialty that may be the subject of intensive questioning and that you do not know cold. It is important that you be familiar with what the major treatises and any relevant current literature say in regard to those areas, because the opposing counsel will be using the information in these materials as the basis for many of his questions on cross-examination.

When you have acquired a working knowledge of all the data, you must have an intensive session with your attorney to review your treatment with him and to allow him to question you and critique your answers so that you understand how to answer properly and do not make vague or misleading answers that would be damaging when read at the time of trial. In addition to giving you general guidelines about testifying and reviewing the danger areas and weak points in your treatment, he should question you himself about sensitive areas of your care and about your specialty. You must know how to field expert questions.

I am not suggesting that your attorney put words in your mouth or suborn perjury. I am suggesting that a good attorney can point out, by asking you questions and critiquing your answers, when you are being ambiguous or unresponsive or are needlessly volunteering information. At this session you should ask whatever questions you have about procedure at the examination before trial.

How to Testify at Your Examination Before Trial

Much of what you need to know on how to testify at your examination before trial is covered in the section on how to testify at your trial, pages 197-214 in Chapter 10. Nevertheless, there are certain points specifically applicable to your testimony at the examination before trial that you should keep in mind.

Physicians are notoriously bad witnesses. For some reason, the scientific mentality required of a physician does not lend itself to the black-or-white reality required by the law. Thus you must make an extra effort to learn how to be an effective witness. Because you must defend your treatment in the legal arena, you must learn to abide by the legal rules.

The examination before trial is not the trial, and you must remember that you are not testifying *to justify* your treatment. There is no judge or jury present to decide whether you are guilty of malpractice. You are there to answer the questions of the opposing counsel as completely and thoroughly as you can, making your meaning clear but not volunteering information outside the scope of the question. You are not there to give lengthy explanations that are not responsive to the questions asked. It is up to the plaintiff's lawyer to be smart enough to ask all the important questions and to obtain all the important information from you he can. If he omits something, it is not your obligation to volunteer it. You will have ample opportunity to tell the complete story at the time of trial. If the opposing attorney fails to ask something important, that is his problem, not yours. If your attorney thinks it is important to raise the matter at the examination before trial, he will do so by asking you about it himself. Your sole job is to answer the questions put to you concisely but without sacrificing completeness. You need not restrict yourself to a yes or a no. If a yes or no will suffice, fine. If qualification or explanation is required to make the answer intelligible and to prevent misinterpretation, you must include the necessary qualification or explanation. What must be remembered is that the answer should be confined as closely as possible to the scope of the question. Do not break new ground for the inquiring attorney when it is not essential to your answer *to the question asked.*

When you ramble on and volunteer information outside the scope of the question, you inadvertently help the opposition by providing to the plaintiff's lawyer (or an opposing codefendant's lawyer) information he might not have thought of asking about. You also lengthen your examination by opening up new areas for him to question about.

The answers to certain questions must be carefully qualified to prevent misinterpretation. This is usually true of expert questions put to you at your examination before trial. The general rule is that you may be asked expert questions within your specialty at the examination before trial. Suppose you are asked about a broad general principle, such as, "Generally speaking, doctor, does good medical practice require the earliest possible evacuation of a subdural hematoma to obtain the best result?" You cannot merely say yes. It is important that your answer make it clear that early evacuation depends on the circumstances involved. Early evacuation of the hematoma may be contraindicated if the hematoma is not causing much damage and the patient's condition is such that he could not withstand such a procedure. If you do not specify your qualifications to the principle enunciated at the time of the examination before trial, you will be confronted with your failure to do so when you try to explain them at the time of trial. The opposing counsel will point out to the jury that when you were asked the same question at your examination before trial you did not mention any of the qualifications you are now trying to explain at the trial. He will read your former answer from the transcript of your examination before trial.

As a witness you must realize that every question asked by an attorney has a purpose that relates to the matter at hand. You must take your time in answering. Give yourself time to understand the question, to formulate your answer, and to allow your attorney to object if the question is improper. Do not interrupt the question or blurt out rapid-fire answers. If you do not understand a question, you must insist that it be rephrased unambiguously so that you can understand it *before you answer it.* This is permitted and is proper.

I very often refuse to allow a client to answer a question I do not understand, feel he does not understand, or consider ambiguous. I insist that it be rephrased until its meaning is clear. Nevertheless, you cannot count on your attorney to do this; nor is he always able to recognize a medical ambiguity contained in a question. *You* are the physician, and if the questioning attorney has put a question that is medically improper, whether inadvertently or purposely, you should not answer it. Ask him to rephrase it until it is medically correct, clear, and unambiguous, so that your answer can be the same. If the attempt at rephrasing is still medically incorrect or ambiguous, continue to ask for a rephrasing until the question is clear and medically correct. This may take four or more rephrasings. It may require enduring the annoyance and exasperation of the interrogating lawyer. Be calm and patient. His histrionics do not matter. What matters is that the question be clear and medically correct so that you can answer clearly and there can be no misinterpretation of the question or the answer later at the trial.

One important rule is never to guess at an examination before trial. If you do not remember something, you should say so rather than guess. "I do not remember" is a perfectly legitimate answer when it is true. It is far preferable to guessing or making up an answer and being convincingly contradicted by other evidence and testimony at the trial. Furthermore, if you speculate, you can be sure that you will later remember the truth as being totally different from your guess. When you have answered that you do not remember something at your examination before trial, it is possible to explain at the trial that your memory was refreshed and then to testify as to what you remember. However, if you have taken a position on the basis of a guess at your examination before trial, you cannot change your testimony without being embarrassed.

Because of their scientific minds and desire for absolute truth, many physicians have difficulty being positive and tend to equivocate when answering. In the minds of the jurors, equivocation has only negative implications and usually results in disbelief. As a witness, therefore, you must consider every factor relevant to your answer and then reach a positive unequivocal conclusion. You must take a stand. It is important to do so in answering both factual and expert questions.

Suppose, for example, that you are an ophthalmologist and that routine preparation for a particular operation is to massage the eyeball to soften it up. You always do so, without exception. Suppose further that you have not read this book, and that your operative note in the case in question states only "routine preparation" in regard to your preparation prior to the operation. Your patient has sued you, alleging that you did not massage the eyeball and that your failure to do so caused the operation to fail. By the time of your examination before trial, you have no *specific* recollection of massaging the eyeball of the plaintiff prior to the operation, which took place five years earlier. In the five years since the operation on the plaintiff, you have operated on hundreds of eyes. The plaintiff's attorney asks you at your examination before trial whether you massaged the plaintiff's eyeball prior to operating on his eye. You cannot answer that you *think* you did. You must consider all the factors *silently*, weigh them, decide where the truth lies, and answer positively one way or another. Saying "I think I did" will be interpreted to mean either that you do not know if you did or that you did not. "I think" means that you do not know, and when read to the jurors will mean to them that you did not. They will reason that you would know if you did massage the eyeball. Such reasoning is unfair to you and can be avoided if you are honest and do not equivocate in your answers. (If you did not massage the eyeball, you should say so and either defend that decision as proper or accept the responsibility for it if it is not.)

If you always massage the eyeball as a part of your preoperative routine prior to the procedure in question, you remember no exception for the case in question, and you wrote down "routine preparation" in your operative note, you should *silently* weigh all these factors and decide what answer has the highest degree of probability of being the truth. Certainly there is more evidence that you did massage the eyeball than that you did not. It is perfectly understandable that you have no *specific* recollection of massaging the eyeball of this particular patient, since the operation took place hundreds of operations ago. With all this in mind, you must give your answer—an answer that will not encompass every negative possibility, because you have no specific recollection of this patient's operation, but that most probably represents the truth given the data you have available. (If you recollected this particular operation, this process would obviously not be necessary.) Doesn't it all add up to an affirmative answer of "Yes, I did massage the eyeball"? Your answer is based on the facts that you wrote down "routine preparation," which always includes massaging the eyeball, that you do not remember an exception for the case in question, and that an exception would be highly unusual and thus not forgettable. The basis for your answer should not be volunteered unless you are asked for it.

By reasoning in the above manner, you have enabled yourself to make an honest definitive answer that you have a basis for and to prevent the unfair and damaging reasoning that flows from equivocation (even if it is innocent). If you are asked about your *specific* recollection of the event, you must admit that you have no specific recollection of performing the massage but that your note, your routine, and the fact that you would remember any deviation from your routine make you positive that you did. (When answering such a question, it is always best to state the affirmative reasoning first and then admit the negative. Doing so insures that you are not cut off before stating the affirmative part.) It is *possible* that you neglected to massage the eyeball in this one case, but anything is possible; such a possibility is pure speculation and very remote in the face of the evidence.

I cannot resist pointing out that if the ophthalmologist in the case (a case I tried) had noted in his operative report what his routine preoperative preparation entailed, the entire lawsuit would have been avoided.

The same method of reasoning must be employed in answering expert questions if your answers are to be meaningful. If the question is whether or not routine preparation for a particular ophthalmological operation includes eyeball massage, you must consider all the pertinent information with which you are familiar and then take a stand. You may know that the major texts specify massage as part of the routine preparation. You may know that most physicians, except for a small group of ophthalmologists at a certain eye institute, do include it. In the face of this information, doesn't the answer have to be yes? If you silently consider the small group of physicians who do not massage the eyeball and then, in an attempt to be honest, answer "Not always," haven't you distorted the truth? The truth is that, generally speaking, routine preoperative preparation for this procedure *does* include eyeball massage. By answering "Not always," you have in effect told the jury that this is not generally true when it is. The jury will interpret your answer to mean that it is just as probable that routine preoperative preparation for the procedure does *not* include eyeball massage as that it does. However, if there are two recognized schools of thought in regard to the subject of inquiry (in this case, massaging the eyeball), this should be noted in your answer when appropriate.

Since the law requires a definitive reply, you must weigh all the probabilities and then answer in accordance with the weight of the probability, not the rare exception. If you need to explain or qualify your answer, you can do so when appropriate. The question is not what *every* physician does in his routine preoperative preparation, but what is generally done. If the vast majority massage the eyeball as part of the routine preoperative preparation, you must answer that the routine preoperative preparation does include eyeball massage. If asked specifically about any exception to the general rule, you can then testify about it.

Basically the question asks for the general rule, not the minority rule or exception. You cannot measure questions in true scientific terms and expect to provide answers that allow for no exceptions or include every possible exception, no matter how rare or unlikely. Strange as it may sound, it is almost impossible to find absolute truth in the courtroom, or anywhere else. The law understands this and attempts to approach the truth as closely as possible by obtaining and considering evidence that reveals the greatest probability of what the truth is. Though in every trial there will be facts that do not add up or fit together, a version of events will emerge that explains what occurred better than any other version. This version may not be the absolute truth, but it is the best we can do and it becomes the truth of the case and the basis for decision.

It is true that some facts will not be disputed or will be supported by tangible evidence that cannot be disputed. Nevertheless, most of the evidence, even written evidence, will be opposed by conflicting evidence. There may be inaccuracies, problems of interpretation, differences in the recollection of events, even among witnesses testifying for the same side, and other ambiguities. Although you swear that your memory is absolutely accurate, another party will swear the same thing and have a very different recollection of what occurred. You cannot both be correct. The absolute truth may lie somewhere in between, but no one can be absolutely sure where. Nevertheless, by considering *everything* brought forward, and considering what is most probable, we can get a pretty good idea of the truth, although we cannot usually pin it down exactly. It is this process that we call justice. Although imperfect by scientific standards, it is the best method we have for settling such factual disputes and attributing fault. This should be kept in mind when you testify at your examination before trial or at your trial (or are called as an expert).

The Format and Scope of the Questioning

The questions asked at an examination before trial are similar to those asked at the trial, except that your attorney should not permit you to be cross-examined. The purpose of the examination before trial is discovery. It differs from the trial, where testimony must stand the test of cross-examination for the benefit of the jury (to allow them to judge the witnesses' credibility). Leading, argumentative, and loaded questions used on cross-examination and permitted at trial are not proper at an examination before trial. If you are being evasive about a fact or an opinion, the attorney is permitted to keep after you, but he should not be permitted by your attorney to be abusive or argumentative or to put questions that are leading or suggestive in form. Your attorney is the best judge of this, and it is his task to object to improper questions. Nevertheless, you should be aware of this rule so that, if your attorney is not objecting and you feel you are being improperly cross-examined, you can at least protest and perhaps wake him up.

The procedure at your examination before trial is that you are sworn in and the plaintiff's attorney questions you first. Your testimony is recorded, by a certified shorthand reporter in most cases, and transcribed for your signature. When the plaintiff's attorney finishes questioning you, the attorneys representing the other parties to the lawsuit—other plaintiffs or codefendants—are entitled to question you, provided they have complied with the procedural requirements of setting up the examination. Sometimes procedural problems prevent an attorney representing one of the parties from questioning. You may or may not be further examined by him later.

When the attorneys representing all the parties have finished examining you, your attorney is also entitled to ask you questions. He will not normally do so unless he feels that something needs clarification or that something was omitted that should be brought out at that time, and in the record. Ordinarily your attorney need not question you, since he knows your story and usually does not want to reveal facts or opinions the other attorney failed to ask about. Remember that your attorney will have ample opportunity at the trial to develop anything omitted at the examination before trial.

Although an attorney is not entitled to be repetitive, when a new attorney questions he is normally entitled to go over material already covered by another attorney. An attorney will not usually do this unless he wishes to clarify something or bring out something new.

The scope of the questioning at the examination before trial is supposed to be defined by the issues raised by the pleadings, especially the bill of particulars. Nevertheless, the trend has been toward liberal disclosure; most courts, following the liberal rules of the federal courts, are quite permissive in regard to what they will allow to be asked. There is a limit, however, and your attorney should object if the questioning attorney goes too far afield, asks irrelevant questions, or attempts what lawyers call a "fishing expedition."

One important guideline is that questions should be asked for the purpose of discovery of facts or opinions relating to the treatment involved. Even general expert questions should have some relevance to the treatment involved. (For example, if the treatment involved is ankle surgery, you should not be answering questions about knee surgery—although you may answer questions about general principles of surgery that apply to both the knee and the ankle.) Questions designed solely to elicit information that may assist in cross-examination, and unrelated to the treatment at issue, are in my opinion improper and outside the scope of the examination. For example, if the lawyer asks you what texts you consider authoritative in your field, or whether you recognize a specific text as authoritative, he is not trying to "discover" anything relating to the treatment; he is trying to establish what texts he can use to cross-examine you at the time of trial.[2] If you provide such information, he will try to use those texts to impeach your opinions. I maintain that the purpose of an examination before trial is not for you to provide this type of information.

Use of Records

As I have said, most notices of examination before trial call for the production of documents and other evidence, about which the witnesses are then questioned. This is *especially* true in medical malpractice cases, which involve office records, hospital records, lab results, x-rays, and other data. A good witness will know how to use this evidence to help him testify.

You are permitted to look at any such evidence to refresh your recollection of events, and you should always do so. Why guess or trust your memory alone when you do not have to? Why take the chance that you might omit something or testify contrary to a note when you do not need to? You should always take the time to look at the applicable note, order, or portion of the hospital record, even if it is only to reassure yourself. Always use the originals if they are present at the examination; let the attorneys use the copies. (The same rule applies at the trial.) Insist that *you* read or consult the originals while testifying. It is your testimony that is being taken. If hospital records are involved and the hospital is a party to the lawsuit, ask your attorney to make sure that the hospital's attorney provides the original records for you to use. Using the actual chart you consulted while treating the patient will make it easier for you to read and locate items within the record. Copies are often hard to read and incomplete.

You must always be careful about the records you produce at the examination before trial. Your attorney may permit the other attorneys to look at and copy them; make sure that they all come back to you *intact* and *complete* and do not testify until you have them back in front of you. You will also need them to consult when you take the stand at your trial.

Sometimes an attorney will try to trick you out of consulting the records before answering by asking you (before you have looked at the record) if you have an independent recollection of the event without looking at the record. In other words, he will stop you before you look at the document or x-ray and ask you whether you can answer from memory without refreshing your recollection. This cute ploy is an attempt to catch you off guard by challenging your memory. The attorney is hoping that you will be affronted by the challenge, take it up, and then make an incomplete or inaccurate answer relying solely on memory. If

---

2. In Chapter 10, see "How to Testify in Court," pp. 197-214, and "The Rule on Textbooks and Articles," pp. 207-214.

this occurs, he may use your answer later at the trial, to suggest that the record is a lie or was made up after the fact or that you are lying.

In my opinion it is always smarter to decline such a challenge and to indicate that you prefer to refresh your recollection from the record before answering. This should be sufficient, but if you are pressed further about your memory without the record, there is nothing wrong with stating that you cannot answer without refreshing your recollection by looking at the record. There is no stigma attached to this response, and it does not necessarily mean that you have no independent recollection of the event. You are merely asserting your right to refresh your recollection by looking at the record. Even if your memory is good and you feel certain of the facts, why give up the advantage of checking yourself by looking at the record? If the questioning attorney tries to embarrass you by suggesting that your request to see the record implies a faulty memory, you should state that you have a good memory but you want to look at the record to make sure all your answers are complete and accurate. The lawyer loses in such an exchange.

Do not let the questioning attorney dupe you by stating that you can look at the records after you answer and then answer again or add what you omitted. If your first answer is faulty in any way, you will have provided him ammunition with which to attack you or the record. The fact that you have amended your answer after looking at the record will be irrelevant.

There will be a great deal about which you will have to testify from memory alone. Use everything you are entitled to use to refresh your memory when you can.

Under certain circumstances it is possible to create an advantage for yourself by asserting your right to refresh your recollection from the records. When records turn up at the last minute, or have not been copied for some reason, or can't be copied on the spot, you can take them away from the questioning attorney by asserting your right to consult them while answering. If you are using the only set of records, the questioning attorney cannot use them to formulate his questions unless he looks over your shoulder or the records are passed back and forth. This is awkward, and many attorneys cannot work this way. It breaks up the flow of questions and gives you a great deal of time to think about your answers, which is not desirable from the questioning attorney's point of view. When this happens, the questioning attorney will sometimes rush through or cut short his questioning about the records. By doing so, he may leave out or miss important or even damaging material he could have questioned you about.

As a general rule, therefore, a smart witness will use and control the records as much as possible when testifying at the examination before trial and at the trial itself.

Objections

If your attorney objects to a question, do not answer it until he tells you that it is permissible to do so. Very often an objection is made and the witness continues to answer. Even when the objection has been made by an attorney representing another party, you should look to your lawyer to see whether he wants to join in the objection or wants you to answer. By not answering, you permit your attorney to protect you. If the question is improper in form, it can be corrected before you answer. When a question is loaded and you blurt out a damaging answer over your attorney's objection, you hurt yourself. The objection would have caused the attorney who asked it to correct the form of the question so that you could respond properly. Remember that damaging answers you give before your attorney can stop you may be used against you on cross-examination at the trial.

Your attorney may object to a question for various reasons. It may be improper. He may want to give you time to think. He may want his objection on the record so that he can object to someone reading the question and answer at the trial. He may object in order to give himself time to evaluate its propriety or to have it repeated by the reporter. No matter what the reason, when you hear him object do not answer or complete any answer you have begun. Think about the question. Your attorney may be trying to alert you to its danger. Do not answer or complete an answer until your attorney has withdrawn his objection or indicated that he wishes you to answer over his objection. (This procedure keeps his objection on the record, which may allow objection at the trial.)

Some attorneys argue that, at an examination before trial, it is permissible to object only to the form of a question (the manner in which it is phrased), not to its content. The rule may vary according to the jurisdiction. Whatever the technical reading of the rule, it is my opinion that your attorney should not permit you to answer questions that are improper in form or content. If the inquiring attorney insists that you answer such questions, your attorney should force him to obtain a court ruling that you must do so. If the questioning attorney does not wish to make such an application to the court (which, depending on the circumstances, can be oral or written), he must either rephrase his questions properly or move on to new material.

An attorney representing another party cannot control you at your examination before trial. That is, such an attorney cannot direct you not to answer, as can your own attorney. Nevertheless, when another attorney does object to a question put to you, you should look to your attorney to see whether he is joining in the objection, permitting you to answer, allowing you to answer over his objection, or directing you not to answer. Do not merely ignore the objection of another attorney. Perhaps this other attorney has a good objection that your attorney had not thought of but wants to use to protect you. If you go ahead and answer because the objection was not raised by your own counsel, you may be losing protection you could have had.

The Testimony of Other Parties

Physicians are busy professionals. However, the failure to spend a little more time on your case can mean the difference between victory and defeat. You should try to make time to be present at the examination before trial of the other parties in your lawsuit. Doing so is very informative and excellent preparation for what lies ahead.

The more testimony you hear the better, in terms of learning how to answer lawyers' questions and be a good witness. And, by hearing the testimony against you, whether it be from the plaintiff or a codefendant, you learn what the crucial issues in the case are going to be. By discussing this testimony and the questions raised by it, you and your attorney will be able to identify the dangerous areas and weaknesses in your case as revealed by the testimony of the other parties. You will be able to point out the falsehoods and other weaknesses in the testimony of the other parties based on your knowledge of the facts and the medicine.

Your presence at the examination before trial of the other parties also puts you face-to-face with your accuser, which can sometimes make it difficult for him to lie or exaggerate. It may prevent a codefendant from trying to exculpate himself by blaming you.

You may also be able to help your attorney by providing him on-the-spot information with which to question the witness. You may be able to suggest important medical questions he would not have thought of himself because he is less familiar with the medicine involved.

If there are many parties to the lawsuit, it may not be possible for you to be present at all the examinations before trial. In such cases you should try to be present for the testimony of the plaintiff and perhaps one or two key codefendants (and certainly for that of any codefendant you expect to attack you). When there are only a few parties to the suit, you should hear all the testimony.

The Recording of Your Testimony

Normally, as I said, your testimony at an examination before trial is recorded by a certified shorthand reporter. Nevertheless, I have run across attorneys who want to tape-record the testimony, and even one who wanted to write down the testimony himself in longhand. I frown on any system other than using a certified shorthand reporter. Tape can be altered or destroyed and is subject to mechanical failure. A certified shorthand reporter must certify that the transcript is a true record of the testimony taken.

Signing the Transcript

After your testimony has been taken at your examination before trial, the reporter's notes are transcribed. Usually this transcript is then sent to you for your signature. Some jurisdictions permit the waiving of the signature of sworn witnesses, but most attorneys prefer to have the witness' signature, so that, if an inconsistency occurs between the sworn testimony at the examination before trial and the testimony at the trial, the attorney can use the signature to attack the witness. By means of questions to the witness, he can point out to the jury that the witness signed the testimony as recorded, signifying that it was accurate and true, although he testified under oath to something different at the trial. The witness cannot wriggle out of the inconsistency by claiming that the reporter incorrectly recorded his answer at the examination before trial and that he himself never read it. Thus the presence of the signature helps the attorney using the transcript on cross-examination to show that the witness swore to the truth of a lie.

Therefore, when the transcript of your testimony is sent to you, it is important that you read it carefully before you sign it in the presence of a notary public. If there are corrections you wish to make in the transcript, they should be typed on a separate piece of paper indicating the page and line of the error and the correction. You are not permitted to change your answers or rewrite them at the time you read over your testimony and sign it. You are entitled to correct errors that the reporter made in recording or transcribing questions or your answers. These are usually matters of spelling, misheard words, grammar, or word transposition. Occasionally a reporter omits something he did not hear or hears you incorrectly. Most certified reporters are good, and the corrections you may have to make should be *minor*. If it turns out that the transcript you receive is substantially different from your testimony, you should contact your attorney so that he can take the appropriate action.

The certified shorthand reporter who records your testimony must certify that you were sworn and that the transcript of your examination is a true record of your testimony. He must further certify that he is not related to any of the parties to the action by blood or marriage and is in no way interested in the outcome of the lawsuit. Given such a certification and the consequences of its violation, substantial variation between the actual testimony and the transcript is unlikely.

9   Settlement

The single dominant topic of discussion in any malpractice suit is settlement. From the moment the claim arises until seconds before the verdict, and sometimes even after the verdict, it is discussed by representatives of the parties involved. There are pragmatic reasons for this phenomenon.

The Considerations

A plaintiff wants to settle a case in order to be sure to recover some money. He wants to avoid the possibility of losing. He wants to make sure that he recovers something for his injuries and their consequences after the attorney deducts expenses and takes his fee. His attorney expends time and money toward the prosecution of the action and wants to insure that he is compensated for his time and recovers his expenses. Both the plaintiff and his attorney want to settle the case as early as possible to avoid any unnecessary expenditure of time, effort, and money. The longer the case lasts, the more effort, preparation, and money it requires.

A defendant wants to settle a case mainly because of the risk of being hit with a verdict greater than the amount of settlement. Time, effort, and expense are minor factors relative to evaluation of the risks of losing and the possible amount of the verdict. If legal expenses are going to amount to the cost of settlement this would be a significant consideration. Such a situation occurs rarely, and only in less serious cases. If the defendant is underinsured or not insured, such factors have to be considered along with the size of any adverse verdict. You may wish to settle within the policy rather than expose the uninsured interest. You may even wish to pay a tolerable amount from your assets rather than risk larger exposure to them. Such circumstances are relatively rare.

In most cases the main factors contributing to the defendant's decision to settle are the weaknesses in his defense, the strength of the plaintiff's case, the verdict potential, and the amount needed to settle the case. These factors can come into play in various ways. The plaintiff may not yet know of certain weaknesses or problems confronting the defense. A destroyed or altered hospital record, a perjured answer, a missing lab report, or a missing witness can create such problems for the defense that the defense attorney may wish to settle the case if the injuries involved are serious and exposure to a large verdict is unavoidable. The ability of the opposing counsel and the quality of the plaintiff in terms of demeanor, appearance, and sympathetic appeal also contribute to the equation. But it is primarily weaknesses or problems in the defense, which strengthen the plaintiff's case and increase the possibility of losing, and the seriousness of the injuries involved, which create the potential for a large award, that cause the pressure to settle. No lawyer worth his salt would ever settle a case merely because of the reputation or ability of the opposing counsel or the favorable demeanor of the plaintiff.

The decision to settle is always the toughest decision for me. My inclination is to fight. If I believe that no malpractice has been committed, I want to take the plaintiff on. I feel that my client and I will overcome our defense problems and convince the jury that my client did nothing wrong. I always feel that, once battle is joined, we will cause problems for the plaintiff and expose unknown weaknesses in his case; the plaintiff's case may look good on paper but it will look less so once the trial gets under way. I believe that any good trial attorney who enjoys his profession and savors trial combat feels this way when he believes in his client.

Despite these feelings, the realities surrounding an individual case may force discretion on your defense attorney. If your expert has abandoned you and you cannot find a new expert in time to testify; if the injuries involved are terrible; if the hospital records are lost or destroyed; if the codefendants have conspired with the plaintiff against you; if your case has not been properly prepared by your prior attorneys, who referred the case to your defense attorney for trial; if the amount demanded to settle the case is low or reasonable under the circumstances; if the other defendants are anxious to settle and have made substantial offers toward settlement, and in similar circumstances, the situation must be weighed very carefully. Such factors *may* cause your attorney to advise settling a case despite his belief that you did not commit malpractice. He may believe that under normal circumstances you would have a good chance to win, but that the odds are stacked against you because of the special circumstances and settlement is advisable.

Sometimes, when discussing settlement, you have to take into consideration that the plaintiff does not yet know a certain fact damaging to the defense, and that the emergence of that fact will drive the price of settlement sky-high. You may not be able to postpone the decision to settle and begin the trial to see how it goes, since you would thus lose the reasonable price of settlement demanded by the plaintiff in ignorance of the damaging information. You must also evaluate the damage the fact can do to your case in terms of winning and the size of a possible verdict. It is not always easy to judge these things realistically.

There may be other difficult considerations for your defense attorney. The expert opinions on your treatment that he has in his file may be conflicting. One expert may believe you have not committed malpractice while the other believes you have. Even committees or panels that reviewed the case may differ in their opinions of the propriety of the treatment rendered. A good experienced defense attorney must sift out the opinions that are realistic and usable in court. Eventually an attorney can tell whether an opinion will stand up from reading the opinion or interviewing the expert. Some physicians lean over backward when reviewing a case to exculpate their colleagues from blame. This approach creates problems for the defense attorney, who may have difficulty convincing the insurance company or the defendant that the opinion is unrealistic and unsellable to a jury and that settlement is advisable. It may even appear that the defense attorney is selling out when he is merely being realistic and trying to choose the correct course.

The opposite can also be true. Sometimes a panel, committee, or even the insurance company wants to settle a case because of the seriousness of the injuries and the reputation of the opposing attorney. They want to give in. Even though the defense attorney believes in the treatment and has obtained a favorable expert opinion, he may have difficulty convincing the insurance company and the defendant himself to do battle. I had this experience under rather peculiar circumstances.

I took over the defense of a case in midstream. The medical facts were rather unusual. The case involved surgical complications, and in particular the method chosen by the defendant physician to stop intestinal bleeding. I was given the file by an associate at a trial conference. Extreme pressure to settle the case was being exerted by the judge, the insurance company, and the attorneys representing the codefendants and the plaintiff. The expert retained by the insurance company stated that the method chosen by the physician to stop the bleeding that occurred after the surgery was not in accordance with accepted practice. On the basis of this opinion, the horrible injuries involved, and conversations with the insurance company adjuster handling the case, my associate who had been handling the file, and the attorneys for the codefendants, I offered to contribute toward the settlement figure on behalf of the defendant I represented.

When I got back to my office, I arranged for an interview with the defendant to discuss the case and secure his consent to the settlement. He had previously insisted that his treatment was proper and had been angry at the settlement posture of the insurance company. He had been adamantly opposed to settlement. I was anxious to speak with him because I still had certain questions about the treatment; the settlement was not final since it was subject to his consent.

The surgery involved was very complicated and I was not sure that I completely understood everything that had happened, although it was clear that the complications that occurred were terrible. The defendant and I sat down with the hospital record and had a long discussion. I asked myriad questions and learned the problems this surgeon had faced in the operating room. I immediately called an expert surgeon whom I knew and respected. With the defendant present, I outlined the facts for my friend and asked him point-blank whether the surgeon's method of stopping the bleeding was consistent with accepted standards of surgical practice. He told me that the circumstances were very unusual, and that although the defendant's choice of treatment was not common it was certainly within accepted surgical practice. This opinion seemed correct to me in light of what I had just learned from the defendant. I called the insurance company to inform the adjuster of my confidence in the defendant's treatment and to have the settlement offer withdrawn. The surgeon had been faced with a difficult situation not of his own making, and the further complications that developed were not related to the defendant's choice of treatment but were inherent in the situation.

Despite my strong feelings about the defendant's treatment, the adjuster wanted to stay with the settlement. He argued that the injuries were bad and the verdict potential large, and that the case was before a terrible judge who would be prejudiced against us and vindictive if we withdrew our offer. I countered with the argument that the amount of settlement was quite large and that I was not afraid of the judge's anger or prejudice. I had dealt with him before; if he erred and we lost, we could appeal. The adjuster wanted to think about it, and I hung up.

I spoke further with the defendant. He explained to me that, because of internal politics at the hospital, he had made an enemy of one of the codefendants in the case and he was sure that this doctor, who had been an assistant at the surgery, would testify against him. I told the defendant that I believed in his treatment as he did, and that I was ready to go to bat for him notwithstanding the adverse codefendant. I explained the time and sacrifice that would be required to defend the case. At this point he did a complete about-face. He said that he was in the process of taking an important position at another hospital and could not afford the time and effort the fight would require. He was also very discouraged by the idea of a codefendant testifying against him. He was sure that this physician would go to any length, including perjury, to make sure that he lost. I asked the doctor about his prior outrage at the settlement posture of his insurance company and repeated that I was willing to defend the case, notwithstanding the problems involved, if he would work with me. I felt that unfair pressure to settle had been applied. He looked at me hard and long but I could see that he was beaten. He declined my offer and told me that he wanted the case settled. I telephoned the adjuster again, told him what had occurred, and asked him to take it all into consideration and call me back with his decision. The settlement was finalized. The insurance company paid a large amount of money despite the opinions of its defense attorney and an expert that there was no malpractice and the case should be defended.

So you see, in addition to the legal and pecuniary considerations involved in the decision to settle, there are such less concrete factors as the mentality of the judge before whom the case must be tried, the posture of the codefendants, and, most important, the mental attitude of the defendant physician. Pride and reputation affect each client differently. You do not want to let your pride and desire to preserve your reputation stand in the way of a realistic appraisal of a case and the desirability of settlement; but these emotions will help you spend the time and effort required to defend your case should you decide on that course of action.

I would be remiss if I did not make it perfectly clear that some cases are simply indefensible. Defense attorneys hate such cases and want to settle them for the best price possible under the circumstances. If the plaintiff wants too much money or the defendant cannot see the light and refuses to consent to settlement (his consent is usually required to finalize a settlement), the attorney will have to try the case. He will be in the unenviable position of not being able to win. The best he can do is try to keep the size of the verdict against his client reasonable, unless the plaintiff's attorney is incompetent and he can turn this into a victory. This situation is rare and cannot, of course, be counted on.

To try an indefensible case that could be settled, simply because the defendant refuses to be realistic and consent to the settlement, is a colossal waste of time for everyone. My advice concerning settlement, therefore, is to try to be as realistic and objective about your case as possible. If the reasons for settlement enumerated by your attorney make sense, act accordingly. If the reasons are not persuasive or fair to your treatment, or if you feel that your case is being settled for reasons unrelated to it and it should be defended, make your feelings known and insist on a defense (assuming that you are in a position to do so under the terms of your policy or that you are uninsured).

Is Settlement an Admission of Liability?

Although I am certainly not trying to make a case for settlement, especially since I lean the other way if at all possible, you should keep in mind that settlement does not constitute an admission of guilt. Settlement is not judgment for the plaintiff or against the defendant. The plaintiff discontinues the action against the defendant and releases the defendant from all liability in regard to the alleged malpractice in exchange for money paid by or on behalf of the defendant. You may feel that settlement is an admission of guilt (otherwise, why would the money be paid?) but technically it is not and is not recorded as such. In fact, the stipulation of settlement will usually include a clause specifying that your settlement in no way constitutes an admission of liability on your part.

Although one often hears about high settlements in the news media, such publicity can and should be controlled as part of the settlement. Your attorney can and should obtain an agreement by the plaintiff and his attorney that they will reveal nothing about the settlement to the news media. This should be included in the stipulation of settlement. This condition should cut down the amount of such publicity.

The Effect of Settlement on Your Insurance

The effect of settlement on your insurance policy will depend on the circumstances. All insurance companies keep records of settlements made on your behalf. A good company will also, however, record the circumstances of any settlement.

When your insurance company and your attorney agree that there is no liability on your part in a case you are being urged to settle for other reasons, you can and should insist that their opinion be noted on your record with the insurance company, so that it will be considered when your record is reviewed for a premium increase or for renewal.

Generally speaking, a high verdict against you is more damaging on your record with the insurance company than a settlement figure that is reasonable on the basis of the facts of the case. If your treatment is very difficult to defend, it is better to settle than to be hardheaded and run up the legal tab only to get walloped with a high verdict by the jury.

10   The Trial

Why a Jury Trial?

The question of whether a physician's (or hospital's) treatment constitutes medical malpractice in any individual case is ultimately decided in a court of law. The trial will be before a judge either sitting without a jury, in which case he decides both the questions of law and the questions of fact, or with a jury, in which case the judge decides only the questions of law and the jury decides the questions of fact. Either party (the plaintiff or the defendant) can demand a trial by jury, and most malpractice trials are jury trials. Why? Usually one or both sides want a jury. Why? There are many theories.

Looking through the plaintiff's eyes, the reasoning seems obvious. The plaintiff, the patient, wants the facts of his case decided by a panel of fellow patients who can sympathize with his plight and put themselves in his place. The plaintiff does not want to leave the decision of his case to the judge, who has been hardened by hearing many stories of horrible injuries; who has experience in evaluating testimony and can ascertain falsity or exaggeration; who may either dislike plaintiff's counsel or be fonder of defense counsel, causing him to favor the defendant; who may know plaintiff's expert to be a professional testifier who will say anything; and who may know some medicine from other similar cases, causing him to question plaintiff's claim. The plaintiff realizes that he can never hope to appeal to the emotion of a judge as he can to that of a lay jury.

Keep in mind that if the case is tried before a jury, it will decide not only the question of the liability of each party but also the amount of damages the plaintiff will recover. Thus the decision to demand a jury affects not only the question of liability but also the possible amount of recovery. The plaintiff knows that the judge is familiar with the dollar value of various injuries from experience and from his knowledge of the law of damages. It is therefore unlikely that a judge will go overboard on the amount awarded if liability is proved. To discourage an appeal, he will keep the damages within an acceptable range that would not be overturned as excessive by an appellate court. Trial judges do not like to have their decisions modified or reversed on appeal, and therefore they are not anxious to have the record of the trials they preside over reviewed by an appellate court.

The plaintiff wants to receive the highest possible award. He would prefer to have a jury return a very high verdict, putting the burden on the defendant to move the trial judge to set it aside as excessive, and, if that fails, to appeal for relief. He knows that the jury's decision is weighed very heavily and that neither the trial judge nor the appellate court will disturb the jury's evaluation of the case unless it is unconscionably high and not commensurate with what the prior case law has established as acceptable for the injuries involved. The plaintiff also knows that these standards change, and that both the trial judge and an appellate court will take into consideration the individual circumstances of the case and inflation in reaching to sustain the jury's verdict on damages. In other words, Nureyev's leg is worth more than John Doe's, and the plaintiff can always hope that both the trial judge and the appellate court will rule that the verdict is not excessive because of the special circumstances of his particular case. In fact, his case might set a new, higher standard of damages for the injuries involved *because of* its special circumstances.

Why then would a defendant ever demand a jury? Good question. Although having a malpractice case decided by a jury of lay persons does seem to be advantageous to the plaintiff at first blush, it can also provide certain real benefits for the defendant. Juries can and often do decide cases on personalities. If the defendant shows the plaintiff to be a liar, the jury may get angry and throw the case out or return a very small verdict. Because a lay jury usually has more in common with the plaintiff than do most judges, it can evaluate his honesty better. Judges often become very opinionated, and are often impossible to convince no matter what the evidence. If a defendant doctor is impressive on the witness stand, there still are jurors who will be favorably affected by his knowledge and expertise. Therefore, many defense lawyers believe that appealing to the reason of six or twelve persons who must agree by a large majority (for example, five-sixths in New York) or unanimously (depending on the rules in your jurisdiction) in order to reach a verdict is preferable to appealing to the reason of a sole judge whose decision governs.

There is a great deal to be said for such reasoning. No one can reliably predict how a juror will decide a case. A juror may sympathize with the doctor rather than the plaintiff. A juror may have a relative or friend who endures pain and suffering similar to or worse than that described by the plaintiff without its being considered anyone's fault and without any compensation; he may therefore not be so quick to blame the defendant solely on the basis of a bad result or to compensate the plaintiff merely because he suffers. If more people decide the case, there is a much vaster body of experience at work; this is fairer and reduces the chance that the prejudice of one person will work an injustice.

When the case is being decided by a jury, there is also the possibility of a mistrial because of a "hung" jury—a jury that cannot agree on a verdict. This outcome means that the parties will have to go through a new trial, which is particularly distasteful to plaintiffs' counsel because it requires a further investment of time and money without any assurance of recovery.

It is my belief that the main reason defense counsel opt for a trial by jury in most medical malpractice cases is that they wish to insure that the defendant will get a fair shake on the facts. The defense lawyer can be almost completely sure the jury has not been reached or tampered with by the opposition. One cannot always be sure of a judge. On occasion a judge will violate his oath and the system of justice by supporting one side for less than honorable reasons. No defense lawyer wants such a judge deciding the entire case; he will have enough detrimental influence as the judge of the law when he sits with a jury. Aside from the risk of having a judge who is opinionated as a result of personal prejudice, there is the possibility of having a judge who is dealing with the opposition.

Dealing takes many forms. Perhaps the judge just wants to help the opposing lawyer, who is an old friend. There may be dealing in favors such as sponsorship of memberships in certain clubs and political contributions or assistance. It may be a matter of picking up the judge's tab at a particular restaurant. It may be a monetary kickback. It may involve helping a judge dispose of cases on his calendar so his record looks good.

I believe that dealing usually (not always) involves attorneys who represent plaintiffs because they stand to win or lose the most monetarily by the outcome of a case. Most lawyers representing plaintiffs work for a contingent fee, which means that they receive nothing if they lose or a percentage (usually about one-third) of whatever they recover for their client if they obtain a verdict in favor of the plaintiff or settle the case. When you consider that the amount of potential recovery in most malpractice cases is quite high, sometimes reaching millions of dollars, you can see why the defense fear of a biased judge is justifiable.

A defense attorney's fee does not depend on the outcome, nor does it involve such huge amounts of money for an individual case.

In light of the possibility of a biased judge, most defense attorneys want malpractice cases decided by juries and demand them. A jury insures a chance of victory, no matter how difficult a biased judge sitting as the judge of the law may make the trial for the defendant. With a jury deciding the facts you can still win, and if the judge makes significant legal error the case can be overturned on appeal.

When the judge and the plaintiff's attorney are "cooperating" and the defense attorney refuses to succumb to their pressure on him to settle he usually incurs the wrath of the judge and may expect that the judge will make it as difficult as he possibly can for the defense. Such judges will usually go to great lengths to punish any lawyer they feel is defying their wishes (power), notwithstanding the merits of the case involved. I have witnessed childish tantrums by judges when I stated that I had no offer of money for settlement but wanted to defend the case. When the trial starts, such a judge will take every opportunity to rule against defense counsel on motions and objections, very often unfairly and incorrectly. He may attempt to help plaintiff's counsel by asking defense witnesses additional questions and attempting to block and interrupt defense cross-examination. I have known such a judge to attempt to interrupt defense cross-examination to rehabilitate the witness!

I had caught the plaintiff's expert in the embarrassing position of having criticized the defendant doctor's treatment without having examined the doctor's office records. I proceeded to go to work on him, inquiring whether he felt it would be important to study the record of the doctor's treatment before criticizing it. I hammered at the blatant unfairness of rendering an opinion against someone without bothering to examine all the information about his treatment. The expert was struggling. He had no satisfactory answers and his credibility was waning fast. Unbelievably, the pro-plaintiff judge attempted to stop my cross-examination and order me to allow the expert to examine the defendant's office chart—*after* the expert had spent the entire morning criticizing the defendant's office treatment on direct examination by plaintiff's counsel. I refused, objected, and opted to proceed with my questioning rather than to stop my cross-examination to allow the witness to read the office record and attempt to rehabilitate himself. Outrageous, you say? Definitely, but the judge just could not stand to see the plaintiff's most important witness being mortally wounded.

If the case is being decided by a jury, however, the defense lawyer can stand up to such improprieties, put in his case, appeal to the jurors' sense of reason and fairness, and make a record for appeal if the judge's bias causes him to make legal error. Doing so takes intestinal fortitude, but allows the defendant to have his day in court before an impartial arbiter of the facts even when his case comes before such a judge. (When the judge is impartial, of course, the whole system can work fairly and mete out justice the way it was designed to.)

You may be wondering about a biased judge disturbing a jury verdict for the defendant. Disturbing the jury's verdict is a question of law and sure to provoke an appeal; a judge will set aside or alter (increase or decrease) a verdict only if it is clearly contrary to the law or "against the overwhelming weight of the evidence." By provoking an appeal, such a judge risks having the entire record of his prejudicial behavior reviewed by the appellate court. Such a review could mean more than having the verdict reinstated. It could mean criticism, a reprimand, or even an investigation and possible action against the judge. It certainly does not help the judge's reputation. For these reasons, most biased judges use their power in regard to motions, rulings on evidence, and even instructions to the jury, but usually they do not disturb the jury's verdict without a proper basis.

Preparation

To win your case before a judge or a jury, you must be credible. You cannot present a credible defense without adequate preparation. This is the *only* way. This means that both the lawyer and the physician must spend a great deal of time alone and together preparing for trial. I am convinced that many cases in which there has been no malpractice are lost or settled simply because, for whatever reason, the doctor or the attorney or both have been unwilling to spend the necessary time in preparation.

Let us assume that you, the defendant physician, have a good attorney who has the time, energy, and will to prepare your case adequately. The efficacy of the defense will in large part, therefore, depend on you. It does rest in part with the experts, but it must start with you, the defendant. After all, it is your treatment that is being judged.

Learning the Medical Data

What must you do? How do you thoroughly prepare yourself? Let us take it step by step. First of all, there is a great deal you can do to prepare yourself without your attorney that will help both of you. You should thoroughly familiarize yourself with all the medical data in the case. This means that you must know not only your own office records, the hospital records, the lab reports, and such, but also any other medical data your attorney may have obtained through investigation and discovery to which you did not have access before. You should also try to recall and reconstruct all the conversations that accompanied the treatment. This thorough preparation will reap unbelievable benefits.

To begin with, it is impressive and comforting to your attorney to discover that you know the sequence of events, what was done when, what was said, and where things are in the records, and that you do not waste time fumbling through the records trying to find this or that to answer his questions. You immediately build your attorney's confidence in you.

While you explain to your attorney the treatment you rendered, he, by asking questions and working with the records, begins to learn not only what happened in the case but also the medicine of the case. He will be asking you all the medical whys. Why was this done? Why wasn't this test taken? Why wasn't that sign or symptom meaningful? Through this process you and your attorney begin to learn your case. You begin to ferret out the little wrinkles in the case, the weaknesses, the strengths, the questions that require more investigation, the things neither of you would have picked up alone. You search each other's mind for the legal or medical significance of certain facts, and you both learn in the process. This review is also the beginning of your training to become an effective witness. You have to answer a lot of questions posed by your attorney. Together you decide what is important, what still must be learned, what reasoning should be stressed to the jury, and what your approach should be.

While your attorney coaches you on how you should explain the medicine so a lay person can understand it, you will be forced to brush up on your medicine. You will probably want to refer to certain texts to make sure of yourself, check statistics that support your reasoning, confirm your position, and learn what the important works that may be used by the opposing attorney say on the subject. All of this preparation will strengthen you for the test of cross-examination that lies ahead.

By examining the entire record of treatment, rather than confining yourself to your own treatment (if we assume there is treatment by others), you will be able to help your attorney fit the pieces together. Doing so strengthens your defense. No matter how experienced, your attorney is not a physician and he may miss an important medical fact in reviewing medical data himself. You can help him understand the treatment the patient received from *all* the parties and determine what your position must be vis-à-vis the other defendants. When another defendant whose treatment is not intertwined with yours has negligently caused the plaintiff's injuries, care must be taken to keep your treatment separate and distinct in the minds of the jurors so that you will not be held responsible for his negligence. Under some circumstances (such as an attack by that codefendant on *your* treatment), your attorney may even have to attack that codefendant's treatment. When, on the other hand, there has been no negligence and the treatment is so intertwined that the defendants stand or fall together, your attorney must understand the other defendants' treatment completely so that he can explain why you agreed with it and take care not to criticize it.

Consider the following case. Several years ago I was called on to defend two internists, one a famous cardiologist and the other a kidney specialist. A patient with severe hypertension and failing kidneys consulted the cardiologist first. The patient did not respond to the medication prescribed by the cardiologist. His blood pressure remained elevated and his kidney function was deteriorating rapidly. The cardiologist asked the nephrologist to see the patient, who was dying. The cardiologist could not determine if the kidneys were failing because of the hypertension or if the diseased kidneys were causing the hypertension.

It was important to determine the etiology of the hypertension in order to prescribe further medical therapy properly. The cardiologist did not want to use strong hypotensive drugs that might damage the kidneys if the kidneys were the culprits. By the same token, he did not want to attack the kidney problem with medication that would aggravate intrinsic hypertension if the kidneys were not the cause of the high blood pressure. A mistake either way could kill the patient. Meanwhile, something had to be done because the man was dying on his own.

After examining the patient and studying the hospital chart, the nephrologist recommended a renal biopsy. This procedure, which would allow microscopic examination of kidney tissue without opening the patient on the operating table, was the only way to make a definitive diagnosis. The cardiologist agreed. The biopsy was performed by the nephrologist. The patient hemorrhaged. Transfusions were given. After many hours and many units of blood, the bleeding came under control and the patient's blood pressure stabilized. After staying with the patient most of the day and a good part of the night, the nephrologist left the patient with the resident on duty and went home. It was about 11 P.M.

In the early morning the patient started to hemorrhage again. Blood was administered. By infusing large amounts of blood, the patient's blood pressure was brought up to an acceptable level. The resident called a surgeon. The surgeon operated, and the patient died on the table while the surgeon was looking for the source of the bleeding. Both internists, the hospital, the resident, and the surgeon were sued.

The treatment of the two internists was intertwined, since both had agreed that the biopsy should be performed. They would stand or fall together in regard to that decision. (The technique used in performing the biopsy was obviously the responsibility of the nephrologist.) The treatment of the two internists was not, however, intertwined with that of the surgeon or the resident. This point had to be understood in order to defend the treatment of both internists effectively.

The last treatment rendered by either internist was at 11 P.M., when the first episode of bleeding had been brought under control and the nephrologist left for the night. Neither physician treated the patient after that time. (Neither was even notified about the second episode of bleeding until after the patient's death.) Nevertheless, both physicians reviewed *all* the treatment rendered, including that of the surgeon, and provided me with valuable information I might not have picked up on my own.

The hospital chart showed that, after the second episode of bleeding, the hospital personnel had managed to elevate the patient's blood pressure to a respectable level by the time the surgeon who had been called in began his procedure. An examination of the operative and anesthesia records showed that the surgeon had probed around for 50 minutes looking for the site of the bleeding, while the blood pressure steadily dropped to zero, before tying off the renal artery and vein, which immediately stopped all bleeding.

My clients discussed this with me in detail. They both agreed that the surgeon should have tied off the renal artery and vein as soon as he realized that he could not readily locate the site of the bleeding. He probed around for 50 minutes trying to save the kidney at the expense of the patient's life. It is true that, had the man survived the operation after the tying off of the renal vessels and the sacrifice of the kidney, he would probably not have lived much longer in his condition. Nevertheless, under the law his life should not have been shortened for any length of time by negligence, and each minute it was so shortened was compensable.

During the trial of this case the surgeon chose to give testimony that was very damaging to the nephrologist in exchange for a promise that the plaintiff's attorney would let him out of the case after the plaintiff had finished putting forward all his evidence. This deal was secret, of course, and became apparent only when the surgeon took the stand. When this unexpected development occurred, I was able to cross-examine him and attempt to discredit his testimony with the information I had acquired from my clients as a result of their review of *all the medical data*. What I had learned about the surgeon's failure to tie off the renal vessels when he could not find the site of the bleeding quickly became ammunition for my unanticipated cross-examination of the codefendant surgeon.

As an adjunct to tutoring your attorney on all the treatment rendered and the medicine of the case, it is always helpful to suggest relevant medical literature he should read and, if possible, to provide him whatever such literature you can.

The more your lawyer knows about the medicine of the case, the better prepared he is to cross-examine any witness who criticizes your treatment, elicit favorable testimony from friendly witnesses, question you so that you can explain your treatment clearly, and argue in support of your treatment to the jury. Knowing the medicine well also helps your attorney establish the necessary "condition precedents" on cross-examination of lay witnesses so that he can draw the desired medical conclusions for the benefit of the jury later in the case, during subsequent expert testimony or even as late as summation. In other words, it will help him establish through the patient, the patient's family, and the other witnesses that the patient did or did not have certain symptoms and signs, which will later justify the treatment you chose or show what the true medical condition of the plaintiff was.

Learning the "Pretrial Testimony"

After you have studied the medical data, you must learn the transcript of your examination before trial. The importance of what most lay people call "pretrial testimony" cannot be overemphasized. You must know what you said at your examination before trial, because contradicting or changing your prior testimony at the time of trial seriously damages your credibility.

Sometimes ambiguous or weak answers that you made at your examination before trial have to be explained or clarified because you are confronted with them on cross-examination at the trial. If you know your prior testimony and have gone over those weak or ambiguous answers with your attorney, you can often explain away the apparent inconsistency the opposing attorney is trying to bring out. Doing so may require explaining how you interpreted the question put to you at your examination before trial, the effect of a misleading word used by counsel, or an important qualification that the opposing lawyer is attempting to gloss over but that distinguishes the question asked at the deposition from that asked at the trial and makes your answer accurate. Obviously, you cannot be sure you will not contradict your prior testimony or be ready to explain it if you do not know it. Your lawyer will go over it with you, point out the weaknesses in it, and help you handle any confrontation with it.

It is always valuable to read *all* the pretrial testimony, even if you heard most of it being given. Testimony has a different impact when you read it. It is easier to work with. You may be able to pick out of the testimony of a codefendant or the plaintiff something important that may have escaped your attorney. Furthermore, reading the testimony against you burns it into your memory and helps you know what to emphasize in your testimony at the trial. For example, if the plaintiff has testified at his deposition that you did not explain any of the risks of the proposed surgery during a particular office visit, you can start focusing your memory on that visit; then, when you relate on the stand what transpired, your testimony will be full of details you have dredged up from your memory. Such detail will show the jury that you do remember the encounter and will lend a great deal of credibility to your testimony about what was said.

Without knowing the testimony of the other parties, you will be less prepared to contradict the attacking party convincingly.

All the preparation I have discussed takes time, which means nights, weekends, and more. As the defendant physician, you must be ready to sacrifice your time if you wish to put forward the strongest defense possible.

Working with Codefendants

In the case just discussed, the two internists learned to work together because their treatment was intertwined. However, when the lawsuit started both physicians became very upset and hired personal attorneys, although both were adequately insured. I was assigned to represent them by their insurance company. The cardiologist initially felt that he should not be held responsible for a complication that developed as a result of a kidney biopsy he did not perform. The nephrologist resented that position and informed me that he performed all the renal biopsies at the hospital; it was, therefore, his position that he merely performed the biopsy at the request of the cardiologist. These positions spelled disaster. The main claim in the case was that the renal biopsy should never have been performed, that the decision to perform the biopsy was negligent. If the two internists stuck to their original positions and kept their personal attorneys, the plaintiff's attorney would have only to sit back and let the two internists throw stones at each other. I spoke to each physician separately with his personal attorney and explained how the treatment of both was intertwined and why, in my opinion, they should work together and present a united defense.

I explained to the cardiologist that he could not wash his hands of the decision to have the renal biopsy performed. He asked the nephrologist to see the patient with this procedure in mind because he was having difficulty treating the patient, who was dying. He knew the risks of the procedure. He would never have agreed to the biopsy if he had felt that the risks of the procedure outweighed the value of the information he would receive from it. He knew that the risk of hemorrhage was very small. He needed microscopic examination of the kidney tissue to help him treat the patient's serious condition. The truth was that he *wanted* the renal biopsy performed under the circumstances and agreed to it. In other words, he had joined in the decision to perform the biopsy. He admitted that everything I said was true.

I explained to the nephrologist that it was unrealistic for him to assert that he was a mere technician performing the biopsy at the request of the referring physician. It was unrealistic because it was untrue. The truth was that he examined the patient, reviewed the patient's hospital record in regard to history and prior treatment, and spoke with the cardiologist about the patient before agreeing that a renal biopsy should be performed. In other words, he applied his expertise to all the information he could gather about the patient before agreeing to perform the biopsy. He had made his own decision, which was in accordance with the decision of the cardiologist, that the biopsy was indicated and should be performed. He too admitted that what I said was true.

After these discussions, the two physicians agreed that their treatment was intertwined in regard to the decision to perform the biopsy and that they should work together to defend that decision, since it was a proper one. (There was no question that the nephrologist's technique in performing the biopsy was his responsibility.) They felt that the best way to present a united defense was to have one attorney represent both of them. Both discharged their personal attorneys and we began working together.

Working together to put forward a united defense becomes more complicated when there are multiple defendants with separate counsel. If the treatment is nonconflicting, the lawyers and physicians should sit down together and do everything possible to iron out any difficulties that exist between defendants. The position of each defendant should be discussed.

The case of the woman who sued as a result of an operation for an ulcer that was nonexistent at the time of surgery, discussed on pages 2-9, is a good case in point. The internist and radiologist could have tried to exculpate themselves by laying all the responsibility at the surgeon's door. This risky tactic would have caused a fight between the defendants (the surgeon would not have taken it lying down) that would have resulted in a verdict for the plaintiff against one or more defendants. Instead, several conferences were held between the attorneys for the defendants, with the defendants participating, and a united position was agreed on. All the defendants believed the treatment was proper, but the conferences were needed to make sure that nobody started throwing stones in order to escape liability or to inculpate others. Sometimes codefendants do this under the pressure of a trial.

As a result of the conferences, the surgeon did not say that the internist was wrong in diagnosing an ulcer or that the radiologist had made a mistake when he saw an ulcer on the films. The internist did not attack the surgeon's decision to perform the surgery or the radiologist's reading of the x-rays. The radiologist stood by his conclusion that the films showed an ulcer. A united defense allowed for a logical picture of careful medical treatment to be presented to the jury.

Protecting Codefendants

When your treatment is not intertwined with that of another codefendant, it is best to disassociate your treatment from his without criticizing or protecting it. However, if faced with questions about the other physician's treatment, it is imperative that you tell the truth. A jury can sense when one defendant is trying to protect another at the expense of the plaintiff, and will often punish the protector as well as the guilty defendant. Juries rightfully resent such behavior.

It is not your responsibility to protect your codefendant in court. You must defend your own treatment and if the hospital (or a colleague) failed in its responsibility (for example, notifying you of a change in the patient's condition) and you are asked about it, you must say so. If you do not, you can never take the position that you relied on the hospital staff to carry out that responsibility properly. Remember that your own attorney may be asking you such questions in order to defend your treatment and explain to the jury why you did what you did. He may also be asking them to explain how the plaintiff was injured. You can inadvertently destroy your own defense if you unjustifiably or unnecessarily try to protect a fellow physician or a hospital.

Helping Your Defense

Aside from testifying in your own defense, you can be an important factor in the presentation of your defense *during the entire trial.* Your presence in court every day has an important effect on the jury. Keep in mind that the injured plaintiff and relatives are in court displaying the injury or mourning the death of the deceased in the presence of the jury at all times. Your presence not only tends to offset the presence of the plaintiff and his family, but also shows that you are just as concerned about the result. The jury is thus made aware that its decision is equally important to both sides. If you come to court only to testify and then disappear, you give the impression that you do not care very much about the result. The jury may conclude that you do not care because you have a large insurance policy, and may use such reasoning to justify awarding the plaintiff a large verdict.

It has been my practice when representing a physician in a malpractice suit not only to have my client in court every day but also to have him sit with me at the counsel table. His presence shows his concern to the jury and allows him to assist me by volunteering information to me or answering any question of mine about the medical testimony and evidence as it unfolds. As an immediate source of medical expertise, he can often be of immense help in the cross-examination of a medical expert or a codefendant. I can always ask him if something that has been said is really true under the circumstances. He can tell me when the expert has omitted an essential distinguishing factor in reaching his conclusion, and I can then confront the expert with this omission on cross-examination to embarrass him and make him recant his conclusion.

For example, if the expert witness states that the defendant should have taken a certain sophisticated test prior to the surgery, the defendant can immediately pass me a note explaining that the equipment necessary to perform the test was not generally available at that time. I can then confront the expert with this fact on cross-examination, embarrassing him and damaging his credibility. The jury will see how hard he is reaching to criticize the defendant unjustly. Without the information immediately provided by the defendant, a damaging piece of cross-examination would be lost and the expert's invalid criticism allowed to rest unchallenged in the minds of the jurors for a substantial length of time. Although I might eventually be able to contradict the expert's testimony with the testimony of the defendant and other witnesses, this is never as effective as destroying the expert immediately on cross-examination. If he recants and admits his error, there is no conflicting testimony for the jury to ponder. It is not a matter of who it is the jurors believe. The attempt of the plaintiff's expert to deceive the jury has been exposed, and whatever else he testifies to will be either disregarded or viewed with suspicion by the jury.

Your presence next to your attorney at the counsel table can sometimes be especially helpful when the plaintiff testifies. It can be disconcerting for the plaintiff to see you watching him and listening to his every word. If he tries to add made-up details to his story, you can tell your attorney at that very moment why the plaintiff's testimony is impossible; your attorney can then use that information on cross-examination. The same thing is true when a codefendant with whom you are at odds tries to add new material unexpectedly.

Even during summations, after all the evidence has been introduced, your presence in court has a good psychological effect on the jury. You should be there when these emotional arguments are made by counsel. It can be very effective for defense counsel to point to the defendant physician who has made a good, honest impression on the jury and has been present with them during the entire trial, and ask the jurors whether they believe that individual, that physician, who dedicated his life to medicine and who carefully explained his treatment, is a liar, as the plaintiff claims.

It is also psychologically advantageous for you to be present when the judge gives his instructions to the jurors and when they finally go out to begin deliberation. The more the jury sees that you care about the result, the better.

The Role of the Judge

As I have pointed out, the judge decides the questions of law in the case. He rules on objections made by counsel throughout the trial. He decides motions made by counsel. The judge thus exerts great influence on the trial. He decides whether certain questions or answers are proper, whether certain evidence is admissable, whether the plaintiff has made out a prima facie case,[1] whether the defendant has proved an affirmative defense, and similar questions.

The judge also "instructs" the jurors on the applicable law for the case they are deciding: He gives them the rules and guidelines they are to use in deciding how to judge the facts and reach a verdict. These instructions ("the charge of the court") explain to the jury the concept of the plaintiff's burden of proof and other legal principles applicable to the individual case.

In his charge, the judge may also choose to review the respective claims of each side as he sees them and to "marshal the evidence." The latter process constitutes a review of the important evidence introduced by each side as the judge recalls it; this review is not binding on the jury. It is my opinion that the judge should not exercise his discretion to review the claims or marshal the evidence, because of the danger of abuse, and encroachment on the jury's function. A biased judge can try to sway the jury by emphasizing, adding, or omitting certain claims or evidence in his review. In other words, the manner in

1. See *prima facie case* in the Glossary.

which he reviews the claims and the evidence may amount to a summation for one side. The facts the judge mentions in marshaling the evidence take on added significance in the minds of the jurors because he is the judge. Even when he tells them that their recollection of the evidence takes precedence over his, the jurors will believe that he considers those facts important and be impressed. Furthermore, the volume and tone of his voice, his facial expressions, and his gestures while discussing a claim, certain evidence, or testimony can have definite and calculated effect on the jury. The trial record will not reflect the judge's demeanor while he was discussing the defendant's testimony or the fact that the judge lowered his voice when he was explaining the claims of the defendant. It will not reflect the face he made when he was speaking of the opinion of the defendant's expert, and so forth. This type of prejudicial behavior on the part of the judge may not be corrected on appeal because the appellate court will not learn what occurred from reading the trial record.

A lawyer may list his exceptions to the charge of the court out of the presence of the jury for the record and for a possible appeal, but doing so will not succeed in overturning the verdict unless the error made by the judge has been a serious one. Since much of the prejudicial behavior can be hidden from the record, and the judge will always cover himself in regard to marshaling the evidence by telling the jurors that their recollection takes precedence over his, most of the error made in reviewing the claims and marshaling the evidence does not become the basis for overturning a verdict on appeal. This is true even if the lawyer attempts to recite the judge's behavior in his exception to the charge.

Though such prejudicial nonsense does take place on occasion, it cannot overcome a clear, honest defense of proper treatment. Keep in mind that the judge cannot limit the evidence too severely because of the likelihood of appeal, and that the jury will decide the case mainly on the evidence. Prejudicial behavior on the part of the judge is ordinarily effective only when there are doubts about your defense.

The Role of the Jury

The jury is the judge of the facts. The jury decides whether or not anyone is guilty of malpractice (liability) and how much the injuries are worth in dollars and cents (damages). These are decisions on the facts, based solely on the testimony and exhibits admitted into evidence by the judge and the credibility of the witnesses. The jurors judge credibility on the basis of the witnesses' demeanor and their own experience in life.

Technically, if the judge directs the jurors to disregard a question and answer and orders the exchange stricken from the record, the jurors are not supposed to take that question and answer into consideration during their deliberations. Obviously, this is impossible. Whatever a juror hears will have some effect; therefore, many attorneys will ask questions or make statements they know are improper, for the effect on the jury. A witness may blurt out an answer for the same reason. No improper statement, whether in the form of a question, answer, objection, comment to counsel, argument to the judge, or argument to the jury, is supposed to be part of the evidence the jury considers in its deliberations.

A juror is supposed to be neutral and objective. He is not supposed to be an advocate or an expert for either side. In selecting a jury, lawyers ask many questions, ostensibly designed to determine whether a particular juror can be neutral, objective, and fair to both sides. Actually, each lawyer is looking for jurors who will be favorably disposed toward his client. Each trial attorney has different theories about jury selection. Some believe that religious, racial, and ethnic considerations are important. Some place more emphasis on economic status and employment. Quite frankly, there is no method for accurately divining a juror's predisposition. Jurors are unpredictable, and many attorneys are surprised by what their selections decide. Jury selection is mostly guesswork based on the attorney's feelings about the individual juror.

Despite your attorney's efforts to obtain jurors favorably disposed to your position during jury selection (known as the voir dire), any juror who indicates either directly or indirectly that he could not be fair to any party will be excused. Unfortunately, some jurors lie in answering questions put to them during selection because they want to sit on the case. Such jurors are sometimes prejudiced and attempt to impose their prejudice on the other jurors. Whenever a juror judges a case on the basis of information other than the evidence introduced at the trial, there is a danger of injustice. There is no way to judge whether such information is correct. The juror may become an advocate or "expert" during deliberations, and cause the jury to reach the wrong conclusion because of his improper arguments or incorrect information. Fortunately, this is rare; such jurors are usually recognized for what they are and ignored by other jurors.

Most jurors are honest and diligent, and work hard to ascertain what they feel is the truth. As a result, most verdicts are reached only after honest deliberation according to the guidelines set by the judge in his charge. The forte of a jury is its ability to sense when someone is lying or has falsified evidence. This ability, based on the collective experience of the many different kinds of people who comprise a jury, allows the jury the inside track on reaching the correct conclusion. This is the reason why complete honesty and candor are essential in presenting your defense.

The Role of the Experts

Medical malpractice cases are unique in that they almost always require expert medical testimony. Even in the rare res ipsa loquitur[2] case, most attorneys representing the plaintiff will prefer to introduce expert medical testimony to bolster the plaintiff's claim of malpractice. The role of the expert is to provide the jurors his expert opinion on the treatment rendered, the effect of that treatment, and the injuries of the plaintiff. This opinion is based on the expert's

2. See res ipsa loquitur in the Glossary.

review of materials provided by the attorney who retained him and on hypothetical questions put to him. The credibility of the expert will depend on his qualifications, demeanor, honesty, and ability to withstand cross-examination. Experts testify for both the plaintiff and the defendant, and they are extremely important witnesses because the lay people who comprise a jury have no knowledge of medicine on which to base a decision concerning malpractice or the cause of the plaintiff's injuries. It should be noted that an examining physician sometimes renders an expert opinion only concerning the plaintiff's injuries and not on the question of improper treatment.

Except in pure res ipsa loquitur cases, expert testimony is absolutely vital to the plaintiff. Because of the jury's lack of medical knowledge, the law will usually not allow the jury to decide the case unless the plaintiff can produce an expert who will testify that in his opinion, with a reasonable degree of medical certainty, the defendant's treatment deviated from the accepted standards of practice and caused the plaintiff's injuries. Thus, except in cases in which "the negligence speaks for itself," the plaintiff must produce a medical expert to support his claims or he will fail to make out a prima facie case and his case will be dismissed.

By the same token, once the plaintiff has produced expert testimony in support of his claim and has made out a prima facie case, it is usually vital that the defendant produce expert testimony to the contrary unless he can introduce strong factual evidence that controverts the plaintiff's version of what took place.

The Opening Statement

The trial has a specific format. The judge may begin with some preliminary instructions to the jurors about the order of things, cautioning them to keep open minds until all the evidence is in and not to discuss the case until after the charge has been given; but the trial really begins when "openings" are heard—when the attorney for each party makes his opening statement. The law gives the plaintiff the opportunity to open first and sum up last; he has the first and last word with the jury. Presumably, this advantage is given to the plaintiff because he carries the burden of proof.[3]

The purpose of the opening statements is to allow the attorneys to outline what they intend to prove or what the evidence will show. As is true of every aspect of trying a lawsuit, there are various philosophies concerning what should be revealed in an opening statement. Every lawyer has his own preference and every case has its own needs, depending on the facts, the opposing attorney, the judge, and other factors. There are no definitive rules. Suffice it to say that the lawyer must weigh revealing his case and evidence to the opposition at this early point against giving up this first opportunity to outline his view of the case and persuade the jurors to see the case his way. Unless surprise is a very important aspect of your strategy, I feel, generally speaking, that it is best to let

3. See *burden of proof* in the Glossary.

the jurors know what you intend to prove, so they can follow the evidence and keep your view of the case in mind as they listen to the evidence introduced by the opposition. Depending on the circumstances of the individual case, you may be able to reveal most of your evidence and your view of the case but still save a few surprises for the trial.

The Plaintiff's Case

After the plaintiff has opened, followed by the defendants in the order in which they were named in the title of the lawsuit, the plaintiff commences his "case." That is, the plaintiff begins to introduce his proof, his evidence. The plaintiff will call his witnesses and introduce whatever medical records or other documents he feels necessary to prove his case. Usually the plaintiff himself will be called to the witness stand, along with any other witnesses with knowledge of events or of the patient's injuries, in addition to the plaintiff's expert. He may attempt to introduce hospital records, medical bills, letters of administration (in death cases), office records, autopsy reports, income tax forms, or other data.

A tactic frequently employed by attorneys representing the plaintiff is to call the defendant himself as a "hostile witness" in the plaintiff's case. This maneuver may be advantageous to the plaintiff in several ways. Often the defendant is not prepared to take the stand so early in the trial, nor has he had the benefit of hearing others testify. If he is flustered, the plaintiff's lawyer can cause the defendant to make damaging statements and admissions. Furthermore, the plaintiff's lawyer can put the defendant doctor's office records into evidence through the doctor himself and then interrogate him on his entries. This evidence can provide fertile information for the plaintiff's expert to work with later when he takes the stand. By using this tactic, the plaintiff and his expert can tailor their testimony to what the doctor has said, rather than giving the doctor the opportunity to hear their testimony first and direct *his* testimony to best oppose and neutralize what they have said when he takes the stand in his own case.

The tactic of calling the defendant doctor as a hostile witness can backfire only when the doctor is thoroughly prepared. A prepared defendant who testifies honestly and well can devastate the plaintiff's case before it gets off the ground. If the plaintiff's attorney goes after him but he makes a good impression and explains why the plaintiff's allegations are wrong, this impression can stick with the jury and prevent the plaintiff from building a case or developing sympathy no matter what his later witnesses say. Such is the value of advance preparation.

Motions for Dismissal at the End of the Plaintiff's Case

Once the plaintiff has completed his case, a motion is always made pro forma by the defendant to dismiss the plaintiff's case on the grounds that the plaintiff failed to fulfill his burden of proof as a matter of law. If the motion has merit and is granted, the case goes no further. That is, the plaintiff's claims are dismissed and judgment is granted to the defendant. After the plaintiff has finished introducing all his evidence (putting in his case), the defendant argues in his motion to dismiss that the evidence introduced is not sufficient as a matter of law to allow submission of the case to the jury for decision. The defendant argues that the proof put forward by the plaintiff does not make out a prima facie case or create material issues of fact for the jury to decide.

Suppose, for example, that the plaintiff's expert testified that "*probably* there was a deviation from accepted practice" by the defendant but admitted on cross-examination that this is not necessarily so and that some physicians might choose the same treatment the defendant did under the same circumstances. Such testimony fails as a matter of law to create an issue of fact for the jury to decide. If the expert can only guess or speculate that there was a deviation from accepted practice, certainly a lay jury cannot be asked or allowed to decide the question. The jurors would have no definitive expert opinion in favor of the plaintiff on which to base a verdict in his favor. Since the plaintiff has the burden of putting forward an unequivocal expert opinion[4] supporting his claims, the failure to do so should result in a dismissal of the case without the defendants' even opening their case or calling a witness. In most cases the plaintiff must produce such expert testimony in his favor to create an issue for the jury to decide (a prima facie case).

Such dismissals at the end of the plaintiff's case are rare. If the plaintiff's attorney has done his preparation, he will be sure to make out at least a prima facie case. That is, he will make sure that he has introduced enough evidence to fulfill the requirements of creating a cause of action—an issue or question of fact entitled to be submitted to the jury for resolution.

It takes a certain degree of courage on the part of a trial judge to dismiss the plaintiff's case at this point in the trial. The usual tendency is to allow the jury to decide the question if at all possible, since such a dismissal by the judge can very often lead to an appeal, which is the plaintiff's last resort under such circumstances. Appeal means that the trial judge's rulings and decision will be scrutinized by the appellate court; and if the higher court finds reversible error—error that substantially prejudiced the appealing party—it will overrule the trial judge and order a new trial.

Even though the appellate court may sustain the trial judge's decision, most judges fear being reversed and therefore either deny dismissal motions made at the end of the plaintiff's case or "reserve decision." Reserving decision means that the judge does not want to decide the motion at the time it is made. He may be delaying his decision because he is unsure and wants to think about it or research it. He may prefer not to make the decision that might create an appeal until after the jury has made its decision. If the jury comes in for the defendant, he will never have to make the decision and the plaintiff has no order of dismissal to appeal from. In other words, the jury eliminates the need and

4. Though it is understood that all medical opinions are made "with a reasonable degree of medical certainty," they must be stated unequivocally.

responsibility for a decision on the defendant's dismissal motion. The plaintiff can now only appeal from the jury's verdict. This situation is completely different. The plaintiff cannot argue that the jury was never permitted to decide his claim. The jury has decided his claim and has come out in favor of the defendant. Appellate courts are usually not inclined to disturb the jury's determination unless there has been some serious legal error on the judge's part that would constitute reversible error or unless the verdict is inconsistent with the facts or the law. Therefore, when there is no decision by the judge denying the plaintiff jury consideration of his case, and a verdict must be overturned for the plaintiff to win a new trial, the plaintiff is not so inclined to appeal.

If the trial judge reserves his decision, forces the defendant to put in his case, allows the case to go to the jury, and the jury returns a verdict for the plaintiff, the trial judge is then forced to make his decision. (The jury has not made it for him.) Of course, the situation is now more complicated. In order to dismiss the case as a matter of law at this point, the judge must set aside the jury's verdict.

When the trial judge reserves on the defendant's motion to dismiss made at the end of the plaintiff's case, he gives the plaintiff the opportunity to cure any defects in his prima facie case during the presentation of the defendant's case, which can be done through cross-examination of witnesses put on the stand by the defendant. This, of course, is unfair to the defendant. Let us suppose that the plaintiff was unable to cure the defects in his case and the judge allowed a legally defective case to go to the jury by reserving on the defendant's motion, but the jury surprised him and decided for the plaintiff. The judge should set the verdict aside and dismiss the plaintiff's case. If he does not, the defendant can appeal. Nevertheless, the judge has created a sticky situation by reserving: A jury's verdict in favor of the plaintiff is now involved, and if he does set the verdict aside and dismiss the plaintiff's case, the plaintiff may be encouraged to challenge the judge's legal decision because of the jury's verdict.

A defendant can always appeal from a judgment in the plaintiff's favor following denial of his motion to set aside the verdict, but the defendant will usually not succeed unless the judge's error is very clear, the plaintiff never corrected the defects in his case, or the jury verdict had no basis in fact or law, because appellate courts do not like to disturb jury verdicts. If the judge grants the defendant's motion at the end of the plaintiff's case, the plaintiff can appeal. If he wins—that is, if the appellate court agrees that the dismissal should not have been granted because the plaintiff made a prima facie case with his proof—there will be a new trial.

When one takes everything into consideration, it is my opinion that the best course for the trial judge is to have the courage of his convictions and to give the defendant the benefit of the rules of evidence, which require the plaintiff to make out a prima facie case before he is entitled to have the defendant come forward with evidence and to have the jury deliberate on his case. If he denies or reserves on the defendant's dismissal motion at the end of the plaintiff's case, merely out of fear of appellate scrutiny, the concept of the plaintiff's burden of proving a prima facie case is subverted and the defendant is forced to put in his entire case, which requires money, time, and effort. The rationale behind requiring the plaintiff at least to make out a prima facie case before proceeding with the trial is to prevent such waste and to weed out spurious claims early. By deciding these motions on their merits when they are made, furthermore, the judge will keep the appellate records shorter and the questions raised on appeal less complicated and easier to decide.

Occasionally a defendant feels so strongly about the plaintiff's failure to make out a prima facie case that, if the judge denies or reserves on his motion at the end of the plaintiff's case, he "rests" without putting in any evidence and renews his motion. This tactic, designed to force the judge to make his decision on the dismissal motion, is extremely dangerous and not advisable. If the judge insists (by denying the renewed motion) that a prima facie case has been made out, the case will then go to the jury solely on the evidence introduced by the plaintiff. If the verdict is for the plaintiff (which is highly probable, in view of the absence of any defense evidence), the defendant's sole basis for appeal is the question of whether the judge erred in his legal decision not to dismiss. If the appellate court agrees with the trial judge that there was enough evidence to allow the case to go to the jury (that is, that the plaintiff did make out a prima facie case), the defendant cannot argue that he never had the opportunity to present his evidence. He gave up that opportunity when he rested his case without putting in his evidence. This is too risky. It is better to put in the defendant's evidence and, if the jury decides adversely and the plaintiff has not cured the defects in his case during the presentation of the defense evidence, to appeal. This approach insures that the jury does not decide the case without considering the defense evidence.

The Defendant's Case

If the plaintiff survives the defendant's motion to dismiss, the defendant must put forward his case, his defense. He must introduce documents, testimony, and whatever other evidence is available to explain the defense position, to prove that there was no medical malpractice, and to rebut the plaintiff's case. Notwithstanding the plaintiff's *legal* burden of proof, in a case involving death or serious injury the *real* burden is on the defendant to explain how such a result could occur *without negligence*. Even so, it should be remembered that the law does not require the defendant to come forward with any evidence whatsoever. It is the evidence introduced by the plaintiff that causes the defendant to come forward with his case.

You cannot gamble that the judge is going to know the law or do what you expect. If the jury is going to decide the lawsuit, you must put in your case. For example, suppose the inference of negligence from res ipsa loquitur does get the case to the jury; the jury *could* decide for the plaintiff on the basis of the inference alone. Thus you must rebut the inference with your evidence. As a rule, if the plaintiff's claims have not been dismissed at the end of the plaintiff's case, the defendant will put in his case.

Possible Rebuttal by the Plaintiff

If something new has come up during the defendant's case about which the plaintiff did not have the opportunity to introduce evidence in his case, the plaintiff has the right to introduce rebuttal evidence on the new matter after the defendant has rested his case. The new matter might involve the credibility of a witness or a new fact brought out by the defense. This right is supposed to be confined to new evidence relating to the new matter brought out by the defense; however, many judges are liberal in allowing the plaintiff to call a rebuttal witness to add an unrelated point or underline a point already made.

Possible Surrebuttal by the Defendant

The defendant, in turn, has the right of surrebuttal: If the plaintiff brings up something new on rebuttal, the defendant has the right to bring forward new evidence to rebut this new matter. Rebuttal and surrebuttal are usually not allowed to go too far.

Motions at the End of the Entire Case

After whatever rebuttal and surrebuttal there may be, both sides rest their case. This means that neither side has any more evidence to introduce. All the evidence is in. Both sides now have the opportunity to make motions to the court. The plaintiff can move for a directed verdict, arguing that he is entitled to a verdict as a matter of law because the defendant's evidence has created no issues of fact for the jury to decide. That is, he will argue that the defense evidence did not controvert the plaintiff's evidence establishing malpractice and the damages it caused.

The defendant can make two motions. First, he can move for dismissal of the plaintiff's case on the ground that the plaintiff's proof is insufficient as a matter of law. His argument will be that the plaintiff has failed to fulfill his burden of proof, has not made out a prima facie case, and therefore is not entitled to have the case go to the jury for decision. He will reiterate the reasoning he offered at the end of the plaintiff's case and add any new points he can, perhaps based on additional evidence that arose in the defendant's case.

The defendant's second motion might be for a directed verdict in his behalf. He may argue that the defendant's evidence so overwhelmed the plaintiff's evidence that there are no issues for the jury to decide, and, as a matter of law, the jury could only find for the defendant. Stated another way: The defendant may argue that the judge would be forced to set aside any verdict rendered by the jury in favor of the plaintiff as against the weight of the evidence; therefore, there is no point in sending the case to the jury, and the judge must direct a verdict for the defendant. (This argument is the opposite of the plaintiff's motion for a directed verdict.)

If the judge reserved on the defense motion at the end of the plaintiff's case, he now has another opportunity to dismiss the plaintiff's case, or direct a verdict. A dismissal at this point in the trial would be called a dismissal at the end of the whole case. The same consequences discussed on pages 183-185 apply if the judge allows the case to proceed, rather than resolving the issues raised by the motions.

Summations

Once the trial judge has reserved or denied the motions made at the end of the case, summations are heard. The last-named defendant's attorney (last-named in the title) sums up first, followed by the next-to-last-named defendant's attorney, and so forth, until the plaintiff's attorney makes the last summation to the jury. The summations constitute the attorneys' final arguments to the jury. Although a certain leeway is allowed counsel on summation, there are some limitations on what can be said.

The attorneys are entitled to make fair comment and argument on the evidence. They are usually allowed to comment on the failure of a party to take the stand or to call a witness who has knowledge of the facts, and who is under the party's control or influence, to testify about those facts. They may comment on the failure of a party to subpoena a witness. If the witness is not subject to the party's control or influence, or subject to subpoena, such comment is not allowed.

The attorneys are not allowed to "testify" during summation and must confine their arguments to the evidence introduced. They are not supposed to paraphrase or summarize testimony incorrectly; however, when objections are raised to such indiscretions, except in cases of severe or repeated inaccuracies, the judge usually just reminds the jurors that it is their recollection of the evidence that controls and that, if their recollection differs with that of the attorney (or the judge), they are to use their own in deliberating. If the attorney's recollection of the evidence is extremely prejudicial, the trial judge should sustain an objection by counsel or object himself and correct the misrepresentation.

The primary guideline to the propriety of comments made during summation is undue prejudice. Verdicts rendered after lengthy trials have been overturned, and new trials ordered, when attorneys have gone overboard in summation and made such prejudicial remarks that the appellate court held that the opposing party was denied fair consideration by the jury. For example, a defendant's attorney who tries to argue that, by rendering a verdict against the defendant physician, the jury will end his career and prevent him from practicing medicine again or a plaintiff's attorney who suggests to the jurors that they should compensate the poor injured plaintiff because he needs the money, and the defendant physician or hospital will really not suffer at all because they are covered by insurance, would be exceeding the bounds of propriety. Prejudicial remarks are sometimes made when an attorney gets carried away attacking the witnesses of the opposition or describing, in an effort to exhort the jury to return a large amount of money in damages, the terrible injuries and suffering his client has endured. The attorneys may not instruct the jury on the law they think applies to the case in summation. Only the judge can instruct the jury on the law.

The Charge of the Court

After the plaintiff has concluded his summation, the spotlight shifts to the judge for his charge to the jury. As I explained earlier in this chapter, in the charge of the court, or the instructions to the jury, the judge attempts to outline the applicable law for the jurors. He gives them guidelines for evaluating testimony and credibility and explains such important principles as the plaintiff's burden of proof, contributory negligence, res ipsa loquitur, informed consent, and proximate cause. The judge attempts to explain the legal principles and doctrines that apply to all cases and those that apply specifically to the case the jurors must decide.

For example, the charge in a medical malpractice case will include general principles that apply to evaluating the testimony of interested witnesses, expert witnesses, and fact witnesses. It will include a discussion of credibility in general. It will explain how to deal with the arguments of counsel, legal rulings, failure to call a witness, hypothetical questions, and the like. Narrowing his focus to the case at hand, the judge will explain the elements of the causes of action pleaded (in the complaint) against the defendant that the plaintiff must prove in order to recover.

As you know, the judge may or may not give his version of the claims made by the plaintiff and the defense. He may marshal the evidence as he sees it. Once he has completed the portion of his charge dealing with the jury's task of deciding liability, he will turn to the subject of damages.

Damages

The judge will usually instruct the jurors that, if they find that there was a deviation from the accepted standards of practice and that the deviation proximately caused the injuries complained of, they must then consider the question of damages—and not before. The jurors are not supposed to give consideration to monetary damages created by the injuries until they have found the defendant guilty of malpractice. In actuality, of course, they probably give a great deal of thought to the severity of the injuries and the monetary damages created thereby while deciding the question of liability, notwithstanding the judge's instructions not to do so. Such thoughts are obviously not appropriate, since if the defendant is not guilty of malpractice it does not matter how grievous the injuries or how great the monetary damages are. How many jurors are able to adhere strictly to this instruction in the face of paraplegia or brain damage is hard to calculate. Many jurors probably do consider the injuries and damages during the liability discussion, but they are also able to put their sympathies aside and decide in favor of the defendant if they are convinced that he did not cause the injuries through his malpractice.

In giving the law on damages, the judge invariably prefaces his instructions by stating that the mere fact that he is doing so is not to be taken as an indication that the court (the judge) feels that damages should be awarded or expects that the jury will even reach the question of damages. This point should be carefully underlined by the judge. He must give the law on damages in every case in which there is a claim for money compensation, and therefore must make it clear when discussing damages that the court has no feelings whatsoever about the case.

There are no specific instructions on how the jury should assign a dollar value to pain and suffering, but there are certain principles the jury must apply in deciding on an amount. For example, if the plaintiff had a preexisting condition unrelated to the claims in the case, the judge will instruct the jurors that they are not to consider any pain and suffering emanating from this condition when evaluating damages. Suppose there was a deviation from accepted practice in the treatment of a leg fracture of a terminally ill patient who died one week after the treatment. The testimony may have been that the fracture was treated improperly, but in terms of pain and suffering setting the leg correctly would not have made any difference, and since the patient died shortly thereafter there are no residual effects. The negligent treatment made no difference to the patient's suffering. Under such circumstances, the deviation from accepted orthopedic standards of practice should not entitle the plaintiff to any money damages.

Almost every malpractice suit involves a claim for expenses and many involve claims for loss of services. The judge must explain in his charge that these are separate claims, one for out-of-pocket expenses allegedly caused by the malpractice and the other for the loss of services to another family member because of the injuries allegedly caused by the malpractice. Service can mean such things as housework, companionship, conjugal relations, and the like. Sometimes plaintiffs' attorneys attempt to help the jury put a dollar value on the loss of services by introducing evidence establishing the cost of replacing the services lost.

The cause of action for pain and suffering very often includes a claim for loss of earnings. Again, the judge will give instructions on evaluating the evidence introduced in support of such a claim (for example, the work life expectancy of the plaintiff).

Wrongful Death

In cases involving wrongful death claims, the judge must instruct the jury on the specific rules relating to damages in such cases as provided by law. Usually the statutory-created action for wrongful death only permits damages for the pecuniary loss to the next of kin of the deceased. There are often special rules in regard to infants. Whether the jury can consider the possible financial contribution to parents after the infant would have reached majority depends on the individual state's treatment. Obviously, the judge must charge concerning the probable life expectancy of the deceased had the alleged wrongful death not occurred. The jury should be told to take into consideration the deceased's previous overall health and any disabilities or diseases unrelated to the claims in the case that may have affected the normal life expectancy of the deceased.

Finally, the judge will instruct the jury on the percentage of its members who must agree to reach a verdict. A unanimous consensus is usually not required. In many states it is sufficient if five-sixths of the jury agree.

Exceptions and Requests to the Charge

Once the charge of the court is completed, the jury is usually excused for a short time to allow the lawyers to make any exceptions or requests to the charge—that is, to object to something the judge said in his charge, to request that the judge charge something the attorney believes he omitted, or both. This is usually done in the absence of the jury so that the lawyers cannot influence the jury by making prejudicial and erroneous exceptions or requests and the jury does not draw any inferences from the denial or granting of an exception or a request. The lawyers should not be allowed to make "points" at this stage of the trial. Occasionally a judge may allow this process to take place in front of the jury. Your attorney should object strenuously, since this is improper.

An exception can refer to a legal explanation, the marshaling of evidence, the stating of a claim or a defense position, and the like. It can refer to any statement by the judge that the attorney believes was prejudicial and improper. Practically speaking, an exception is made both to convince the judge to correct his statement and for the record, so that if the judge does not do so it can be used as a basis for an appeal. Exceptions may refer not only to statements the attorney feels are objectionable but also to objectionable omissions the attorney believes the judge made. Most exceptions are denied, because the judge usually feels that he covered everything fairly and is not anxious to correct himself or emphasize any point by making additional remarks.

Despite most judges' reluctance to agree with an exception and correct their errors, a judge will sometimes omit something important or misstate a point that could be crucial to a party's position and affect the jury's determination. On occasion, a judge's ego gets in the way of admitting an error and he denies the exception pro forma. This is, of course, a travesty, and can cause an appeal and new trial if the appellate court considers the error serious enough. Unfortunately, such an error may sometimes have a prejudicial effect on the jury's thinking yet not be considered important enough by the appellate court to require a new trial. Because it is impossible to know what a juror will focus on or what point will turn the tide, it is of the utmost importance that neither ego nor personality stand in the way of a charge that is fair to both sides.

There are usually certain points of law that the attorney for each party will want the judge to include in his charge, and these will be submitted in the attorney's requests to charge. This is true whether or not an exception has been made (although it is true that exceptions do bring on requests to charge). The most common procedure is for the attorneys to submit written requests to charge to the judge before he charges, so that he can decide on the respective requests before charging. Very often these requests can be helpful to the judge. When a lawyer feels that he must protect the record (for appeal) in regard to certain requests that were not charged by the judge, he will make them again formally after the charge is completed. The written requests themselves can be made part of the record as a court exhibit. The judge will then either deny or grant each request. An attorney may also make orally any request he deems appropriate at the completion of the charge. This process can occur in connection with an exception; or, if the attorney thinks of a request that he did not include in his written requests to charge, he can add it at this time.

If the judge denies all the exceptions and requests (or if there are none) the jury will be called back from the jury room, perhaps given some last-minute instructions (such as a reminder that they can call for the evidence to examine or have a witness's testimony read), and sent out to begin deliberation. If there are any exceptions that the judge agrees with or requests to charge granted, the judge will make whatever additional remarks or instructions are required before sending the jury out to deliberate.

It is crucial that exceptions and requests to the charge be made even if your attorney knows that the trial judge will deny them, because doing so will show the appellate court, should there be an appeal, that he felt they were important points likely to affect the jury and thus worth mentioning to the judge. Without the exceptions and requests on the record, the appellate court will not usually consider the point reversible error. In other words, the appellate court reasons that if the trial attorney did not consider the point important enough to raise to the trial judge by means of an exception or a request to charge, there is no reason for it to consider the point important enough to upset the entire trial and order a new one.

Mistrials

If there is misconduct by a witness, the judge, or a juror, or some other event that could prejudice the outcome or prevent the jury from reaching a fair verdict, the trial judge may order a mistrial. He can do so at any time before the verdict is reached, on his own volition or on motion by any attorney. A mistrial means that the trial is concluded without result and that there will have to be a new trial because the jurors' minds have been so poisoned they could not reach a fair verdict.

The testimony taken during the aborted trial can be used for purposes of cross-examination in the new trial (in the same manner your testimony at your examination before trial is used), since it is still sworn testimony, but, in effect, the entire effort that went into the trial is wasted and battle will have to be joined another day. Depending on the circumstances and strategies involved, a mistrial can be a small advantage to one side or another because the attack or the defense of one side has been revealed, allowing the other side to prepare for it the next time around. Sometimes, for this reason and because of the time and expense involved in a new trial, the case is settled before a new trial actually takes place.

A good attorney will always make a motion for a mistrial if something untoward occurs during the trial that could possibly prejudice his client. Doing so protects the client in two ways. If the motion for a mistrial is granted, the case will not be decided by a jury that may be prejudiced against him. If the motion is not granted, its presence on the record will have the same effect as an exception or request to charge, should there be an appeal, in that it will show the appellate court that the attorney considered the event prejudicial at the time it occurred; therefore, it may be important enough to be the basis for overturning the verdict and granting a new trial.

The Verdict

Supposedly the jurors have not deliberated at all when they receive the case from the judge for decision. In reality, they have probably discussed a great deal of evidence in pairs and small groups. In any event, once they receive the case your work is over, except for the ordeal of waiting. This can often be the worst part of any lawsuit. A great deal of second-guessing and looking back always occurs as you wait. There is also a sense of relief because the case is finally in the hands of the jury.

One rule of thumb about the length of time it takes the jury to reach a decision is that a verdict reached quickly is a verdict for the defendant. This is not always the case, however, and it is frankly impossible to guess what the jurors will do. Sometimes they will stay out a long time to try to convince one holdout to join the rest so they can present a unanimous verdict, despite the fact that unanimity is not required. Sometimes, if they are angered by the defendant's conduct, they will come in quickly with a verdict for the plaintiff in the amount he asked for in summation (assuming such a request is permissible) or in a large amount selected without much debate.

I find that the period of waiting can be the time when attorney and client enjoy each other's company the most because, despite the worrying, the tension of the battle is over. The lawyer is not preoccupied with tactics, the next witness, cross-examination, or subpoenaing a document, and the client need no longer worry about his own testimony, the evidence to come, or the opposing attorney's summation. All the two can do is wait and relate to each other, about anything from the trial to personal matters. Remember that the period of waiting can go on for a long time, sometimes twelve hours or more. It is an interesting interlude. From a lawyer's point of view, it can only feel good when he knows, win or lose, that he did a good job. From a doctor's point of view, you can only feel satisfied that you presented your best defense if you know that you prepared yourself, were honest, and helped your attorney refute the plaintiff's claims against you.

Juror Requests or Questions

The jurors are entitled to see everything admitted into evidence and to have the testimony of any witness read to them. They make their desires known through notes to the judge. These notes are marked as court exhibits. The jurors can also ask the judge questions about the law or anything else in the charge they did not understand. Such requests and questions often arouse great consternation and speculation as to which way the jurors are leaning. Such speculation is fruitless, since the question or request might be solely for the purpose of convincing a holdout or to reassure themselves that the conclusion they have reached is correct.

For example, I was involved in the defense of a case in which the jury asked a question about causation, which had been clearly spelled out by the judge in his charge. The jury's question was: "In order to find for the plaintiff, do we have to find that the tetanus the deceased suffered from was contracted as a result of the defendant's negligence?" The judge repeated his instruction that the jurors had to find that the defendant's negligence was a "substantial factor" in causing the deceased to contract tetanus. It was hard to understand how the jury could ask this question when the judge had been so explicit in his charge. The manner in which the question was phrased also worried the defendants. Approximately fifteen minutes later, the jurors came in with a unanimous verdict in favor of the defendants.

In speaking with the jurors after the verdict, I learned that they had decided not to consider the conflicting testimony as to whether there was negligence, but rather, to focus directly on the question of causation. They felt that the evidence was insufficient to connect the contracting of tetanus (the disease that had caused the patient to die) to the alleged negligence, even if they believed the plaintiff's version of what took place. They had asked the question of the court to reassure themselves that it was proper to hold in favor of the defendants on the basis of the fact that the plaintiff failed to prove causation.

Polling

After the foreman or forelady of the jury has reported the jury's verdict, the losing party can request that the jury be polled. The clerk of the court polls the jury by asking each juror in open court what his or her verdict is. This procedure supposedly allows a wavering juror who was railroaded by the others one last opportunity to rebel and change his vote. Thus polling is supposed to insure that the foreman or forelady is accurately reporting the true wishes of the jurors. Polling can be requested by any losing party, if there is more than one. I have never seen or heard of a juror changing his vote as a result of being polled.

Post-verdict Motions

After the verdict, the attorney for the losing party will almost always automatically move to set aside the verdict as against the weight of the evidence and for judgment in favor of his client. He can also move for a new trial. If the plaintiff is not satisfied with the amount of the verdict in his favor, he can move to set it aside as inadequate. Similarly, the defendant can move to set aside the verdict on the ground that it is excessive.

In response to such motions, the trial judge has a variety of options. He can set aside the verdict and grant judgment to the losing party. He can reduce or increase the amount of the verdict. He can set aside the verdict and grant a new trial. He can deny the motions and allow the verdict to stand. Such motions are usually made orally immediately after the verdict. If a motion is denied or only partially granted from the bench, the attorney can usually still remake his motion on papers within a specified time, determined by statute, after the verdict. Legal action to collect (execute) the judgment is not permitted until this period has expired.

If the judge does not wish to decide a motion from the bench, he can reserve his decision and order the attorneys to submit papers in support of and in opposition to the motion by certain dates. He may also order additional oral argument to be made on a certain date. Again, no action will be taken on the verdict until the motion is decided. There is a right of appeal from the decision on a motion and the judgment (based on the verdict or the decision of the judge).

The Format of the Questioning

The format of questioning at the trial is not exactly like that at an examination before trial, as you might expect. The trial is not for discovery. It is to ascertain the truth, to resolve the disputes between the parties, and to mete out justice. There is cross-examination, and a definite format for questioning and accompanying rules that play a large part in determining what testimony is elicited at the trial.

Direct Testimony (Examination)

When an attorney calls a friendly witness to the stand to testify in support of his client's case, he is eliciting "direct" testimony. A witness is called "friendly" when he is friendly to the position of the party calling him to the stand. An "adverse" or "hostile" witness is not friendly to the position of the party whose attorney is questioning him. When an attorney is questioning a hostile witness, he is permitted to cross-examine the witness. Cross-examination is the opposite of taking direct testimony (direct examination). A party may call both friendly and hostile witnesses to the stand in his case. For example, if the attorney for the plaintiff called you, the defendant, as the first witness in his case, you would be a hostile witness; thus the rules of cross-examination, not direct examination, would apply.

The classic example of direct examination is the plaintiff's attorney questioning the plaintiff in the plaintiff's case (or your attorney questioning you). When he begins questioning the plaintiff, he does so under the rules of direct examination. The plaintiff's answers become his direct testimony. Obviously, the plaintiff's lawyer has gone over the plaintiff's testimony with him before he takes the stand and thus knows what he will say. (This is usually true of any friendly witness an attorney calls to the stand for direct examination.) Consequently, the attorney is not permitted to "lead" his own witness (the plaintiff) on direct examination. In effect, this rule prevents the attorney from putting the answer he wants the jury to hear in the question, requiring the witness merely to say "Yes" or "No" without putting anything in his own words.

For example, if the plaintiff's lawyer asks the plaintiff, "Did the doctor then pull with great force on your ankle?" he is leading the witness. Words are being put into the witness's mouth. A proper way to put the question would be "What did the doctor do then?" The question is not supposed to contain the answer on *direct* examination. The reason for this rule is obvious: The witness who tells his story in his own words will probably adhere more closely to the truth. He will not necessarily put the gloss or emphasis on the aspects his attorney would highlight to make the story sound better. He might say that the doctor "slowly manipulated" his ankle rather than that he "pulled with great force" on the ankle. The jury should hear the version the witness remembers, not the version desired by the attorney. If the plaintiff does attempt to lie or embellish on his own, he will be doing so without his attorney's words; thus his testimony will be easier for the jury to see through and for opposing counsel to destroy on cross-examination.

A certain amount of preliminary leading may be permitted on direct examination, but once any witness begins to testify about the facts or to give opinions, objections to leading questions should be made by opposing counsel and upheld by the trial judge.

There are many rules of evidence that deal with testimony, and this book does not purport to be a primer on the rules of evidence. However, you should know that the story elicited by an attorney through direct examination of his own witness is the story the interrogating party will be bound by. The attorney will not be permitted to impeach his own witness unless he convinces the court that the witness has turned hostile. This is usually done by showing that the witness has made prior statements that are inconsistent with his testimony on the stand.

Cross-examination

Once the direct examination of a witness is completed by the attorney who called him to the stand, the attorneys representing the other parties in the case have the opportunity to cross-examine the witness. If the witness is, in effect, appearing for more than one party, more direct testimony may be elicited by the attorneys representing other parties whose interests do not conflict with the party who called the witness. True cross-examination is done by opposing counsel.

Opposing counsel are attempting to tear down the testimony of an adverse witness. Because of the difficulty of this task, more latitude is permitted in the questioning designed to achieve this end. The basic principle is that a truthful witness will be able to weather cross-examination. Thus a cross-examiner should be permitted to lead the witness in order to trip him up and catch him in a lie. He should be permitted to be argumentative and persistent, within reason (at the discretion of the trial judge).

On cross-examination an attorney can try to impeach the witness with his prior testimony or with any other evidence the attorney has found that is inconsistent with the witness's testimony on direct examination. The cross-examiner may use medical journals and texts *recognized by the witness as authoritative*[5] to impeach the witness's opinions. The court (judge) will sometimes allow the cross-examiner to go into tangential subject matter for the purpose of impeaching the witness. The degree of latitude permitted on cross-examination is in the judge's discretion. On direct examination the questioning is supposed to be limited to relevant material.

Because the judge controls what is permitted on cross-examination, he can greatly influence the effectiveness of cross-examination. Truth is supposed to emerge from this crucible of fire, and it is my belief that the ability to hold up well under cross-examination does tend to vouch for the veracity of one's testimony. This test of veracity is not foolproof, mind you, but it does weed out a great deal. Notwithstanding the important function of cross-examination, many judges tend to restrict attorneys in their attempts to tear down opposing witnesses. Incessant badgering certainly cannot be allowed, but the effectiveness of cross-examination should not be sacrificed to an undue desire to move the case along, finish the case, help the witness under fire, or help a particular side. It often takes a little time to set an effective trap on cross-examination, and this cannot be done if the judge is rushing the attorney or not permitting half of his questions. An unbiased experienced judge will know where to draw the line. Cross-examination is supposed to cover only the material covered on direct, although a certain amount of leeway is permitted at the discretion of the judge.

In view of the importance of cross-examination and its function in establishing your veracity, you can see why preparation to stand up to cross-examination is essential.

Redirect Examination

If after cross-examination points brought out or new material allowed into evidence during cross-examination needs further explanation, in the opinion of the attorney who called the witness on direct, there will be redirect examination. Strictly speaking, redirect is supposed to be limited to matters brought out on cross-examination, but some leeway is usually allowed; redirect is very often abused to repeat or underline points made on direct after the cross-examination has drawn attention away from them or called them into question. Sometimes this tactic can rehabilitate a point, but if the cross-examination has cut deep and exposed untruths or an attempt to deceive the jury, it will not succeed.

Recross-Examination

Again, if something brought out on redirect needs further clarification from the opposing party's point of view, or if something new has been allowed to sneak in on redirect, the attorney for that party has the right to recross the witness on these matters. Recross-examination is limited to matters covered on redirect examination, and the trial judge will usually adhere strictly to this rule in order to end the questioning.

5. See "The Rule on Textbooks and Articles," pp. 207-214 in this chapter.

The process of questioning is complicated and it is lengthened when there are multiple defendants or multiple plaintiffs, or both. If new matters brought out by a coplaintiff or codefendant affect another party, that party has the right to question concerning those matters. In such situations the judge will usually hold the examiners more strictly to the rules of questioning, allowing no new matter to be introduced once the original direct examinations and cross-examinations have been completed. He will exercise his discretion as fairly as possible to end the questioning of each witness after each attorney has had an opportunity to interrogate.

How to Testify in Court

Because of differences in personality, some people are naturally better witnesses than others. Nevertheless, keeping certain principles in mind will always help you be a better witness. Preparation, which has already been covered, is always a must. If we assume thorough preparation and familiarity with the medical data and examinations before trial, the manner in which you field the questions and handle your interrogator is crucial if you are to be a good witness and impress the jury. (The same thing is true of your examination before trial, since, if you are a party to the suit, the entire transcript of your deposition may be read to the jury and you may be confronted with portions of it when you are cross-examined at the trial.)

Since your own attorney (or the attorney representing a party with whom you have no conflict) will be questioning you gently, the following discussion of how to testify in court applies mainly to cross-examination, the real test of a good witness.

Keeping the Interrogator Honest

The first goal of every good witness is *to keep the interrogator honest* in his questioning. Often an attorney will ask a general or vague question that could *possibly* apply to the facts of the case involved, push for an answer favorable to the party he represents, and then argue later that you have admitted that the principle established by the answer applies to the case in question. Or he may use the answer later to embarrass you when you try to explain why the principle does *not* apply to the case in question. The attorney might shout, "But doctor, didn't you tell us before that it *is* good practice in general to x-ray under these circumstances? And now you say that you do not have to do it in this case?" Let us consider an example.

Suppose you are a neurosurgeon testifying in a case in which surgery was delayed. You are asked, "Doctor, isn't it true that if one sees a patient, and x-ray diagnosis and identification of an aneurysm are made, surgery should be performed as soon as possible?" Generally speaking, the answer to this question might be "Yes." But if you merely answer "Yes," you are asking for trouble. Obviously, the decision to perform surgery under such circumstances depends on many factors. Certainly it might be conceded that under optimal conditions the earlier one goes in, the better the result; but the question as asked is so general that it cannot and should not be answered without qualification. It is my understanding that the scheduling of aneurysm surgery depends on the physical and neurological condition of the patient, whether there has been a recent bleed, the location of the aneurysm, the type of aneurysm, and other factors. Apparently, if there has been a recent bleed, if the chances of arterial spasm seem high and the patient has a headache and nuchal rigidity, a neurosurgeon would *not* operate right away despite x-ray diagnosis and identification of an aneurysm.

So what should your answer be? There is no perfect answer, but you must force the questioning attorney to put in the information necessary to make the question accurately answerable in terms of the medicine involved. For example, you could say, "Counselor, that question cannot be answered properly without knowing more about the history and the medical signs and symptoms the patient is manifesting at the time he is seen. It may not be proper to go in immediately." Or: "It may not be proper to perform surgery immediately. It depends on a host of other factors and circumstances that I must know in order to be able to answer your question honestly." Thus the attorney's attempt to have you state that, in general, one should perform surgery on an aneurysm as soon as possible (thereby indirectly criticizing the decision of the surgeon in the case) has been foiled without denying or affirming the proposition directly. He has been kept honest. In addition, you have made the jury aware that the decision to operate on an aneurysm is a complicated one depending on many factors. The questioning attorney will now be forced to include the relevant factors in his subsequent questions.

Attorneys often lay traps by leaving vital information out of their questions. Careless answering of such questions will result in an apparent logical syllogism that leads to a damaging incorrect conclusion. This outcome is prevented when you keep the interrogator honest and do not permit improper postulates. A good witness must insure that all the necessary information is included in *the question and the answer*.

In a wrongful death case involving cervical cancer that I tried, the plaintiff's attorney used this type of questioning in an attempt to establish that it was bad medical practice, after obtaining one suspicious Pap smear reading, to take a repeat smear before taking any further steps. For example:

Q It's true, doctor, is it not, that tissue diagnosis is always more accurate than diagnosis on the basis of a Pap smear?

A Yes.

Q And one common way to take tissue from the cervix is to perform a punch biospy, correct?

A Correct.

Q So, if a physician obtained a suspicious Pap smear, it would be good gynecological practice to perform a punch biopsy to ascertain whether or not the patient really has cancer, would it not?

A Yes.

Q In fact, it would be a *deviation* from good gynecological practice *not* to perform a punch biopsy on the patient, since, as you told us, tissue diagnosis is more definitive than a diagnosis based on a smear, and, therefore, a diagnosis based on the tissue taken from a biopsy would be more definitive than a diagnosis from a repeat smear, right?

Where does the witness go from here? What is his answer? He has cornered himself by answering carelessly. Under the circumstances, is it a deviation from good gynecological practice to take a repeat smear before performing a punch biopsy? If the witness answers in the negative at this point, doesn't he appear to be contradicting his own prior testimony? Why wouldn't it be a deviation from good practice not to take the *most* definitive test for *cancer* after obtaining one suspicious smear? How can the jury believe his answer? If this witness is the defendant in the case, he may have caused the case to be lost. His answers to the questions suggest that the most accurate method of diagnosing cancer is to obtain tissue by means of a biopsy or some other method, and that good practice requires that this be done after obtaining one suspicious smear. To do anything less, such as to take a repeat smear, would appear according to his testimony to be a deviation from good practice.

The cross-examining attorney is leading the doctor down a tricky path, and it takes an astute, knowledgeable witness to keep the attorney accurate and avoid reaching the wrong conclusion in front of the jury or looking foolish by denying what appears to be the logical conclusion of a syllogism his own prior answers set up.

The expert gynecologists in this case informed me that it is perfectly good and accepted gynecological practice for a physician to take a repeat Pap smear when the initial smear is reported back as suspicious or Class III. Many doctors will do so before subjecting their patient to a punch biopsy, because the initial suspicious smear could be accounted for by such benign factors as taking a smear too soon after menstruation, menopausal changes that have caused the shedding of abnormal cells, lab error, mixed-up slides, or taking insufficient material for the smear. Furthermore, a punch biopsy involves a certain amount of discomfort, a minor risk of hemorrhage, and, of course, expense. I was told by my experts that there is no harm in immediately taking a repeat smear when the first smear is read as suspicious and then, if the repeat comes back as suspicious or worse, performing a biopsy. If the repeat smear comes back negative, the prudent thing to do is to take a third smear in order *to verify the negative finding.*

The attorney for the plaintiff tried to argue that taking a repeat smear instead of an immediate biopsy was malpractice and caused the death of the patient. This was not true; immediately taking a repeat smear is *good* practice. Let's see how a sharp defendant or expert might handle the cross-examining attorney's questions:

Q It's true, doctor, is it not, that tissue diagnosis is always more accurate than diagnosis on the basis of a Pap smear?

A *Generally speaking,* tissue diagnosis or examination of tissue under a microscope will give a more definitive diagnosis than diagnosis based on a Pap smear.

Q And one common way to take tissue from the cervix is to perform a punch biopsy, correct?

A One way to remove tissue from one area of the cervix *when it is indicated* is to surgically punch a hole in the cervix with a punch biopsy tool, which will then yield tissue for microscopic examination.

Q So, if a physician obtained a suspicious Pap smear, it would be good gynecological practice to perform a punch biopsy to ascertain whether or not the patient really has cancer, would it not?

A Assuming that the physician has taken a confirmatory repeat smear and is still suspicious on the basis of the second smear, it would be good practice for him to subject his patient to a punch biopsy under anesthesia to confirm a diagnosis.

Q But, doctor, since you told us that tissue diagnosis is more definitive than diagnosis based on a smear, wouldn't it be pointless and, in fact, bad practice to take another smear rather than immediately perform a punch biopsy?

A Since as medical practitioners we are aware that there are many harmless reasons why one smear might be reported as suspicious—such as lab error, which does occur; insufficient specimen; abnormal cells from menopause, and so forth—a careful physician would not subject his patient to a biopsy that requires anesthesia and some risk, not to mention discomfort and cost, on the basis of an initial suspicious smear. He would take a repeat smear to confirm the finding of the initial smear before performing a biopsy.

What has happened here? By answering carefully and qualifying each answer to make sure that all the relevant factors are included, the witness has turned the line of questioning around to make *his* points rather than the attorney's. He has pointed out that Pap smears can sometimes be unreliable and require repeating before subjecting the patient to the discomfort, risk, and cost of a biopsy.

Common Mistakes

As I have said, doctors are notoriously bad witnesses. Physicians often testify as if they had no confidence in their treatment and are guilty of malpractice because of the patient's poor result. This guilty feeling is transmitted to the jury. A guilty feeling is also transmitted to the jury by a physician who feels he has to justify his every assertion, decision, or opinion with statements such as "The literature says. . ." "Many in the profession agree. . ." and "Other doctors will agree. . ." instead of, "On the basis of the clinical picture *I* decided that surgery was indicated." The literature does not decide the treatment you render. *You* decide, and you must convey that what you did was *your* best judgment after considering all the factors and that it was definitely within accepted standards of practice, whether or not in hindsight it caused a disastrous result.

Another common reason why physicians err on the stand is that they forget where they are. They forget that they are in a court of law before a jury of lay persons, not before a group of their peers at a medical meeting. When a question is asked about the relative medical probabilities of a general medical proposition, most physicians search their brains for the one case reported in New Zealand that did not follow the norm and proceed to answer contrary to what is usually the case. It is not only a physician's scientific mind that causes him to do this, as I proposed in Chapter 8; it is also his failure to understand the mentality of the people judging his case and the black or white reality of the legal process. It happens time and time again that a doctor defendant tells his lawyer one thing concerning the medicine of the case during the preparation of the case, and then on the witness stand he says the opposite due to his scientific training and his failure to understand his judges and the process they must use to decide his case. In an extreme search for absolute truth, the physician denies what is true in 99.9 percent of the cases, and thus destroys his defense.

Suppose a physician tells his attorney that the normal recovery period for the surgery involved in the case is three weeks. This point is important in defending his postoperative care, since the plaintiff is claiming that the defendant physician discharged him too soon or allowed him to walk on his leg too early. The physician is then asked by his own attorney on direct examination, "What is the normal recovery period for this surgery, doctor?" Much to his lawyer's surprise and dismay, the physician answers, "Anywhere from three to ten weeks." The lawyer must show no emotion in front of the jury, but inside he cringes and wants to choke his client. Why? Why? Why does the physician do this? He has just taken the oath to tell the truth and he is nervous. He remembers a rare case in which recovery took ten weeks, and wants to include this exception in his answer in an attempt to be completely honest. However, by answering this way he has made the jury think that the recovery period for the surgery is ten weeks as often as it is three weeks. This misconception, in turn, calls the doctor's postoperative treatment into question. It is more than likely that the case of the ten-week recovery involved special circumstances not germane to the case under scrutiny, but the jurors do not understand this because it has not been explained to them. The physician's attorney wanted his client to tell the jury the normal recovery period, so that the jury could understand why the physician discharged the plaintiff from the hospital when he did, or let the plaintiff start walking when he did. The defendant's attorney is trying to have his client establish the normal recovery period, so that he can show that the defendant allowed the normal recovery period to pass before discharging the patient or allowing him to start walking on his leg. If there were no special factors that should have alerted the physician to delay discharging the patient or allowing the patient to start walking on his leg, this may be the physician's entire defense.

This syndrome is often coupled with failure to listen to what is being asked and the desire to show the range of his knowledge. Imagine that in an orthopedic case the defendant is being criticized for not using metal fixation in treating the plaintiff's leg. He is asked by his attorney, "Doctor, what is the significance of a history of a 12-year-old compound fracture of the leg with drainage and osteomyelitis in terms of your decision not to use a metal fixation device in the same site?" The answer the attorney expects, on the basis of his prior discussions with his client, is that such a history would be a contraindication to the use of metal because of the possibility of reactivating the osteomyelitis. However, the physician adds, "Except there was a series of cases in a study by the staff at the Hospital for Special Surgery in which metal devices were used if the prior osteomyelitis was more than ten years old." Why mention the study? Who cares about one study? The defense attorney is trying to establish generally accepted standards of practice and to demonstrate that the defendant's decision not to use metal was within those standards. Through the physician he is trying to explain to the jury that fear of reactivating a dormant osteomyelitis is a recognized contraindication to the use of metal in treating a fracture in the same site as the prior infection. This would make the defendant's decision clearly within the accepted standards of orthopedic practice. The study does not establish the generally accepted standards in this regard, nor does it lend anything to what the defense is trying to prove. In fact, volunteering the statement about the study could be very detrimental. It confuses the issue and could be interpreted by the jury to mean that the accepted standard followed by the best physicians is to use metal if the osteomyelitis is more than ten years old or that fear of reactivating an osteomyelitis more than ten years old is not a recognized contraindication to the use of metal.

Another common error physicians make on the witness stand is almost the opposite of what I have just described: They sometimes become so outraged that they have been sued and have to be in court that they become obstreperous, argumentative, and aggressively defensive. This demeanor has a terrible effect on the jury. Such a physician comes off as an untrustworthy partisan, instead of an objective and fair physician trying to explain the medicine of the case and the reasons why his treatment was within the accepted standards of practice. This overly defensive attitude is best exemplified by the unwillingness of such a physician to concede any points to the opposing counsel, no matter how minor or obvious. This attitude can also afflict physicians called as experts.

The case involving Pap smears and biopsy can serve as an example. In that case it was clear that certain obviously correct premises had to be admitted. There is no point in denying that tissue from a punch biopsy studied under a microscope is more definitive than lab analysis of a Pap smear. In general this is true. An angry, overly partisan witness might try to deny the basic validity of this proposition by saying that the punch biopsy is sometimes taken from the wrong part of the cervix and that tissue study is therefore misleading and not as definitive as a smear. Although there may be some validity to such an argument—if we assume that the punch biopsy is taken from the wrong part of the cervix and that the smear is taken properly and at the proper time—it is reaching, not generally considered true, and not convincing. Even if you can be misled by a biopsy because the tissue removed does not contain the cancer present on the cervix, the accepted standard is apparently that, if we assume the biopsy and the smear are taken properly, the tissue study will yield more definitive results. Even if these assumptions are not spelled out, they are obviously assumed in the question. It is a mistake to stretch the truth in order to oppose every proposition put to you by the opposition; your effort becomes obvious and you lose your credibility. You should agree with true propositions put to you by anyone, as long as they are accurate and the assumptions contained in the question are clear. You can make them clear by stating them in your answer. For example, you can answer that, generally speaking, if one *assumes* that the tissue has been taken from the proper place, tissue diagnosis is more definitive than diagnosis based on a smear. This answer makes the point that obtaining cancerous tissue from a punch biopsy can be tricky and that diagnosis based on tissue from a biopsy is thus not foolproof. You must show the jury that you are trying to give them the most accurate information, and not fighting for your cause no matter what the truth is.

Expert Questions

Defendants as well as expert witnesses have to deal with expert questions. This is a special area of questioning that requires the utmost care, because it is here that many legal questions concerning the sufficiency of the proof arise and much of the argument to both the jury and the judge is concentrated. Again, since your own attorney or the attorney who calls you as his expert will be a friendly interrogator, the following discussion applies mainly to dealing with expert questions on cross-examination by an opposing attorney.

Expert questions are posed in various forms. One of the most dramatic is the long hypothetical question in which the interrogator asks you to "assume" certain facts already in evidence and then to render an opinion based on those assumptions. Such a question can be extremely dangerous and misleading if it misstates or omits important facts. When answering such a question, you must be extremely careful to keep the interrogator honest by correcting erroneous statements or omissions in the hypothetical question and by qualifying your answer if necessary. For example, if the hypothetical question leaves out information necessary to the formulation of a medically accurate opinion, you must ask the interrogator for this information and indicate that the question cannot be answered without it.

If you disagree with the truth of the assumptions contained in the hypothetical question but the interrogating attorney insists that you assume their truth, make it clear in your answer that your opinion is based solely on the assumption that all the givens posed in the hypothetical question are true—which you do not believe—and that your answer would not be the same if you were not required to make such an assumption. A good expert witness will answer a hypothetical question that contains an incorrect recitation of the facts in this fashion:"If everything you asked me to assume were true, which I disagree with (or find very unlikely), my opinion would be . . ."

In explaining your opinion, be sure to note all the relevant reasoning and data that led to your opinion. Doing so not only shows the jury your knowledge of the medicine involved and of the case, but also gives substance to your opinion and lends it credibility in the eyes of the jury.

Not all expert questions are asked in hypothetical form. The hypothetical aspect can be omitted when asking an expert opinion about general medical principles. For example, in the case involving Pap smears and a punch biopsy, the witness was asked whether, in general, tissue diagnosis is more definitive than diagnosis based on a smear. Sometimes the witness may be asked to state his opinion on the basis of his review of materials provided to him and any other information he is aware of: "Doctor, based on your review of the hospital records, the defendant's office records, and your physical examination of the patient, do you have an opinion with a reasonable degree of medical certainty as to whether Dr. Smith's treatment of Mrs. Doe's arm was in accordance with accepted standards of medical practice?" After the witness answers that he does have an opinion, he will be asked what the opinion is. In stating his opinion, the expert will be free to use any of the data made available to him to support his opinion. When you, as an expert or defendant, are stating your opinion, you should thus always support your opinion by citing the relevant medical information and medical principles and explaining your reasoning. The more thorough and convincing you are, the more strength your opinion has. In most cases you will be asked to give your expert opinion about your own treatment.

When you are being asked expert questions interspersed with other questions, you must be careful of the quick little expert question that can be slipped in among nonexpert questions to catch you off guard. Your careless answer to such a question could cost you the case. Consider the following sequence:

Q Doctor, it is good practice to take preoperative electrolyte studies in this kind of a case, isn't it?

A Yes.

Q You examined the hospital record, correct?

A Yes.

Q No electrolyte studies were taken before the procedure, correct?

A Correct.

Q That wasn't in accordance with accepted practice, was it?

If you are not careful, you can be trapped into rendering an expert opinion against yourself or another defendant that you did not intend. The fact that it is good practice to take preoperative electrolyte studies may not mean that there was a deviation from accepted practice in the above case merely because no such studies are recorded in the hospital record. The tests may have been performed immediately prior to admission in the office of the patient's local physician. The procedure involved may be so minor as not to require such studies. Other tests, such as electrocardiograms and blood studies, in the face of a normal clinical picture may have obviated the necessity for electrolyte studies. A good witness might have answered the same questions as follows:

Q Doctor, it is good practice to take preoperative electrolyte studies in this kind of a case, isn't it?

A It is not always required but, generally speaking, it is good practice.

Q You examined the hospital record, correct?

A Yes.

Q No electrolyte studies were taken before the procedure, correct?

A None were recorded in the hospital record as being performed in the hospital.

Q That wasn't in accordance with accepted practice, was it?

A In my opinion the circumstances of this case did not require that such studies be taken in the hospital, in view of the fact that they had been recently taken at the office of the patient's local physician and found to be normal. There was no reason to expect any change in the readings in the short time between the taking of the studies and the performance of the procedure. In other words, there was no deviation from accepted practice in regard to the taking of electrolyte studies in this case.

It is important to remember that, when you wish to qualify your answer, as in the response to the first question above, it is best to state the qualification *first*. Thus it is better to state, "It is not always required" first and then admit that it is generally considered good practice to take preoperative electrolyte studies. If you give the affirmative part of the answer first and then try to add the qualification, you run the risk of being cut off by the questioning attorney before you finish. If you answer, "Generally speaking, yes, but . . ." the attorney may stop you there and say, "Thank you, doctor, that answers the question." When this happens the qualification can only be stated later, maybe not until your attorney (or another friendly attorney) has the opportunity to question you. By that time the qualification has lost effect and has taken on the character of an afterthought, not to mention the possibility that a whole series of questions were asked and points developed by the opposing attorney on the basis of the answer he interrupted. If the qualification comes first, interruption is unlikely because the attorney will want to salvage the favorable part of the answer.

If you fail to state your qualification first and are cut off before you can add it, make a direct appeal to the judge to be allowed to finish your answer. This tactic shows the jury that you have not completed your answer and is often successful because the judge may not wish to deny such a request in front of the jury. However, be advised that it cannot be used repeatedly and will not be successful at all if the judge is pro-plaintiff. He can deny your request by telling you that you can add what you wish when your own attorney questions you. A direct appeal to the questioning attorney to be allowed to finish your answer might succeed on occasion but will usually be shunted aside in a similar fashion; he, too, does not want you to add your qualification.

When discussing untoward developments that occurred during the treatment, you must watch very carefully for sneaky expert questions. Suppose a bone has separated or fractured during the insertion of a prosthesis. After asking you about what happened, the plaintiff's lawyer may try to sneak in a question such as "That can happen only if too much force is applied, right?" or "That doesn't normally occur when the procedure is done properly, does it?" The correct response to this type of loaded question is that the complication can occur even with the best care when everything is done properly. It is a known risk of the procedure. Despite the obviousness of this type of response, many physicians are caught off guard and respond with something like "Well . . . excessive force *can* cause it" or "Well, that's right, normally this does not occur." Such thoughtless slips can seal your fate. The clear implication of such answers is that the complication would not have occurred unless excessive force was used or the procedure was done improperly. No matter what you say thereafter, you may never be able to erase that answer from the jurors' minds. You can be sure that a good plaintiff's attorney will attempt to obtain the maximum effect from your answer. He may or may not use it on further cross-examination (depending on whether he believes you might be able to explain your way out of the answer in responding to further questions on the subject), but he surely will harp on it on summation. Can you hear him exclaiming to the jury? "And remember when I asked that quick little question that the doctor answered before thinking about what he was told to say. His *only* truthful answer came out before he could catch it. Sure, he and other witnesses tried to deny it later. They tried to explain it away but it remains to haunt him. By his own words, this physician admitted on the stand that the fracture that causes Mrs. Jones, my client, to be in a wheelchair for the rest of her days would not have occurred if the procedure had been done properly."

Why do physicians make such mistakes? They do not think like witnesses. Obviously, a fracture is not supposed to occur when a prosthesis is being inserted, but if you focus on the usual success of the procedure you will give an answer that implies negligence. When you think about the question for a minute, it becomes evident that the occurrence of a complication is not necessarily related to incompetence or negligence. For example, the fracture that occurred as the prosthesis was being inserted could have been caused by the weak nature of the bone itself, which is impossible to determine in advance. The answer to such an improper question should be that such a fracture can occur despite the fact that everything is done properly by the most skilled hands.

Sometimes physicians fall for even more blatantly loaded questions, such as, "The breaking of the bone surely isn't consistent with good practice, is it, doctor?" You must be alert to the reasoning behind the question, which is totally unfair. Your analysis will lead you to an answer such as, "Certainly this can happen even when the highest standards of practice are followed. There is no way to be certain in advance how every bone will react to the procedure. Unfortunately, sometimes the bone itself is not strong enough to withstand the insertion of the prosthesis."

You must keep in mind when rendering an expert opinion that the law only requires you to opine with a reasonable degree of medical certainty and that being a physician entitles you to have an expert opinion. Your qualifications in terms of training, hospital affiliations, teaching positions, and the like add weight to your opinion, but equally or even more important is the manner in which you state your opinion. If you have formulated your opinion and state it clearly, unequivocally, and without hedging, the jury will want to believe you. When you are being cross-examined, you must not fight about minor points that do not matter. Be sure to put the necessary qualifications in your answers so that your honesty cannot be challenged. Remember that your expert opinion is *your* opinion. No one can take it from you, whether you are the expert called by a party or a defendant answering expert questions.

It is up to you to make your expert opinion as convincing as possible. Once you have formulated your opinion, taking into consideration all the pros and cons, you must support that opinion 100 percent and allow no doubt or equivocation to creep into your voice or your answers. There will always be some negative factors working against your opinion. These must be thought over and worked out in advance so that you can explain why they do not invalidate your opinion when you are confronted with them. The reason the law requires that expert opinions be definitive is obvious. If you, an expert, are unsure and cannot make up your mind, how can the lay jurors be expected to reach a decision? When the jurors are given the case to decide, they must have definite opinions to choose from. Therefore, if an expert opinion is too equivocal or speculative, it may be stricken from the record and from the jurors' consideration by the judge. Jurors are not supposed to guess. The case is not to be decided on the basis of speculation. Aside from the legalities, even if the opinion is allowed to stand by the judge it will carry no weight with the jurors when it is not strong and definitive.

The Rule on Textbooks and Articles

One way to impeach the opinions of an expert witness on cross-examination is to attack the physician's qualifications and expertise. Another method, which can be devastatingly effective, is to attack the expert's opinion with the contrary opinion of a published authority recognized by the expert. This tactic requires the use of medical literature.

Before an attorney can confront an expert with contrary medical opinions from medical texts, journals, or other publications, certain legal prerequisites must be met. The publication must contain an opinion contrary to that expressed by the witness. The witness whose opinion the cross-examiner wishes to impeach must recognize the publication as authoritative, or its author as an authority, in the field. If you are familiar with the work or author but do not recognize either as authoritative, the cross-examining attorney is not permitted to use the contrary opinion to impeach your opinion. You are not compelled to recognize any publication or author, no matter how widely used or famous. Remember that the jury does not know if a text is obscure or the bible of the field. You, as a witness, must decide about the contents of the work, its authority, and how you will deal with the opinions expressed. It is advisable to base what you consider authoritative on the contents of the work rather than the prominence of any particular author. Always ask what work of the author is being referred to. Recognizing an author as an authority when you do not know the work referred to or disagree with its contents is foolish, since you will be confronted with the contrary opinions contained within the work.

If you feel that you must acknowledge a certain text as authoritative in the field, you must always be sure to make it clear that you do not agree with all the opinions expressed in it. While admitting that the work is authoritative, add something to the effect ". . . but I do not agree with all the opinions expressed in it." When you are then confronted with an opinion in the text that is contrary to yours, you can explain that this opinion is one of those that you disagree with. Of course, this response is still somewhat damaging, and you are much better off if you can distinguish the facts of the court case from those on which the author's opinion is based. Explaining why the author's opinion does not apply to the case in question, and is therefore not contrary to your opinion, can actually strengthen your opinion in the minds of the jurors. This excellent means of thwarting what might otherwise be an effective method of impeaching your opinion can be used more often than most physicians realize. Very often the opinion in the authoritative text is expressed in general terms and does not really apply to the case at hand. If you are prepared and astute, you may be able to explain why the opinion is true in general but inapplicable to the facts of the case in question.

Obviously it is preferable for an opinion contrary to yours never to reach the ears of the jurors, but there will in many cases be authoritative texts you will feel compelled to recognize. You should always be familiar with the contents of the texts you recognize; it is very dangerous not to be. For example, without being familiar with the section from which the contrary opinion is being quoted it is very difficult to distinguish the opinion properly and to explain why it does not apply to the case in question. It is also impossible to show that the author agrees with your opinion in a later passage. Thus it is best not to recognize unfamiliar texts (or authors); there is then no possibility of their use against you. (Remember that if you recognize an author as an authority, the cross-examining attorney can use any text by him against you if it contains a contrary opinion.)

One method attorneys use to attempt to embarrass a physician who will not recognize certain texts as authoritative is to pile a large number of texts on the counsel table and to pick up each one and ask him whether he recognizes it as authoritative in the field. If the physician refuses to recognize the text, the attorney then reads him the author's titles, affiliations, and positions, which usually sound impressive, and asks the physician if he recognizes the "distinguished" author as an authority. If this process is repeated a sufficient number of times and the witness refuses to recognize any of the works or authors without adequate explanation, the jury may think either that the physician does not know his field of expertise or that he is trying to put something over on them. It is important, therefore, that you know how to field questions about medical works and their authors in the proper fashion. Remember that an opposing attorney may collect a number of medical texts that are not authoritative at all in an attempt to embarrass you with this technique.

If you are aware of the text the attorney questions you about, it is always a good idea to indicate your knowledge of its existence (being careful that nothing you say can be construed as recognition of the work as authoritative) and then to inform the interrogator that although you know of the book you do not recognize it as authoritative in the field. If the text is passé, you might explain that it was once authoritative but no longer is, and that therefore you do not recognize it. If the text the attorney is trying to confront you with is considered inferior or misleading, you should make this clear in your refusal to recognize it. There is nothing wrong with embarrassing the cross-examiner by stating, "That book is considered to be one of the worst ever published in this field. No one who knows anything about medicine would recognize it as authoritative or an authority." If you have never heard of the text or its author, say so definitively: "I am familiar with all the major periodicals in my field and I have never heard of that magazine, that article, or that author." Answers such as these prevent negative inferences from being drawn as a result of your refusal to recognize the medical work you are being asked to recognize. They may even show the jurors that the attorney is trying to deceive them with inferior medical publications. In fact, such answers can enhance your credibility and prevent the cross-examiner from indulging in a song and dance about your refusal to recognize the work. Keep in mind that your awareness of, or even familiarity with, a text does not permit the cross-examining attorney to use it on cross-examination (in other words, to read from it). It may be used only if you recognize it or its author as an *authority*.

Whenever an attorney attempts to cross-examine you with a medical text, you should always ask him the date of publication and the identity of the author of the *chapter* or *article* that contains the opinion the attorney wishes to question you about. If the date of publication (the copyright) is old, your refusal to recognize the medical work as authoritative on the ground that it is out of date is strengthened. If the date of publication is more recent than the date of the treatment in question, your attorney (or the attorney who called you as a witness) can object to the use of the text as inapplicable to the treatment; if he doesn't, you can always explain that the opinions expressed in the text were not developed or accepted as good practice, whichever is the case, until after the date of the treatment in question.

Many medical books are edited by one physician but include chapters written by many different physicians as contributing authors. When it is appropriate, you should admit that you recognize certain *chapters* in a given text as authoritative because you recognize their authors as authorities in the field, but that you do not recognize the author of the chapter in question as an authority, and therefore do not recognize that chapter as authoritative. When you make such distinctions, you must spell out what you mean very carefully, so that your answer cannot be misconstrued to permit the attorney to read a contrary opinion from a chapter written by someone you do not recognize as an authority in your field.

Consider the following series of questions you could be confronted with when the cross-examining attorney wishes to use a medical text to impeach your expert opinion. The answers are those an experienced witness might give in refusing to recognize the text:

Q Dr. Smith, do you recognize McLaughlin's *Trauma* as an authoritative work in the field of orthopedics?

A Which edition of Dr. McLaughlin's book are you referring to?

Q The 1959 edition.

A I know the book to be written by many contributing authors. Which chapter are you referring to and what is the name of its author?

Q I am referring to Dr. Lord's chapter on vascular difficulties.

A I know Dr. Lord well—in fact, we play tennis together—but I do not recognize that chapter or him as a definitive authority in this area.

The attorney, hearing the word "definitive," might feel that he has struck on a weakness in your answer and pursue it further:

Q Doctor, do you recognize him as an *authority*?

A He is a fine physician but I do *not* recognize him as an authority.

Q Isn't it true, sir, that he is a diplomate of surgery, an attending physician at various prominent hospitals, and a professor of vascular surgery?

A Yes, I said I considered him a fine physician, but there are many fine doctors with such qualifications whom I do not consider authorities in the field although I respect their work. They probably feel the same about me.

This witness has effectively thwarted the use of a medical text he does not recognize, and that contains an adverse opinion he disagrees with, without appearing ignorant or false.

Dr. Jere Lord, when I used him as an expert witness in a case I was defending, refused on cross-examination by the plaintiff's counsel to recognize as authoritative his own chapter in Dr. Harrison McLaughlin's *Trauma*, explaining that the opinions he expressed when he wrote the chapter had been revised prior to the dates of the treatment involved in the case in which he was testifying, and that therefore he could not consider the chapter authoritative with respect to the treatment in question. It was an amazing statement, but his sincerity and honesty were apparent. As a result, the plaintiff's attorney was prevented from reading to the jury Dr. Lord's written opinion, which was contrary to the opinion expressed in his testimony.

A good cross-examiner will often attempt to browbeat you into recognizing a given medical text as authoritative:

Q Doctor, you recognize Dr. Gray's book *Anatomy* as an authoritative work, do you not?

A No.

Q Well, doctor, isn't this the book used to teach medical students at the medical school where you teach?

A Yes.

Q Isn't this book considered the bible in regard to anatomy?

A Yes.

Q And you recognize it as such, don't you?

A Yes.

Q And therefore it is considered by the medical community and yourself as an authority, is it not?

A Well . . . yes.

Now the lawyer can read an opinion from the text that is contrary to your opinion and ask whether you agree or disagree with it. This is a device to impeach your opinion by having the jury hear the contrary opinion of an authority you recognize.

The browbeating technique is often used when the attorney wants you to recognize a journal article that really should not be recognized as authoritative. The lawyer will pressure you by attempting to make you agree that, since medical periodicals are subscribed to and read to keep abreast of developments in the field, they are authoritative. This reasoning is fallacious. The appropriate answer, of course, is that medical periodicals are subscribed to and read to keep apprised of new studies, theories, and proposals, but the contents of the articles in the periodicals are not necessarily authoritative in terms of the *accepted* standards of practice. For example, such articles very often introduce new ideas and theories on the basis of inconclusive studies. These theories are eventually either accepted or rejected by the medical profession, but they are by no means the accepted standards of practice at the time of publication.

You may be wondering how one might handle the series of questions about Dr. Gray's *Anatomy*. One of the many ways to handle such questions is as follows:

Q Doctor, you recognize Dr. Gray's book *Anatomy* as an authoritative work, do you not?

A No.

Q Well, doctor, isn't this the book used to teach medical students at the medical school where you teach?

A We use many texts to teach medical students at the medical school. One of them is Gray's; another is the medical dictionary. While such general texts are important for the instruction of medical students, that does not make them authoritative to the trained physician.

Q But, doctor, isn't this book considered the bible in regard to anatomy?

A Absolutely not. It is a good general text on the subject, but not necessarily authoritative in any one area.

Q You mean to say you don't recognize Gray's as the bible on anatomy?

A Absolutely not.

Q Isn't it considered by the medical community as such? As an authority?

A Most physicians are familiar with the work, since it is a general text used in teaching, but no expert would accept it as the bible or as authoritative in this field.

By answering in this fashion the physician has established that his opinion is based on his expertise, training, and experience, and is not easily challenged by a general text. He concedes certain points about the text, but he is standing firm on his refusal to recognize the book as an authority. This stance keeps him honest in the eyes of the jurors. It also impresses on them the scope of his knowledge and the weight he puts on his own opinion.

You may fear that the cross-examining attorney will cut you off before you can complete an answer such as that made to the second question. A good witness will get his message across one way or another; if not in a given answer, in the next one. For example, you might answer the second question in this way:

A It is true that we use the text for beginning students, but that does not make it authoritative for a highly trained expert. It is too general.

There are many ways to answer a question. This is what makes the duel between a good cross-examiner and a good witness so interesting to the trained observer.

Sometimes a cross-examining attorney can embarrass a physician into recognizing an article or a text by flaunting its author's credentials in front of the jury, causing the witness to be embarrassed into recognizing as authoritative an author he does not know.

Q Oh, come now, doctor, surely you recognize Dr. Charles K. Friedberg, former chief of cardiology at Mount Sinai Hospital, professor of cardiology, president of innumerable associations in his field, whose book on cardiology has been translated into eleven languages and who has written so many articles and papers in the field of cardiology, as an authority in the field?

Such a build-up is tough to handle, but if you feel the work should not be recognized you can refuse to do so on the grounds it is outdated or not authoritative on the particular subject in question. Thus you might say that you acknowledge Dr. Friedberg's expertise in the area of *medical* treatment of heart ailments but not in regard to the *surgical* treatment of such ailments, and therefore refuse to recognize him or his work in this area.

A Dr. Friedberg was a great physician. However, he was not a recognized expert in regard to the *surgical* treatment of the heart, and I cannot recognize him as an authority or that part of his text referring to that area of the field of cardiology as authoritative, despite the fact he was well recognized in the *medical* treatment of the heart.

As I stated earlier, if the work you are confronted with on cross-examination should be accepted as an authority, accept it; then, if possible, distinguish the facts applicable to the opinion in the work from the facts of the case at trial, so that the opinion expressed in the work can be understood as not contrary to your opinion. Otherwise, you can only identify this opinion as one of those in the work with which you disagree and state why. (If the cross-examiner does not permit you to state why, you will have to wait until you are questioned on redirect examination by your attorney or the attorney who called you as a witness.)

Your decision about recognizing a medical work as authoritative (or its author as an authority, which amounts to the same thing) must be made with honesty and discretion. Remember, you should never generally recognize an author as an authority but always ask specifically what work is being referred to and base your recognition on the contents of that specific work. No one can quarrel if you do not recognize a work or its author, but your refusal must not appear deceitful, obstreperous, or ignorant. When you do recognize a work as authoritative (or its author as an authority), you must know the work and always leave yourself the option of disagreeing with portions of it. When something is read from it that you cannot place or are not familiar with, you should always request to see the passage. Examine the book or article and read the passage yourself. You may request this of the questioning attorney or, if he balks, of the judge. Most judges will permit you to look at the work. By doing so you may be able to place the passage in a larger context and explain the author's intention and the reasons why the opinion read is not contrary to your opinion. The cross-examining attorney may have read the passage out of context or omitted a qualifying sentence that puts the opinion in the proper perspective. Sometimes a lawyer will leave out the sentence that enumerates the exceptions to the opinion expressed. Your attorney should be watching out for such omissions, but you cannot count on him to pick them up and should be vigilant yourself. Sometimes the omission can be as subtle as failing to read a chapter heading or subheading that qualifies the opinion expressed. Just such an omission was attempted by the plaintiff's attorney when cross-examining a defense expert in a case involving vascular surgery that I tried.

The plaintiff contended that surgery on a stab wound should have been performed immediately. The defense contended that since the injury was to a minor vessel and there appeared to be no major vessel damage, the best course of treatment was to wait and observe the patient rather than spread the contamination of the dirty wound by surgery. In cross-examining the defense expert, a prominent vascular surgeon, the plaintiff's attorney attempted to read, from a text recognized by the expert as authoritative, an opinion from a section entitled

"Injury to Major Vessels" without including the section heading. The opinion in the passage quoted was that, for injury to the vessel, immediate surgical intervention is advisable to prevent loss of limb. The omitted heading was on the flip side of the page from the one the attorney was quoting, so I did not spot the omission despite the fact that I was reading the text over the shoulder of the plaintiff's attorney. The expert was familiar with the text that he had recognized and exposed the omission. The attorney's trick failed and the expert was able to reemphasize his opinion that the injury involved was to a *minor* vessel, not a *major* one, so that the opinion read did not apply. He made further points by stating that he agreed with the text in regard to injuries to major vessels, and that if the attorney read the text further he would see that the author agreed with him about the proper treatment of injury to minor vessels, which was, in fact, the treatment rendered by the defendant. Such moments are pure joy to the defense attorney. They are also, unfortunately, rare.

Generally speaking, if you are aware of the rule on the use of medical literature and familiar with the major works in your field, you should be able to handle cross-examination with medical literature.

Your Conduct with Others during the Trial

Sometimes a defendant will unwittingly prejudice his defense because he does not know how to conduct himself during the trial. Cases have been lost because of thoughtless behavior.

There is a great deal of activity before the trial begins for the day, during the breaks in the trial day, and after the trial day has ended. Conversations go on between lawyers and other lawyers, clients, witnesses, investigators, and prep men (those who help the attorney prepare during the trial). There are opportunities to converse with all of these people. The attorney for the plaintiff or a codefendant may be very personable and fraternize with you when the court is not in session. After the amenities, conversation may turn to what has just occurred on the witness stand, an item of evidence, or a medical point in the case. A naive defendant may inadvertently educate the attorney for the plaintiff or a codefendant who is an opponent in regard to some medical aspect of the case or other fact that he was not aware of. Such a physician may reveal the name of a witness or information about a witness that allows his opponent to prepare more thoroughly for cross-examination. Sound melodramatic? Maybe so, but it happens.

Suppose a gregarious attorney approaches you during a break and says something like "Isn't it ridiculous what Dr. Jones said about using a cast on the plaintiff's ankle to treat the fracture?" You may carelessly reply, "Of course. The operation was performed to repair the patient's torn ligaments, not for the fracture, which was undisplaced. A cast can't hold the ankle bones sufficiently together to allow the ligaments to heal. You have to use internal fixation." The attorney nods in agreement, smiles, excuses himself, and leaves. He may not have realized that the main injury was the torn ligaments and that it was their repair, not the fracture, that required the internal fixation. He may not have understood why casting alone would not have been sufficient. Now he can make use of the information you have inadvertently provided in the manner most beneficial to his client, which may be prejudicial to your defense. He may attack a different area of treatment. He may dig to find literature containing opinions contrary to your opinion for use in cross-examination. In sum, he now knows more about your position and can act accordingly.

Even revealing the identity of a witness who may be sitting in court listening before taking the stand can mean a great deal. It is common for an attorney who sees a new face in the courtroom (assuming the usual sparseness of spectators) to approach the individual on a break or before the court is called to order and ask him his identity. He wants to find out if the person is a witness so he can ask the judge to excuse the witness to prevent him from hearing the testimony of the other witnesses. If he finds out the witness is an expert, he may also be able to have the witness investigated. He can send his prep man or call his office to have an associate find out everything he can about the witness in the hope of learning something he can use in cross-examination. He may learn that the expert testified for your attorney in several other cases. Perhaps one of the other attorneys in his office knows or has cross-examined the witness and can supply information about his testimony in other cases, his weaknesses as a witness, or his lack of qualifications. Some offices keep files containing information on expert witnesses and transcripts of prior testimony they have given. The cross-examining attorney may be able to call his office and obtain prior testimony rendered by the expert in another case that is inconsistent with the position he is now in court to support. Despite the desire of an opponent's attorney to learn the identity of everyone in court, circumstances sometimes make it very difficult for him to do so. Several strangers may come in simultaneously. A stranger may enter just as the court is being called to order. The person he approaches may decline to speak to him (as all witnesses should be instructed to do), which will signal to him that the person is a witness but will not reveal his identity. (In other words, he will be able to have him excluded but not investigated.) Under such circumstances the attorney may approach you for the information.

Suppose the clerk is calling the court to order and your expert, Dr. Smith, walks into court and sits down. The plaintiff's attorney sees him, suspects he may be a witness, but does not have time to approach him. As he is taking his seat at the counsel table opposite you, he smiles and asks innocuously, "Isn't that Dr. Jones who just came into court?" You unwittingly reply, "Oh, no, that's Dr. Smith from Mount Sinai." You have done it. Dr. Smith will be excluded from court on the request of the attorney, losing the benefit of hearing other witnesses testify and lawyers question, and the opposing attorney will do everything he can to have the witness investigated.

Sometimes several people enter the court simultaneously and the opposing attorney does not suspect that your expert is among them. He may be very busy with other matters or just not notice. Never acknowledge the witness or volunteer that he has arrived. Why signal the opposing attorney that your witness has arrived so that he can ask for your witness to be excluded? Even if you do not volunteer the witness's identity, you will deny him the advantage of listening to testimony before he takes the stand. I have actually seen defendants introduce the plaintiff's attorney to their experts or warmly greet their experts in court in front of the lawyers for other parties. This behavior not only revealed the identity of the witness and caused his exclusion from court until he was called to the stand, but also caused him to be accused on cross-examination of testifying out of friendship.

Consider for a moment the advantage to your expert of hearing testimony. If your expert can hear what the plaintiff's expert is criticizing and the reasons the expert is giving to back up his opinions, your expert can direct his testimony to speak to the points made by the plaintiff's expert and to explain why the plaintiff's expert is wrong. Hearing any witness being questioned will give your expert a feel for the trial, the manner in which the various attorneys interrogate, and what the judge is like and will allow. He can learn from the mistakes made by other witnesses. He starts to think like a witness and prepares to answer like one. To deprive him of all this because you cannot keep quiet or are trying to be civil or friendly is ridiculous. Let the opposing attorneys in the case learn what they can on their own, not with your help.

In general, it is best to refrain from talking to any of the attorneys in your case, except for amenities. Listen carefully to the instructions your attorney gives you. He will want you to be on the lookout for physicians you recognize who are in court to testify for other parties. Do not fraternize with witnesses who are in court to testify for you or anyone else unless doing so has been cleared by your attorney. If the jurors see you fraternizing, they may draw damaging inferences. Your trial is not a social event.

I make it a practice to have my expert meet the defendant and me at a designated place out of sight of other lawyers and the jurors, so that we can discuss testimony without being disadvantaged. Intense discussion in front of a juror outside the courtroom may give the juror the impression that the expert is being told what to say. If the juror sees obvious displays of friendship between you and the witness, he may decide that the witness cannot be objective. If the expert is in court undetected, he is always instructed to leave the courtroom on his own at any break and not to approach me or the defendant. If I wish to speak with him, I will signal him to meet me at a place where we cannot be seen. If the break is for lunch, I instruct the witness to meet me and my client on the way to or at the restaurant. After the witness has taken the stand, separate exiting is not necessary; but heavy discussion should be conducted away from the other attorneys and areas where jurors might roam on a break, like the men's room or an elevator.

If a juror is spotted anywhere, such as in the elevator or at a restaurant, discussion of the case must cease and a quiet exit must be made. Acknowledging the juror is permissible, but further contact should be avoided. The jury is not to be wooed, courted, or spoken to; this is totally improper conduct.

The rules that apply to conversing with attorneys also apply to other parties in your suit. A codefendant may by your worst enemy in a trial, and it is important not to arm him against you inadvertently. If your attorney is also representing another defendant, you will be able to work closely to further your mutual defense. If your attorney and the attorney for another defendant agree to work together, consult your attorney as to exactly what degree of cooperation and revelation on your part is proper. As a general rule, you should keep silent and allow your attorney to do the talking unless you are asked by your attorney to discuss something. As I noted in the case involving an ulcer operation, it often takes a great deal of discussion between attorneys for codefendants whose positions at first do not seem consistent to reach full cooperation. It is important that you as a defendant do not reveal important information until your attorney is sure that the codefendants are united in interest and can work together. Otherwise, you may be giving the others ammunition to hurt your defense.

Negotiations during Trial

In recent years there has been more and more emphasis on settling malpractice cases. Judges with crowded calendars want to move cases, and settlement is the best way to do so in terms of time and effort. Insurance companies want to dispose of many cases in this manner to avoid spending more money on defense and in order to release reserve money committed to the cases. The plaintiff's attorney wants settlement so that he is assured of being compensated for his time and effort and so that he can move on to the next case. Many defense attorneys are overly concerned with pleasing their clients (insurance companies or hospitals as well as physicians), and if they can achieve a reasonable settlement and avoid the possibility of losing big, they too desire settlement. All these factors, in conjunction with factors peculiar to each case (such as a limited policy, high risk, serious injuries, weak witnesses, or missing evidence), guarantee that there will be considerable pressure to settle in every case.[6] Negotiations will be carried on both before and during the trial.

During these negotiations you must keep your discussions with your attorney confidential. The discussion of amounts and the reasons why settlement might be beneficial to one party are delicate matters. It is sometimes very difficult to convince the plaintiff or a codefendant to settle, despite the fact that it is the wisest course of action. Inadvertent remarks can ruin a settlement that would have saved you a great deal of money, time, and effort.

As I noted in the chapter on settlement, there are cases that should be settled. Once this conclusion is reached, the next task is to settle for the best price possible. This process involves intensive negotiation and bluff and counter-bluff. An inadvertent remark by you can upset your attorney's efforts to settle the case for the lowest price the plaintiff's attorney will accept and the insurance company will pay. If there are many defendants, it will mean obtaining the proper amount of contribution toward the settlement from each defendant. This requires even more complicated bargaining and psychological warfare. If there are multiple plaintiffs the situation becomes even more complex.

6. See Chapter 9, pp. 161-166.

On the other hand, if you and your attorney decide after careful consideration that the case should be defended, and if your insurance company concurs, the right to a trial should be preserved at all costs, notwithstanding the pressure to settle. Your attorney should not allow this right to be abrogated by an ambitious judge trying to make a name for himself by disposing of cases, a threatening or powerful plaintiff's attorney, or anyone else. I have had judges and lawyers attempt to coerce me by every method they could think of to settle cases that I (and my client) determined should be defended. They have used insults, threats involving future cases, calls to the insurance company insuring my client, calls to the referring attorney, and the like. Such pressure only succeeded in angering me, because I believe that your right to defend yourself by means of a jury trial is an essential right that must not be lost.

When a judge can make no headway with your attorney, he may request that you, the defendant, come into his chambers so that he can attempt to persuade or pressure you to authorize a settlement. I resist this tactic as a usurpation of the attorney's right of representation. But if your attorney accedes to the judge's request or demand to speak directly to you, even though you, your attorney, and your insurance carrier have agreed that a trial and full defense are the proper course of action, you must stand firm and not be awed or overcome by the doom predictions of the judge. This is not to say that all risks, including whatever weaknesses or dangers the judge points out, should not be considered. Everything, including whatever valid arguments the judge or other attorneys raise, should be discussed and weighed with your attorney. But if, after that process, you and your attorney decide you want a trial, you should demand it and have it, no matter how angry his honor or anyone else gets. (I actually had a judge tell me that he did not have four days to try my client's case, that my office had other cases on his calendar, and that he wanted the case settled. He wanted to get to the next case, which would bring him publicity because of the interest it had generated. I had to tell him that this was not my problem, that I did not understand his remark about "other cases on his calendar," that I would not contribute toward a settlement, and that my client and I were ready to go to trial.) Remember that the judge may make it difficult for you during the trial, but it is the jury you must convince[7] and jurors are not blind to unfair treatment by a judge. There is also the right of appeal. Your right to defend yourself should not be abrogated by the personal desires of the judge or any attorney, and it will not be if you and your attorney stand up for that right.

7. See "Why a Jury Trial?" pp. 167-170 in this chapter.

11   Appeals

After the attorney for the losing party has had his post-verdict motions for a new trial and for judgment notwithstanding the verdict denied, he can appeal if he feels that there has been sufficient error to have the result reversed in his favor or a new trial granted. This means that the entire transcript of the trial, including copies of all the materials admitted into evidence, will be printed as "the record on appeal," and briefs will be submitted by the attorneys on both sides arguing the law as to what occurred. There may or may not be oral argument before the appellate court.

The appellate court will then decide whether there was sufficient error to permit it to interfere with the jury's verdict or the action taken by the judge (if, for example, he set aside the verdict). As a rule, appellate judges do not like to interfere with the decision reached by the jury "down below" in the trial court, because they feel that the jurors who have heard the case firsthand have a better idea of the truth than they can glean from the *written* record on appeal. They also put great weight on the trial judge's evaluation of the importance of any incident that occurred during the trial, because he was there on the scene. Nevertheless, the appellate judges will disturb the jury's verdict if something has occurred that they decide constitutes "reversible error"—that is, something prejudicial enough to one side to affect the outcome improperly. They may also interfere if, on review of the record, they find the jury's verdict inconsistent with the facts or the law. They may interfere if they find the jury's verdict to be excessive or inadequate, in which case they can either reduce or increase the verdict or order an entire new trial. An appellate court can also direct a verdict for the losing party (usually the appealing party) if the judges feel that the evidence is so overwhelming as to dictate such action, notwithstanding the conclusion of the jury.

Whatever the appellate court does, there is *usually* a right to appeal from its decision to a higher appellate court. (In certain instances this right may be limited, depending on the laws of the jurisdiction.) This appeal is again based on the printed record on appeal, which will include the decision of the interim appellate court. New briefs are submitted and there may or may not be oral argument. (Oral argument will depend on the rules of the jurisdiction and the requests of counsel.) Sometimes such an appeal involves only one legal question raised by the lower court; in other words, part of the interim appellate court's decision can be accepted and part appealed to a higher court. Generally speaking, the higher appellate court accepts the facts as found by the lower appellate court and focuses on the questions of law raised.

12   Conclusion

The number of malpractice suits being brought and the amounts of money involved in judgments, settlements, and legal defense have been increasing steadily. States such as California and New York find themselves with physicians in rebellion because of the tremendous rise in premiums caused by this phenomenon. Various experiments to handle malpractice claims are being tested. Panels of judges, doctors, and lawyers are being formed to make recommendations concerning the claims. Sometimes the recommendations are binding; most often, not. Sometimes the panel's finding can be introduced at the trial, if there is one. Such panels represent an attempt to avoid the cost of trial, to settle liability cases early, to eliminate spurious claims, and to keep the amount of recovery reasonable. There are also proposals ranging from arbitration to some kind of no-fault system. It is my position that panels and the other proposals are fraught with danger in terms of fairness to both you and the patient. The right to sue and defend need not and should not be so compromised. The present system of settling and trying malpractice suits is the fairest and most beneficial system in terms of patient care, if it can be brought under control.

The effect of the right of a patient to sue for medical malpractice has been both beneficial and detrimental. It has finally forced the medical profession to face up to incompetence in its community and to begin to police itself. It has forced physicians to keep up with the times. It has made physicians more aware of their patients' rights and caused them to deal more openly with their patients.

At the same time, because of the excessive number of medical malpractice suits and the astronomical amounts of money sometimes involved, the patient's right to sue has caused physicians to retire early, order unnecessary and redundant tests that drive up the cost of treatment, join group practice to escape the cost of insurance, go exclusively into research, and hesitate to use new and perhaps better medications or modes of treatment. The high premiums have put a tremendous cost burden on all physicians, especially new practitioners. (They may even discourage students from pursuing medical careers.) The increase in premiums has not only caused an increase in the cost of treatment but also put pressure on some physicians to see more patients daily, thereby diminishing the quality of their care.

I believe that the beneficial effects of the patient's right to sue can be maintained, the detrimental effects greatly reduced, and your right to defend yourself in a trial preserved if the medical profession educates itself about malpractice and applies its knowledge to the treatment of patients. This process will reduce the number of malpractice suits and the amounts of recovery and increase the success rate of defending malpractice suits—which in turn will reduce the cost of malpractice insurance to tolerable levels, improve patient care, and allow the physician and the patient to maintain all their rights. Thus both can continue to use the fairest system to resolve their disputes, instead of accepting some alternative that either is more vulnerable to bias or automatically provides for some type of award to be granted.

It is my belief that if you as a physician know what is contained in this book and attempt to follow its suggestions you can substantially decrease the chances of being sued and, if you are sued, you will be in a better position to defend yourself successfully. I also believe that if the medical profession as a whole does this, the result will be a significant reduction in the number of suits and the amounts of money expended. If so, the present system, which is the most equitable, will continue to exist and become manageable.

Glossary

admissions Damaging statements by a party of the lawsuit.

burden of proof The burden of coming forward with evidence or failing to win the issue. For example, the plaintiff has the burden of proving a prima facie case. A defendant may have the burden of proving contributory negligence. The term also refers to the *quality* of evidence one must produce to prevail on an issue. For example, in a civil case the burden of proof is less than in a criminal case, which requires proof "beyond a reasonable doubt." Usually all that is required in a civil case is to prove "by a fair preponderance of the evidence." This is the burden applicable to a malpractice case. It means that, weighing all the evidence, the party with the burden of proof has tipped the scales (of justice) somewhat toward his side. That tipping constitutes a fair preponderance of the evidence. If the party who has the burden of proof fails to tip the scales in his favor, or if the scales remain even or tip toward the other party, he loses on that issue because he has failed to sustain his burden of proof.

cause of action A specific claim; for example, a cause of action for lack of informed consent.

comparative negligence The system of apportioning negligence between the parties. Apportionment can be done by the jury or the judge. Under some systems the plaintiff cannot recover if the jury finds that he is 50 percent or more responsible for his injuries.

contributory negligence Negligence on the part of the injured party making the claim (that the defendant is guilty of negligence), which may bar him from recovering for his injuries from the defendant.

directed verdict A ruling by the trial judge that as a matter of law the verdict must be in favor of a particular party. Such a ruling can occur before or after the jury has reached its verdict. In conjunction with directing a verdict for a given party, the judge will then grant judgment to that party. This action has the same effect as the granting of summary judgment in favor of a given party. A verdict is usually directed as a result of a failure in proof. See *summary judgment.*

hearsay Testimony about statements of a non-party to the lawsuit. Hearsay is not permitted under the rules of evidence unless the circumstances fit one of the rare exceptions to the hearsay rule.

mitigation Reduction. This term is usually used in conjunction with damages. For example, the fact that the plaintiff has a shortened life expectancy will mitigate the amount he can collect for pain and suffering. It is also possible for the term to apply to liability.

prima facie case The quality of evidence the plaintiff must come forward with in order to defeat the defendant's motion to dismiss at the end of the plaintiff's case and allow the case to go to the jury for decision.

release Relinquishment of one's right to assert a claim against another party, as in the case of a legal release. The term can also refer to a legal document authorizing the release of privileged information, sometimes called a medical (hospital) authorization.

res ipsa loquitur "The thing speaks for itself"; the principle that there is an inference of negligence from the very facts themselves, without any expert medical testimony. Common experience must show that the incident would not have occurred without negligence. This inference can be rebutted by evidence introduced by the defendant. In order to invoke this inference, the plaintiff must usually identify the instrument that caused the injury and establish exclusive control of that instrument by the defendant or defendants. The inference sought should be the only one that can fairly and reasonably be drawn from the facts as proved. If there is a plausible alternative, the inference should not be permitted. Defendants in medical malpractice cases argue that res ipsa loquitur cannot be invoked very often in regard to the human body because it is rare that common knowledge is sufficient to show that the incident would not have occurred without negligence.

statute of limitations The period within which the plaintiff must sue in order to assert a medical malpractice (or any other) claim. Once this period expires, the plaintiff is barred from suing you if you assert the defense of the statute of limitations.

summary judgment The granting of judgment in favor of one party as a matter of law. Usually summary judgment is granted because of a legal deficiency, rather than a failure of proof. For example, if the plaintiff has failed to sue the defendant within the applicable statute of limitations, the judge will grant summary judgment to the defendant if he moves for it and introduces sufficient evidence of the plaintiff's failure to sue in time.

vicarious liability Legal responsibility for the acts of someone else through the law of agency or partnership. For example, a hospital is vicariously liable for the acts of its employees.

wrongful death A cause of action asserted by the next of kin of a deceased patient for the pecuniary loss incurred as a result of the negligent treatment that killed the patient. Wrongful death is a cause of action created by statute, and it permits compensation only for pecuniary loss to the next of kin as a result of the death (that is, loss of income). It does not include any right to recover for the pain and suffering of the deceased or the anguish of the next of kin. A cause of action for the pain and suffering of the deceased patient can be alleged separately. A cause of action for wrongful death has its own statute of limitations.

Index